Brian Pinto is that rare economist who is abreast of theoretical research on economic growth and has also participated in policy design and implementation during crucial periods in several countries. This account of his experiences from his long career with the World Bank will be of interest to everyone who thinks about economic growth.

—*Robert E. Lucas, Jr., The John Dewey Distinguished Service Professor in Economics, University of Chicago, 1995 Nobel Prize in Economics*

I have followed Brian Pinto's economic work since his days in Poland in the early 1990s. His fascinating book takes us on a trip that starts in Poland at the outset of its transition, and then continues in Russia before its 1998 financial crisis, before bringing us to India ten years after its sweeping reforms were implemented, and finally to Kenya during its improving economic performance prior to the 2007 elections. In this journey, a growth policy "trio" repeatedly pops up: the combination of hard budget constraints, market competition, and competitive exchange rates. This micropolicy trio forces firms to innovate in order to survive. Firms' dynamism generates growth and tax revenues that place government debt on a sustainable path. And this in turn lowers interest rates, which further encourages firms' innovative investments. Through these lenses, the book revisits the recent history of developing and emerging market economies and points to misdiagnoses from academics and international financial institutions involved in policy advice to these countries. I strongly recommend this insightful book to researchers and policymakers interested in growth and development.

—*Philippe Aghion, Robert C. Waggoner Professor of Economics, Harvard University*

Brian Pinto brings a unique combination of passion, personality, knowledge of the latest economics research, and good common sense to his vibrant discussion of the interaction between sovereign debt and economic growth. He draws on personal experience from his work at the World Bank on Kenya, Poland, India, and Russia to formulate broader policy lessons about critical issues that arise repeatedly in emerging market countries. The exposition is refreshing and insightful, and it makes the practical implications of economic research come to life.

—*Gene Grossman, Jacob Viner Professor of International Economics, Princeton University*

Pinto argues that "country economics" is in effect a separate branch of economics. Economic theory and the "conventional wisdom" offer only starting points. He succeeds admirably in offering insights about what drives the growth experiences of developing countries, and points out the perils of conclusions drawn hastily from afar. Understanding the linkages between a country's sovereign debt dynamics and its microfoundations of growth is the core of his investigation.

—*Robert J. Shiller, Arthur M. Okun Professor of Economics, Yale University, 2013 Nobel Prize in Economics*

Brian Pinto brings country economic policy to life and shows what it means to practice it. The stories in his insightful book resonate very strongly with me as a practitioner on the ground. His analysis of the linkages between growth and sovereign debt is spot on. Brian was one of the best economists I worked with at the World Bank—and this book is a fun read too!

—*Ngozi Okonjo-Iweala, Coordinating Minister for the Economy and Minister of Finance, Nigeria, and former Managing Director, The World Bank*

This is a special and rare book, which builds on Brian Pinto's deep experience. It shows how one uses theory, country knowledge, and practice, to analyze the world and make policy recommendations. It is a pleasure to read; the style is relaxed and clear, and the boxes are good.

—*Olivier Blanchard, Economic Counsellor and Director of the Research Department, IMF*

# How Does My Country Grow?

# How Does My Country Grow?

## Economic Advice Through Storytelling

BRIAN PINTO

OXFORD
UNIVERSITY PRESS

UNIVERSITY PRESS

Great Clarendon Street, Oxford, ox2 6DP,
United Kingdom

Oxford University Press is a department of the University of Oxford.
It furthers the University's objective of excellence in research, scholarship,
and education by publishing worldwide. Oxford is a registered trade mark of
Oxford University Press in the UK and in certain other countries

Published in the United States of America by Oxford University Press
198 Madison Avenue, New York, NY 10016, United States of America

British Library Cataloguing in Publication Data
Data available

Library of Congress Control Number: 2014936654

ISBN 978–0–19–871467–5

Printed and bound in Great Britain by
Clays Ltd, St Ives plc

To Claire Agnes Pinto
*You sing now in heaven, but I hear you still.*
A tribute of love from your sorrowing father

# PREFACE

Economic truth is, by nature, more episodic than universal. The two episodes defining this book are the transition to a market economy in Central and Eastern Europe, which began in 1990; and the emerging market crises between 1997 and 2001, and their aftermath. The book's focus is on the reforms and policy debates these episodes inspired in connection with economic growth and sovereign debt. I learned about these topics from various on-the-job country experiences between 1990 and the onset of the global financial crisis in 2008 while at the World Bank. This is an institution which offers a high measure of intellectual freedom that can be taken advantage of if one resists the temptation of being politically correct and is willing to go where the evidence leads. I attempt to share that learning and a distillation of the growth policy lessons in this book.

In 1990, I left Washington DC for Poland to become the World Bank's economist there. Endogenous growth theory was just about hitting its stride, following the pioneering contributions of Robert Lucas and Paul Romer. I studied it long after returning from Warsaw. Only much later was I able to see how the hard budget constraints, import competition, and competitive real exchange rates implemented by the legendary Leszek Balcerowicz fitted in with growth theory. In early 1998, I found myself in Moscow. The country had substantially completed privatization and inflation was heading inexorably to single-digit levels. Yet Russia endured a massive macroeconomic collapse that August in spite of a large international rescue package. For me, the 1998 Russian crisis rewrote the book on stabilization policy. You don't forget the lessons you learn during a crisis.

I worked on several other emerging market and developing countries, discovering that *country economics* is, in effect, a separate branch of economics. One may be a great, even eminent, academic economist, but a flop when it comes to the rough and tumble of a real-world country situation. Ours is a profession where there is a growing chasm between academic and country economics—mainly because country situations require a time-consuming, integrative approach whereas academics has been heading toward fragmented specialization.

While each country situation is unique and demands an open-minded approach, certain basics are indispensable. Whether you are working on poverty or gender or rural development, it helps immensely to know what the country's growth story and strategy are. The way a country is run—or "governed"—is most visible in the way it manages its public finances. No wonder it is usually the picture of the Indian Finance Minister clutching the budget in his briefcase at the entrance of parliament that graces the front page of the *Financial Times*, not the minister of rural electrification or petroleum or education or health—all undeniably important as well. The point is, no matter what you study in a developing country, it helps to know what it means when someone says that the government's debt is on an unsustainable trajectory; or that the real exchange rate is competitive; or why a country economist should care about neoclassical and endogenous growth (she should).

I try to weave these and other basics into the book, which is divided into three parts: Part One covers growth theory from the prism of policy. Part Two includes country stories on Poland, Kenya, India, and Russia. Part Three looks at the major policy debates of the last decade flowing from the emerging market crises of 1997–2001 and how they were resolved, and ends with a list of lessons. I hope you enjoy the book, even though I do not expect you to agree with all of it!

# ACKNOWLEDGMENTS

I have been fortunate enough to work with and learn from several outstanding economists over the last 30 years. They include Joshua Aizenman, Christophe Chamley, Homi Kharas, Saúl Lizondo, and Sweder van Wijnbergen. I share a special bond with Marek Belka and Stefan Krajewski because of our work together during the heady early days of transition in Poland, which led to an enduring friendship. My soulmates, Jamil Baz, Indermit Gill, Lester Seigel, and S. Subramanian, were always available for a word of encouragement. Philippe Aghion, Armeane Choksi, Bob Flood, Zia Qureshi, Vito Tanzi, Alan Walters (now sadly deceased), and John Williamson were incredibly generous in taking my work seriously, giving me the fortitude to keep going. In this context, I must single out Olivier Blanchard and George Perry. They know what I mean.

In many ways I grew up at the World Bank, where I spent close to 30 years. It gave me the opportunities that led to the learning that is documented in this book. I had the good fortune to serve as an adviser to the inspiring Ngozi Okonjo-Iweala from 2008 to 2010 when she was managing director at the Bank. It was while working for her that I began this book.

I want to thank the following economists for taking the trouble to read and comment on different parts of the book: Joshua Aizenman, Christophe Chamley, Shanta Devarajan, Gene Grossman, Ravi Kanbur, Eduardo Ley (rest in peace, amigo), Rakesh Mohan, Mona Prasad, Francis Rowe, Apurva Sanghi, Luis Servén, Alex Tabarrok, and Faraz Usmani. To the creative and boundlessly enthusiastic Adam Swallow as well as Aimee Wright of Oxford University Press, my gratitude for bringing this manuscript to fruition. I thank Elizabeth Stone for her excellent copy editing, and Saipriya Kannan and Deepa John at Newgen for an outstanding job in producing the book.

My wife, Nancy, and my children, Alex and Alma, made this worthwhile. They put up with me. Claire was my muse. My mother, Praxedes, now 90, was my first and best teacher. I can never adequately express my gratitude to them.

# CONTENTS

List of Figures                                                    xv

List of Tables                                                     xvii

List of Boxes                                                      xix

1. Country Economics is Different                                  1

**PART ONE: What Do We Tell Policymakers about Growth?**

2. Growth Theory from the Prism of Policy                          19

3. In Search of a Growth Policy Package                            32

**PART TWO: Country Stories**

4. Why Poland Beat the Odds                                        55

5. Kenya's Achilles Heel                                           77

6. India's Unanticipated Growth Takeoff                            95

7. Russia Rewrites the Book                                        115

**PART THREE: Policy Debates and Lessons**

8. Emerging Market Crises of the Last Decade: A Watershed          141

9. Self-Insurance and Self-Financed Growth                        162

10. Lessons for Low-Income Countries                              182

## ANNEXES

Annex 1  Key Features of Neoclassical Growth                              205

Annex 2  Assessing Government Debt Sustainability                        211

Annex 3  The Russian and Argentine Debt Swaps                            217

Annex 4  Three Generations of Crisis Models                              221

Annex 5  The Sovereign Debt Restructuring Mechanism (SDRM)               225

Annex 6  IMF's Flexible Credit Line                                      227


References                                                               229

Index                                                                    241

# LIST OF FIGURES

| | | |
|---|---|---|
| 2.1 | China and India: National Savings and Growth 1990–2008 | 27 |
| 5.1 | Kenya: Primary Deficit and Interest Payments 1992–2008 | 82 |
| 5.2 | Political Risk, Investment, and Debt Dynamics | 92 |
| 6.1 | India: Investment-to-GDP (%) 1985/6–2007/8 | 107 |
| 6.2 | India: Corporate Profit and GDP Growth Rate 1993–2007 | 108 |
| 6.3 | India: Government Debt-to-GDP (%) 1991/2–2004/5 | 110 |
| 8.1 | Brazil: Net Public Sector Debt-to-GDP (%) 1995–2007 | 155 |
| 8.2 | Brazil: Primary Surplus and EMBI+ Spread 1995–2007 | 157 |
| 9.1 | Why Turkey's Exchange Rate-Based Stabilization Failed | 166 |
| A1.1 | Effects of Capital Account Liberalization | 208 |

# LIST OF TABLES

3.1 The GC and the Washington Consensus 35

4.1 Quarterly Trends in Underlying Profitability 63

4.2 Managers' Responses to Questions on Motives for Restructuring 70

5.1 A Pleasant Kenyan Surprise 80

5.2 Factors Explaining Falling Indebtedness 1996/7–2006/7 88

5.3 Firm Perceptions of Major or Severe Constraints to Business 89

6.1 Economic Timeline for India 1985–2007 99

6.2 Fiscal Adjustment 1985/6–2006/7 102

6.3 Factors Accounting for Rising Indebtedness 1985/6–2006/7 105

7.1 Public Finances and Economic Growth in Russia 1995–8 123

7.2 Trends in Default and Devaluation Risk Premiums prior to the August 17, 1998 Crisis 125

8.1 Bank Bailout Cost during the East Asian Crisis 145

8.2 Crisis Models—Essential Features and Consequences 146

9.1 Self-Insurance: A Package Deal 172

A2.1 Fundamentals, Market Signals, and International Liquidity 215

# LIST OF BOXES

| | | |
|---|---|---|
| 1.1 | The Importance of Anecdotes | 8 |
| 2.1 | Key Results from Neoclassical Growth Economics | 20 |
| 2.2 | The Savings Rate for a Given Growth Target | 28 |
| 3.1 | Debt Sustainability, Solvency, and Overhangs in Emerging Markets | 37 |
| 3.2 | A Refresher on Macroeconomic Accounting | 39 |
| 3.3 | János Kornai's Hard Budget Constraint | 44 |
| 3.4 | Competitive Real Exchange Rates | 46 |
| 3.5 | Prominent Themes in Volatility | 48 |
| 3.6 | Nigeria—Managing Volatility Better | 51 |
| 4.1 | Poland—Analytical Interlude | 60 |
| 4.2 | The Importance of Being Earnest | 66 |
| 4.3 | The Virtue of Policy Consistency | 74 |
| 5.1 | Kenya—Analytical Interlude | 79 |
| 5.2 | Decomposing Debt Buildups or Reductions | 87 |
| 5.3 | Vignettes from Interviews with Private Sector Firms, July 2006 | 91 |
| 6.1 | India—Analytical Interlude | 97 |
| 6.2 | What Exactly Does "Unsustainable Debt Dynamics" Mean? | 104 |
| 7.1 | Russia—Analytical Interlude | 117 |
| 7.2 | Stabilization and Growth: The Thinking before the Crises of 1997–2001 | 119 |
| 7.3 | Russia's July 1998 Rescue Package | 126 |
| 7.4 | Russia 1998 and Argentina 2001 | 134 |

8.1   Diaz-Alejandro (1985)—Déjà Vu All Over Again        147

8.2   Living with Debt        149

9.1   Arithmetic of the One-Way Bet        165

A3.1  Argentina's Mega-Swap        218

A4.1  The ERM Crisis of 1992–3        223

# CHAPTER 1

# Country Economics is Different

*It is generally considered unprofessional for economists to base their analyses on stories.*

—Akerlof and Shiller (2009, p. 55)[1]

Suppose, after close to 30 years as a practicing economist, I was invited to address a room full of leaders anxious to make their countries grow. This is, in itself, a victory of sorts because not every leader wants economic growth and a better future for their country. It would be a stretch to argue that Ferdinand Marcos wanted the Philippines to grow at its maximum potential during the 21 years he was in power from 1965 to 1986, or that Sani Abacha wanted the same for Nigeria during the five years he ruled the country from 1993 to 1998, to cite two examples; the devastation of Zimbabwe under Mugabe over the past decade is another, albeit extreme, example. Policymakers and the political elite have to *want* growth if growth is to occur. There may be exceptions, such as during an oil price boom; but, without good governance and fiscal policy, the resulting growth accelerations are likely to be short-lived and the country could end up deeply indebted and stagnate, as happened to Nigeria in the 1980s and 1990s following the windfall associated with the Organization of the Petroleum Exporting Countries (OPEC) oil price hikes of 1973–4 and 1979–80.

I could start by telling them that fast growth is elusive.[2] Just look at the difficulty developing countries have been experiencing in converging to income levels in rich countries. This is an uncomfortable reminder of something they already know. I could say it is not factor accumulation that drives long-run per capita growth, but technology and total factor productivity, a growth fact unearthed in Robert Solow's seminal work. They would point to their shoddy infrastructure and obsolete capital equipment and say: "We need large increases in public and private investment. That's what every investment climate assessment done by the World Bank tells us." Truth be told, I am aware that growth miracles based on high growth rates of total factor productivity are extremely rare; most countries catch up by growing the old-fashioned way, by increasing national savings and investment, and by increasing exports. I then point them in the direction of governance and institutions.[3] That's ultimately what distinguishes developed from developing nations. Once again, they know this. They are probably sick of hearing that, if only their quality of governance rivaled Sweden's or New Zealand's, their per capita income would be several times higher. In fact, apart from a few failed states, economic governance has improved hugely in the developing world over the past 15 years or so.

This leaves me at my wits' end because the three points I just made—on the difficulty in achieving income convergence, on the centrality of total factor productivity growth, and on the supremacy of governance and institutions—captures the bulk of what we know about economic growth. I take a stab at sovereign debt, drawing on the burgeoning literature on cross-country regressions to warn them that debt has harmful effects on growth once the debt-to-GDP ratio crosses a threshold of x percent. But the stab is perfunctory because I know such regressions are hard to interpret: is it higher indebtedness that is driving low growth or vice versa? Besides, many of the low-income countries represented in my captive, but increasingly restive, audience have had their sovereign debt slashed as a result of the Heavily Indebted Poor Countries (HIPC) Initiative and the Multilateral Debt Relief Initiative (MDRI).[4] The question for countries which have had their debt slates recently wiped clean is: What next?

And then I pull out my trump card. I decide to tell them a bunch of stories on how countries actually did it; not necessarily success stories, just the challenges they faced in improving their growth prospects and how they responded. This is usually a winner because everyone wants to know what everyone else did right or wrong. One feature emerges clearly: country experiences with growth are intertwined with their sovereign debt experiences;

in particular, with the occurrence or avoidance of debt crises, a harsh reality even advanced economies in the Eurozone are being forced to admit.

That's what this book is about. It contains a set of developing country stories on growth and sovereign debt informed by two episodes: the transition to a market economy in Central and Eastern Europe; and the emerging market crises of 1997–2001 and their aftermath. The period covered extends from 1990 to the onset of the global financial crisis and Great Recession of 2008–9 (which I shall refer to as the "global financial crisis").

The stories and the macroeconomic policy debates are brought to life by what I learned on the job as a World Bank economist. While the mechanical linkages between debt and growth are obvious—a country's capacity to carry sovereign debt or its debt sustainability improves with faster growth—the policy linkages and the dynamics are subtle and vary substantially from country to country. This appears to be as true for advanced economies as it is true for developing countries: the book's completion has coincided with a major sovereign debt crisis engulfing the Euro area, which has infected their banking systems and stands in the way of a full recovery from the global financial crisis.

A look back over the decade preceding the global financial crisis would find emerging markets, or those developing countries with access to the international capital markets, in the throes of macroeconomic crisis during the years 1997 to 2001. In addition to reversals in capital flows from advanced economies, emerging markets endured a string of prominent public debt crises. These crises began with Thailand and East Asia in 1997 and then relentlessly marched on to Russia (1998), Brazil (1999), and Argentina and Turkey (2000–01). While their origin—whether in unsustainable public finances or in the private sector with the effect transmitted to the public finances via bailouts—varied, the affected countries had two features in common: open capital accounts; and exchange rates which were typically fixed to the US dollar either explicitly or implicitly.

The emerging market crises of 1997–2001 were the last straw that broke the camel's back. Fed up of dealing with constant volatility and vulnerability, these countries engineered a remarkable change in government behavior and economic policy. They reduced public indebtedness, strengthened fiscal and financial institutions, built up foreign exchange reserves, and shifted toward flexible exchange rates. Emerging markets learned to formulate macroeconomic policy and navigate the turbulent international capital markets the hard way—from their own mistakes and in the face of profound investor skepticism, as we shall see. While the nature of the mistakes made varied, with East Asian economies deemed better managed and more inclined to bounce back quickly from crises, emerging markets as a group were being seen in a much more favorable light when the global financial crisis hit.

In fact, developing countries proved remarkably resilient during the global crisis, and by 2010 more than half of global growth originated in these countries. This fueled the idea that they might be decoupling from the advanced economies and become the new engine of global growth. Not by accident did countries like Brazil and Turkey, with a long history of unstable public debt dynamics and exchange rate and banking crises, receive multi-notch credit upgrades during the global crisis itself when the economies of rich countries and their stock markets were floundering. Emerging markets could actually begin to dare to think about optimal debt (or how to better align their public finances with faster growth) instead of just sustainable debt (or how to avoid disruptive crises).

Alas, the triumph proved short-lived. By mid-2013, many prominent developing countries had their growth forecasts substantially lowered. The proximate cause was the then-expected tapering of the US Federal Reserve Board's extraordinary quantitative easing (QE) program. The Fed had embarked upon QE via a massive asset purchase program in order to shore up the prices of various financial securities and put a lid on mortgage rates and long bond yields once its short-term policy rate reached the dreaded zero lower bound in December 2008. QE injected a huge amount of liquidity into the global financial system, a substantial part of which found its way to emerging markets in a grab for yield, enabling huge cuts in policy interest rates in these countries, frequently to negative levels in real terms. Possibly seduced by the exceptionally low interest rates permitted by QE and a sense of invulnerability because of their resilience during the global financial crisis, emerging market policymakers slowed the momentum of reform.

I shall not dwell on this post-global financial crisis episode involving emerging markets because it is evolving and deserves a book in its own right. While numerous PhD dissertations will no doubt be written on what exactly happened in developing countries between 2008 and the Fed decision to taper, there is no gainsaying the substantial progress on reform and the turnaround in emerging markets prior to the global financial crisis. Documenting the lessons for growth and sovereign debt is important for two reasons: first, history has a habit of repeating itself and declarations of victory tend to backfire, indicating the importance of remembering the lessons. Just ask the advanced economies, which have become embroiled in their biggest sovereign debt and banking crisis since World War II so soon after influential policymakers were extolling the virtues of the Great Moderation and categorically ruling out disruptive crises![5] Or emerging market policymakers following the onset of the US Fed's QE tapering, for that matter.

The second reason is to share the emerging market experience with low-income countries, or developing countries with only limited access to the international capital markets, which constitute the next wave of emerging markets. By 2005, an impressive critical mass of low-income countries was making substantial progress and growing at rates faster than ever before, especially in Sub-Saharan Africa. That year, many of these countries had their government balance sheets substantially purged of debt as a consequence of HIPC–MDRI. Subsequently, many of these low-income countries began eyeing the international capital markets as a source of additional government finance, until the global financial crisis put their plans on hold. These countries are accustomed to operating in the sheltered environs of official creditors while emerging markets have been subject to the unforgiving rigors of a market oftentimes accused of being myopic and prone to herd behavior. Low-income countries can learn from the mistakes of emerging markets as they join their ranks. In particular, I shall argue that much of the basis for dispensing macroeconomic policy advice, and certainly the thinking on external financial integration, needs to be re-examined because of the emerging market crises of 1997–2001.

To convey its ideas, this book relies on the experiences of India, Kenya, Poland, and Russia. I deliberately chose these countries because my work at the World Bank allowed me to spend a considerable amount of time studying them: as the next section sets out, being a country economist calls for a disposition quite different from that for an academic economist. The growth and sovereign debt experiences of these countries inform the key insights in this book. The episodes in India and Russia overlapped with the emerging market crises of 1997–2001. These crises fueled a series of policy debates on growth, long-run fiscal sustainability, and the management of sovereign debt. In addition to the four countries above, I draw on the rich experience of Brazil and Turkey in shaking off their bad inflation and credit histories to illuminate these policy debates.

In setting out a framework for looking at the economic experiences of the countries named, I include a self-contained refresher course on public debt sustainability, some national income accounting, and an overview of the growth and macroeconomic crisis literature. This is a compendium of results that, with the wisdom of hindsight, I wish I had been acquainted with when I embarked on my voyage as a country economist at the World Bank.

## Country Economic Analysis

When I joined the Bank in the mid-1980s, the developing country economic scene was dominated by three unfolding events: the debt crisis in Latin America, which by then was halfway through its so-called "lost decade"; the ravages of Dutch Disease, which were becoming apparent after the collapse in oil prices in the early 1980s and which were particularly evident in low-income oil exporters like Nigeria; and black markets for foreign exchange, which had become pervasive in Latin America and Africa. Economists at the Bank and at the IMF were preoccupied with high inflation, macroeconomic instability, and sovereign debt crises. Attention had gone beyond simply "getting the prices right"—essentially, importing world prices by liberalizing trade—to structural reform, because of the recognition that there were impediments other than distorted prices to more efficient resource allocation and higher output levels. Then, in 1989, the Berlin Wall fell and the momentous transition from central planning to a market economy began in Central and Eastern Europe, with Poland playing a pioneering role.

By the mid-1990s, the Brady deals to resolve the 1980s debt crisis by writing down the sovereign claims of the money center banks were completed; but this did not prevent Mexico from suffering yet another crisis, starting in late 1994. Turkey had suffered a similar crisis around the same time, but, in our profession, crises in Latin America tend to receive much more attention than emerging market crises elsewhere. Brazil was just about succeeding in its attempt to tame hyperinflation after several unsuccessful campaigns. Then the East Asian crises began in 1997 in Thailand and spread quickly.

Russia endured a massive crisis in 1998, followed by Brazil in 1999, and then Argentina and Turkey in 2000–01.

I was thrown headfirst into this mix. In early 1985, I found myself on an airplane to Lagos, then the capital of Nigeria, to look at the country's policy options in addressing Dutch Disease. A year later, I was asked to prepare a taxonomy of exchange rate regimes in Africa. The task took me to countries like Ghana and Sierra Leone, and I soon realized that a satisfactory framework for understanding the macroeconomics of black markets for foreign exchange did not exist. Working on live economic problems in real countries was an alien environment for someone who had just finished a PhD in economics. At the beginning of 1985, I would have been hard-pressed to even define a real exchange rate.[6] But you learn quickly when you know that your results are going to feed into policy recommendations for countries affecting millions of lives, not to mention the profound embarrassment of coming up short. Besides, it is an immense help to have the World Bank's resources at your disposal: colleagues who are deeply interested in how developing countries work; the luxury of traveling to distant countries knowing that a local office will arrange meetings with policymakers, as well as with private firms and banks putting their money on the line. My learning adventure took a big step up when I was sent to serve as the Bank's economist in Poland in 1990. Given the unprecedented nature of its transformation, there was no off-the-shelf framework you could pick and apply to the country. Later that decade, I became the Bank's economist in Russia, just in time for its 1998 crisis.

I made five discoveries as the result of being thrust into complicated country situations, each of which was unique. First, academic economics works.[7] But applying it to specific countries requires getting your hands dirty for a prolonged period of time in the country itself. A desk exercise will not simply be insufficient but prone to serious error. Second, *country economic analysis* is, in effect, a separate branch of economics which is complementary to academic economics. You saturate yourself with information about a country, talk to people, lose sleep, keep winnowing your hypotheses down, and hope that things fall into place one day, with serendipity often playing a role. Anecdotes help. Box 1.1 provides an example from my early experience on Nigeria, which forever underlined the importance of intelligent listening to non-economists. Third, country economic analysis is integrative by nature.

**Box 1.1** The Importance of Anecdotes

In September 1986, the black market exchange rate in Nigeria, at a little over 5 naira per dollar, was at a premium of 230 percent over the official rate of 1.5 naira per dollar. Import licenses rationing Nigeria's oil dollars were issued at the official rate. Everyone recognized this as a distortion which needed elimination because it led to rent-seeking and misallocated resources.

Floating the exchange rate was an option gaining ground; but there were two concerns. First, what rate would emerge from the float; and second, would it lead to a burst of inflation. On the first, there was a more-or-less unanimous position in the Bank and IMF that the exchange rate to emerge from the float would be much closer to the official rate than the black market rate because oil proceeds, which accounted for over 90 percent of exports, were sold via import licenses at the official rate. Therefore, the inflationary consequences would be limited. Notwithstanding this intuitively appealing argument, there was reason to believe that a float might produce a rate closer to the black market rate. An earlier Bank study had shown that the local price of traded goods reflected the black market and not the official rate: an imported good costing one dollar was more likely to be sold for 5 naira than 1.5 naira. Ironically, this would *also* mean zero inflationary consequences, notwithstanding the potential depreciation of 230 percent in the official exchange rate upon floating, because it was irrelevant for prices!

Formal analysis supported the latter, less intuitive, outcome.[a] I was one of the few who took this position—but not before testing it out with a trader who was a beneficiary of import licenses. "Suppose," I asked him, "the central bank were to float the naira. Wouldn't there be a huge burst of inflation?" Unfazed by the magnitude of the premium, he instantly replied, "You don't understand. The inflation has already taken place through the black market. All they will be doing is slashing my profit margin!"

He was absolutely right. The float produced a market rate within 1 percent of the black market exchange rate and there was no burst of inflation. What increased the trader's credibility was that it was in his interest to warn about the inflationary consequences of a float so that he could preserve his profit margin!

---

[a] This is available in Pinto (1990, 1991).

You cannot say, "Sorry, I'm a macroeconomist," or "I'm a trade theorist," or a specialist in labor markets, or something similar. Fourth, path dependence in countries is deeply entrenched. Bad policy habits and institutions die hard, and it could take a long time to turn things around—much longer than can be accommodated in the traditional regressions run by economists. Fifth, the hallmark of a good country economist is someone who questions the conventional wisdom and goes where the evidence leads. A good country economist will refrain from using as an excuse: "Oh, eminent economist X already figured that out, so we don't need to worry about it."

Let me provide four examples to make the point about country economic analysis being different and integrative. The first two are drawn from India and Russia while the next two have a bearing on the debates reviewed in this book as informed by actual country experience.

## India's "Fiscal Profligacy"

This example illustrates the meandering path economies can take and the long time that could elapse between the start of reform and the appearance of the desired economic benefits. In the late 1990s, the real interest rate the Indian government paid on its debt began to catch up with, and then exceed, the real growth rate of GDP. Since primary fiscal balances were negative, this meant that that the debt-to-GDP ratio was, by definition, on an explosive path,[8] fueling fears by the early 2000s that India was heading for a macroeconomic crisis of major proportions. And why not? India's fiscal and debt indicators were far worse than in countries like Russia and Argentina, which had actually endured major crises. Had one adopted a purely macroeconomic approach and extrapolated from the experience of other countries, one would have concluded that India was on the verge of a serious crisis—as did many well-known observers of the Indian economy in 2003. Ironically, growth rates doubled that very year: a performance that was sustained until the global financial crisis. Closer examination revealed that India was different from Russia and Argentina, as we shall see in Chapter 6. The reality proved more complicated and more hopeful. The government's debt dynamics had deteriorated *not* because of the "fiscal profligacy" eminent observers of India's economy were complaining about, but because of the fiscal costs of reforms in connection with converting India from a relatively closed to a much more open economy. It took 12 years after the reforms first began, in 1991, for the benefits to appear in the shape of sustained faster growth.

## The Curious Rise of Barter in Russia between 1995 and 1998

Russia's experience between 1995 and 1998 illustrates the pitfalls of being drawn to conclusions about how an economy works because you find them convenient, and then proceeding to design an international rescue package based on these conclusions.

Imagine the major manufacturing US corporations selling their products through barter deals instead of for dollars, and paying their workers in the goods they produce—tires, bubble gum, ketchup, underwear—instead of in cash. They even settle their taxes and energy bills in kind. This is what happened in Russia as the government was trying to reduce inflation to single-digit levels via a stabilization program launched in mid-1995. Clifford Gaddy and Barry Ickes (1998) came up with a seemingly ingenious explanation for all how this hung together: a culturally based interpretation which they dubbed the *virtual economy*. They developed a numerical example to show that unviable manufacturing companies could fetch a higher price if they engaged in barter, effectively letting them pay their taxes and energy bills at a discount. Everyone, they argued, went along with this pretense because they all benefited from it. And the government tolerated it because the alternative would be to deal with the chaotic social effects of mass bankruptcy in the manufacturing sector.

It was easy to show from Gaddy and Ickes' own example that not everyone benefited from barter, meaning that the system could not last.[9] But it was a convenient story to go along with because it vindicated those attributing the difficulty in reforming Russia's economy to lack of political will (the government was turning a blind eye to high-profile tax delinquents epitomized by the fabulously rich gas monopoly, Gazprom) and the difficulty in changing a mindset inherited from the Soviet times (recall the Soviet-era joke: "They pretend to pay us and we pretend to work").

Even Paul Krugman signed on, dismissing Russia's economy at the time of its 1998 crisis as a "Potemkin Economy," a reference to the antics of the chief minister of Catherine the Great of Russia, who went ahead of her when she was touring the country "setting up false fronts that made wretched villages look prosperous.... Ever since, the term 'Potemkin village' has been used to refer to apparently happy scenes that are in reality nothing but facades..."[10] Except, as even a brief visit to Russia and conversations with company directors and bank managers would have readily convinced him, it was all wrong. The rise of barter and noncash transactions over the 1995–7 period was not the result of culturally ingrained pretense but of cripplingly high real interest rates accompanying the stabilization program that had pushed enterprises to desperation. The government itself was spearheading the drive to economize on cash.

As Chapter 7 will show, attributing the rise of barter to weak political will and tax evasion resulted eventually in a flawed international rescue package for Russia, which collapsed less than a month after it was announced in July 1998. Ironically, the collapse of the package set the stage for a quicker economic recovery than anyone had imagined, providing enduring insights into how the microfoundations of growth are affected by the macroeconomic environment. Russia never went back to barter.

## Debt and Growth—Different for Developing Countries?

This example illustrates why country economists should be wary of rules of thumb derived from cross-country studies or the examination of historical episodes. These are fine for defining priors, but not much more.

Carmen Reinhart and Kenneth Rogoff have undertaken much-publicized recent work on the connection between government debt and growth, based on two centuries of data for 44 countries including 20 advanced economies.[11] They conclude that debt affects growth only weakly for debt-to-GDP ratios below 90 percent; but above this threshold, median growth rates fall by 1 percentage point and average growth falls much more. This result applies to both emerging markets and advanced economies. Reinhart and Rogoff use this finding to argue that those who regard levels of government indebtedness in advanced countries today as benign are wrong: in many cases debt is above 100 percent of GDP. For the post-World War II period, they find that only 8 percent of the annual observations on debt-to-GDP ratios of advanced economies are above 90 percent, attributing this to the harmful effects of growth on debt: "If debt-to-GDP levels over 90 percent are so benign, then generations of politicians must have been overlooking proverbial money on the street."

While most would agree that politicians would go for easy money, is it concerns about growth that detain them beyond debt-to-GDP ratios of 90 percent? Or is the inhibiting factor the exorbitant interest rates the market would demand? Most developing countries would probably suffer a crisis, precipitated by slowing growth and taxes and rapidly rising interest rates, long before the 90 percent threshold was reached. Russia's 1998 crisis and

Argentina's 2001 crisis occurred when government debt was about 50 percent of GDP, lower even than the Maastricht criterion of 60 percent.[12] Countries would therefore be well-advised to heed signals on default risk as reflected in market interest rates *irrespective* of their debt levels. Such feedback is likely to be more helpful in guiding policy than a rule of thumb like the 90 percent threshold identified by Reinhart and Rogoff. Interestingly, there has been a definite change for the better in government behavior in emerging markets, which shows up in their comprehensive and persistent response to the crises of 1997–2001. This will be evident in Chapters 8 and 9. This change may not last forever, but I would bet on it for the foreseeable future.[13]

### The "Bipolar View" of Exchange Rate Regimes

This example captures the fragmentation in our profession. By June 2001, we had witnessed the East Asian crises of 1997–8, the Russian crisis of 1998, and the Brazilian crisis of January 1999, while Argentina and Turkey were still in the throes of their economic crises. That month, a paper was published in *Finance & Development* on how countries were shying away from so-called intermediate exchange rate systems and gravitating toward one of two polar extremes: hard pegs, as in Argentina's constitutionally mandated peg to the US dollar; or pure floats. The article, written by Stanley Fischer, concludes: "The trend away from softly pegged exchange rate regimes toward floating rates and hard pegs appears to be well established, both for countries that are integrated into international capital markets and those that are not. This is no bad thing and it looks set to continue."[14]

The article was broadly accurate in its characterization of how exchange rate arrangements were changing. The euro was in the process of replacing several national currencies in Europe, constituting a switch from floating rates to a hard peg in the Eurozone countries.[15] But prominent emerging markets were in disarray. Not only was Fischer's normative conclusion that "This is no bad thing and looks set to continue" unfortunate in its timing— the Argentine hard peg was on its last legs even as the article was being published—it was divorced from the broader economic challenges with which emerging markets were then grappling. The choice of the exchange rate regime was not an end in itself. It was more likely driven by the requirements of building up foreign exchange reserves as a buffer against shocks, and prodding the private sector to reduce currency mismatches on its balance sheet. Flexible exchange rates would then be more appealing. Ironically, countries like Russia and Turkey, which had adopted pegs to the dollar as a classic strategy to lower inflation, ended up stabilizing after abandoning their pegs to the US dollar! How did they do this? By giving top priority to placing government debt on a sustainable trajectory. Exchange rate arrangements were only one, and not necessarily the most important, part of a much bigger policy package emerging markets were pursuing as a result of the learning from their own crises, as discussed in Chapters 8 and 9.

## Country Stories

The country stories in this book are all very different. But they converge to common ground, perhaps unsurprisingly, given the common history of macroeconomic instability and debt crises in developing countries. The nucleus is the interdependence between strong microeconomic foundations for growth and a healthy government intertemporal budget constraint, thought of as sustainable debt dynamics. As an *analytical* construct, this interdependence, which I shall refer to as "macro–micro linkages," is obvious if not trivial; as a *policy or institutional* construct, nurturing these linkages presents profound political challenges.

Let me elaborate. Sustainable government debt dynamics would foster reasonable real interest rates and real exchange rates that would underpin faster growth. For example, if you look at Kenya's Vision 2030, published in 2007, which aims at a 10 percent growth rate for 25 years, the following receive prominent mention: macroeconomic stability in terms of low fiscal deficits, inflation, and interest rates and a stable exchange rate; achieving a total factor productivity (TFP) growth rate of 2.5 percent (which would constitute a growth miracle); and doubling national savings rates to 30 percent (a much higher national savings rate would probably be needed were TFP growth to be, say, 1.75 percent, which would still be a formidable performance).

How would the requirements for attaining 10 percent growth (assuming it is feasible) be integrated into a coherent whole? The experience recounted in this book indicates that macroeconomic stability, interpreted as what the Ministry of Finance and Central Bank jointly achieve on controlling fiscal deficits and inflation, would not suffice for strengthening the microfoundations for growth, interpreted as the requirements for faster TFP growth. Specifically, competitive real exchange rates, import competition and hard budget constraints would also be needed to prod firms to innovate and move up the technology ladder, thus raising TFP growth.[16] *This is where the battle for faster growth is likely to be won or lost because increasing import competition and hardening budgets quickly gets into the rocky terrain of political economy and vested interests.* Losing this battle would impede the faster growth and higher future taxes required for sustainable debt dynamics for the government, thereby foiling the best-laid macroeconomic stabilization plans of the Ministry of Finance and Central Bank.

It is worth emphasizing that if the Ministry of Finance and Central Bank are unable to deliver on their goals, private firms and banks would be reluctant to make long-term investments and invest in better technology, while portfolio investors would demand high risk premia on government debt. The failure to get these basics right is itself likely to be symptomatic of deeper institutional and societal failures. Ultimately, developing country governments must find a way of managing the macro–micro linkages spelled out in this section if they are to entertain any hope of making progress in areas of vital interest to human beings, such as poverty alleviation and a better life.

## Notes

1. Akerlof, George A. *Animal Spirits.* © 2009 by Princeton University Press. Reprinted by permission of Princeton University Press.
2. The reference is to Easterly (2001).
3. The erudite tome on why nations fail by Daron Acemoglu and James Robinson (2012) appears set to become the gold standard in this area, with its emphasis on political institutions.
4. Commonly referred to as HIPC–MDRI. For an overview, see IDA and IMF (2011).
5. The canonical example is Fed Chairman Ben Bernanke's February 2004 speech on the Great Moderation (Bernanke 2004).
6. The well-known economist Sebastian Edwards was visiting the Bank in 1985 when I began my study of Nigeria. After discovering how deficient I was in open economy macroeconomics and development economics, he asked bluntly why the Bank had ever hired me. He nevertheless helped me by pointing to chapter 2 in Dornbusch's textbook (Dornbusch 1980), which contained one of the few systematic treatments of open economy national income accounting.

7. This stands in contrast to views of academic economists after the global crisis. See DeLong (2011), in which he claims economics is in crisis. Economists, perhaps, but not economics.

8. A precise statement of what this means will be provided in Chapter 3 and Annex 2. The primary fiscal surplus, or primary surplus, is defined as total government revenues minus non-interest spending. It is, by construction, the surplus available for servicing government debt.

9. For a refutation, see Pinto, Drebentsov, and Morozov (2000 a, b).

10. Krugman (2009, p. 132).

11. Reinhart and Rogoff (2010 a, b).

12. According to the Maastricht (European Union) Treaty signed in 1992, EU countries wishing to join the euro currency would have to ensure that gross government debt was no more than 60 percent and the ratio of the fiscal deficit no more than 3 percent of GDP, among other conditions.

13. Argentina is an exception.

14. Fischer (2001).

15. The euro replaced the European Currency Unit as an accounting unit on January 1, 1999 in 11 Eurozone countries and entered circulation on January 1, 2002.

16. "Hard budget constraints" refer to financial discipline, the absence of politically motivated bailouts of firms and a strong governance framework for banks. More in Chapter 3 and Box 3.3.

# PART ONE

# What Do We Tell Policymakers about Growth?

Developing-country policymakers who want fast growth are unlikely to be acquainted with growth theory. But they would readily accept the ideas that faster growth is going to require higher investment rates; that large current account deficits (that is, borrowing from abroad to augment investment) cannot be indefinitely maintained without enhancing risk; and that the public finances have to be on a sustainable trajectory to permit reasonable interest rates on government debt and an attractive cost of capital for the private sector.

Pursuing the preceding objectives will raise the steady-state output *level* by increasing accumulation, bolstering macroeconomic stability, and lowering the cost of capital; but will it also enable a faster *long-run growth rate*? The latter will call for policies that increase total factor productivity (TFP) growth, for which there is ample scope in developing countries. Besides, the faster TFP grows, the smaller will be the increase in the investment rate needed for a given long-run growth target. This, in turn, means a smaller increase in national saving rates—clearly helpful for developing countries, which might find it difficult to raise saving rates in short order.

What do policies capable of spurring TFP growth look like? My experience with diverse developing countries converges to a compact list: hard budget constraints for firms and banks; competition, domestically and especially from imports; and competitive real exchange rates. Implementing this innocuous-sounding list—which I christen the *micropolicy trio*—successfully could make the difference between a good growth experience and a dismal one; but the quest is rife with political economy challenges. The overall context is defined by good governance, which finds its most immediate expression in a sound government intertemporal budget constraint, and the ability to manage volatility from domestic and external sources. Chapters 2 and 3 demonstrate how this package, inspired by live country experience, fits in with neoclassical and endogenous growth theory, and with the constant search for effective growth policy packages.

## CHAPTER 2

# Growth Theory from the Prism of Policy

*Gross output per hour of work in the U. S. economy doubled between 1909 and 1949; and some seven-eighths of that increase could be attributed to "technical change in the broadest sense" and only the remaining eighth could be attributed to conventional increase in capital intensity ...technology remains the dominant engine of growth, with human capital investment in second place.*

—Robert M. Solow, Nobel Prize Lecture, December 8, 1987,
© The Nobel Foundation 1987

An enduring insight emerged from the pioneering neoclassical growth accounting results of Robert Solow (1957) and Edward Denison (1962): that the lion's share of long-run per capita growth is explained by technical change as captured by rising total factor productivity (TFP). Ever since, the emphasis in growth has been on TFP. With capital marked by diminishing marginal returns, sustained per capita growth over the long haul must ultimately come from rising productivity, or more output per unit of input, rather than factor accumulation. Box 2.1 contains the key ideas in neoclassical growth economics and defines TFP.

An immediate *policy prescription* emerges from Box 2.1: opening up the capital account will speed up convergence in income levels as capital flows from richer countries with relatively high capital–labor ratios to poorer countries in search of higher marginal returns. This is where the neoclassical model begins to fall apart. As Paul Romer points out in his 1994 survey article

**Box 2.1** Key Results from Neoclassical Growth Economics

Gross domestic product, Y, is a function of capital $K$ and labor $L$, as in (i) with $0 < \alpha < 1$:

$$Y = A(t)K^{\alpha}L^{1-\alpha}. \qquad \text{(i)}$$

In equation (i), $A$ stands for technological progress and is shown as a function of time to capture its exogenous nature in the neoclassical Solow–Swann growth model. Algebraically, $A = \dfrac{Y}{K^{\alpha}L^{1-\alpha}}$, which is simply output per unit of input measured as a geometric average of $K$ and $L$. Hence, $A$ is a generalized measure of productivity or efficiency, and is called total factor productivity or TFP. Under perfect competition, $a$ equals the share of national income going to capital.

From (i), it follows that that the growth rate of output depends upon the growth rates of labor and capital inputs, and of TFP. While labor input growth is assumed to equal the exogenously given population growth rate, capital input growth is endogenous and is determined by savings adjusted for the depreciation of capital. Both labor and capital inputs are subject to diminishing marginal returns (captured in (i) by the assumption that $0 < \alpha < 1$). While this assumption is absolutely crucial, as Robert Solow (1994) notes, that of constant returns to scale merely helps simplify the algebra: equation (i) can be written in "per worker" terms by dividing both sides by $L$.

The preceding structure leads to *three main conclusions* (which are algebraically presented in Annex 1):

- Convergence in output per worker ("per capita income") levels will happen automatically as poorer countries (those with lower initial output per worker) grow faster than richer countries. In addition to diminishing marginal returns to capital, critical to the "Convergence Hypothesis" are the assumptions of identical savings rates and technology—and if you wanted to be punctilious, identical population growth rates and depreciation rates as well.
- While a rise in the savings rate will result in faster growth during the transition to a new steady state *and* in a higher *level* of steady-state per capita income, it will not result in a faster steady-state rate of growth of per capita income. This counterintuitive result is driven by diminishing marginal returns to capital.
- The steady-state rate of growth of per capita income will be zero (total output will grow at the *natural rate* defined by the population growth rate) *unless* there is persistent, exogenously given, TFP growth.

Weak empirical support for income convergence across countries and the persistence of positive long-run per capita income growth in the rich countries led eventually to endogenous growth, with the breakthrough provided by Paul Romer in 1986.

in the *Journal of Economic Perspectives*, convergence is not supported by the evidence. Besides, the model leads to certain implausible inferences about the level of savings and investment rates in rich countries relative to poorer ones, as Annex 1 shows.

What does this mean for development? First, most country economists would suspect that, compared with an advanced economy, a developing country would have simpler technology (a smaller $A$, see the production function in Box 2.1), be less capital intensive (a lower amount of capital per worker), and poorer, but boast higher returns to capital (a higher marginal product of capital or *marginal product of capital*). But the last is not guaranteed because a higher TFP level in a rich country could offset the impact of a higher level of capital intensity on the marginal product of capital (see equation (A6), Annex1)! Therefore, what might have seemed like a simple prescription of "Open up the capital account!" under the neoclassical model with its assumption of identical technology in order to spur growth and convergence may lead to capital flows in the wrong direction, as Robert Lucas observed in his 1990 paper (Lucas 1990). He brought in human capital (the difference in capital–labor ratios between rich and poor countries is much smaller when based on *effective* labor units, reflecting the superior human capital in richer countries) and externalities associated with it to argue that marginal returns to capital in rich countries could be higher than in poorer countries, especially when adjusting returns for political risk.[1]

But *even if the marginal product of capital is higher in the poorer country*, as posited by the neoclassical growth model, opening up the capital account may not take a developing country far along convergence in income levels if technology is more advanced in the rich country (that is, its TFP level is higher) as illustrated in Figure A1.1. This point is made tellingly by Pierre-Olivier Gourinchas and Olivier Jeanne (Gourinchas and Jeanne 2006). They model the increase in consumption that could be secured as a result of instantly liberalizing the capital account in a developing country versus keeping it closed forever: the production function is neoclassical, with technology exogenously given but with a higher TFP level in rich countries. The gains are modest, equivalent to a permanent increase in consumption of about 1 percent. Capital mobility equalizes the *marginal returns to capital* across rich and poor countries but does not necessarily equate *TFP levels*, which is where the true action is. If the same developing country contrived to erase 25 percent of its productivity gap as compared with the USA, the welfare benefit would be 50 times larger (Gourinchas and Jeanne 2006, p. 716)! In a similar vein, Krugman notes in his 1994 article on the East Asian miracle, that even though China at the time was a poor country, "its population is so huge that it will become a major economic power if it achieves even a fraction of Western productivity levels" (Krugman 1994, p. 75).

It is an open question whether opening up the capital account will help with the convergence of TFP levels; all we know in the neoclassical model is that it should hasten an equalization of the *marginal* returns to capital and raise capital intensity in poorer countries in the process. Intuitively, one would expect foreign direct investment to help with higher TFP because of the better technology it brings. But foreign investors from the richer countries may not be inclined to locate in a developing country even if its measured marginal product of capital is higher. Bad governance, poor policies, weak institutions, and macroeconomic instability can lead to a situation where returns adjusted for risk may be much lower. Inadequate infrastructure, which needs to be paid for and has profound implications for the public finances, is another reason: if electricity is erratic, the ports inefficient and riddled with corruption, and the roads full of potholes, firms may be deterred from investing. Lastly, emerging markets which opened up their capital accounts tended to suffer macroeconomic crises instead of enjoying faster growth, rendering the liberalization of the capital account among the most controversial of policy prescriptions ever for developing countries.[2]

## Neoclassical versus Endogenous Growth

The original Solow model came under attack because of its alleged inability to replicate international variations in per capita growth rates and the absence of convincing evidence on convergence in income levels.[3] Besides, the only way to explain positive steady-state per capita growth over long periods in rich countries like the USA would be to assume exogenous technological progress or TFP growth. A well-known effort to salvage the Solow model following the endogenous growth onslaught launched by Paul Romer (1986) and Robert Lucas (1988) is contained in a 1992 paper by Gregory Mankiw, David Romer, and David Weil.

Mankiw, Romer, and Weil's defense can be presented in four steps. First, there is no earthly reason for poor and rich countries to converge to the same level of per capita income *even in the original Solow model* because countries have different saving and population growth rates. Second, Mankiw, Romer, and Weil calculate, from a cross-country regression using data from 1960–1985, that the effects of the savings and population growth rates on income per capita in the steady state are much larger than what one would infer from the original Solow model applying the observed share of capital in national income of 1/3. The implied share from their regression is closer to 0.60. In their regression, the left-hand-side variable is real per capita GDP in 1985, with the savings rate measured as the average investment rate and population growth rate measured as the growth rate of working-age population over the period 1960–85. The initial level of technology, its growth rate, and the rate of depreciation are assumed to be common across countries. Third, to remedy the problem caused by the difference between the observed share of capital in national income and the share implied by their regression, Mankiw, Romer, and Weil bring human capital into the production function—but without invoking any externalities. They rerun their regression with a measure of human capital included and find that the results are consistent with a capital elasticity of output of 1/3 (equal to its observed share in national income accounts and assuming perfect competition), labor elasticity of 1/3, and human capital elasticity of 1/3.[4] They call this the "augmented Solow model." Fourth, the speed of convergence to the steady state in the augmented Solow model is about half that in the original Solow model. The fact that that countries converge to their *own* steady states defined by their unique education levels, savings rates, and population growth rates—a phenomenon Mankiw, Romer, and Weil label "conditional convergence"—allows for international variation. And countries with similar savings and population growth rates will converge to the same income per capita, but much more slowly than predicted by the original Solow model. Unless one brings in human capital, one is liable to confuse slow convergence with the absence of convergence.

A final point: Mankiw, Romer, and Weil are able to explain international variation in per capita incomes and the seeming lack of convergence without abandoning the assumption of diminishing returns to capital: the sum of the elasticity of output with respect to physical and human capital is less than 1 in the augmented Solow model.

In their refutation of Mankiw, Romer, and Weil, Gene Grossman and Elhanan Helpman (1994) note that their most impactful results come from differences in investment rates and population growth rates between rich and poor countries. Grossman and Helpman argue that the higher investment rates observed in rich countries must be partly driven by a faster pace of technological progress. Therefore, "we believe that the assumption [in the Mankiw, Romer, and Weil regressions] of a common rate of technological progress in all 98 [rich and poor] countries over a 25-year period is simply indefensible."[5]

In the same set of survey articles, Howard Pack notes that "most empirical research...has tested earlier [neoclassical] growth models, rather than testing endogenous growth itself" (Pack 1994, p. 55), and that even though endogenous growth has considerable intellectual appeal, it has "led to little tested knowledge" (p. 69). Ultimately, then, if one is wedded to the neoclassical model with its assumptions of diminishing marginal returns to capital, exogenous technology, and perfect competition, one can always find a modification to it, as Mankiw, Romer, and Weil did, that will sit more easily with the empirical evidence.

## The Country Economist's Dilemma

Why should the country economist care about whether growth is neoclassical or endogenous? Because the policy implications and the nature of the growth challenge differ. In the original Solow model, a developing country can converge to the income level of a rich country simply by accumulating more capital per worker. This process can be speeded up by attracting capital from the rich country based on higher marginal returns in the capital-scarce developing country. But four impediments arise. The first, emphasized by Pierre-Olivier Gourinchas and Olivier Jeanne is that technology may not be identical with the richer country boasting a higher level of TFP. Marginal returns to capital may be equalized, but not income levels. The second and third impediments are those identified by Robert Lucas: human capital is superior and risk much lower in rich countries, so that capital may flow in the "wrong" direction. The fourth brings us to nature of endogenous growth. As set out by Paul Romer and Robert Lucas, various forces may come into play that result in non-diminishing returns to human and physical capital accumulation, contriving to keep richer countries ahead. Growth policy, therefore, must focus on a combination of accumulation, lowering country risk, and eliminating the barriers to better technologies while inducing firms to adopt them.

Robert Lucas latches on to the power of technology. The starting point of his eloquent 1988 critique of neoclassical growth theory is that it was constructed to fit the 20th-century growth experience of the USA but fails as a theory of development *because* it cannot reproduce the international diversity in income levels and growth rates. Besides, its prediction that free capital mobility and trade should equalize capital–labor ratios and hence factor prices across countries patently does not hold in practice. Lucas singles out the one factor he believes has the potential to explain diversity in international growth experience: technology. He uses this as a segue into human capital, including it in the production function together with physical capital and labor, with the argument that the ability to exploit technology requires skilled human beings. Human capital production exhibits constant returns and there are positive externalities associated with the stock of human capital, a crucial contrast with the approach of Mankiw, Romer, and Weil. In Lucas' framework, initial conditions determine the particular income level a country attains in steady state with equal growth rates across countries; there is, therefore, no convergence in income levels. Further, the marginal return to physical capital will tend to be equal across countries, so that there will be no systematic reason for capital to move from rich to poor countries. Introducing two goods distinguished by the human capital needed to produce them, which is acquired on the job, could also lead to persistent differences in growth rates across countries, completing the picture.

Lucas's conclusion may appear depressing because it implies poor countries may not catch up; but he offers a glimmer of hope by suggesting that the constant introduction of new products and trade might give poorer countries an opportunity to alter their product mix and grow faster. He conjectures that such trade-induced shifts in growth rates might have played a role in the East Asian growth miracle.

Not so fast! Alwyn Young's 1995 evisceration of the Asian growth miracle—showing that its growth was driven primarily by factor accumulation and not by TFP growth rates high above those observed in other countries, as many presumed—leads us back to square one. In fact, Young concludes his paper by noting that his results validate the neoclassical framework with its emphasis on income levels explained by capital–labor ratios. Raising savings and capital accumulation rates will lead to a one-time upward shift in steady-state income levels without fostering persistent growth. Therefore, catching up will call for massive increases in savings rates and factor accumulation. Figure 2.1 on China and India, the two fastest-growing developing countries, indicates that this is more than a theoretical curiosity. In both cases, savings rates have increased steadily while growth rates have tended upwards on more volatile trajectories.

Box 2.2 shows that a persistent *rise* in the savings rate may be required just to *maintain* the growth rate at a high level in a developing country, defined as one that exceeds the long-run (steady-state) growth rate. In a Solow-type model, the latter would be determined by TFP and human capital growth; and demographics. Diminishing returns to capital plays a crucial role.

The significance of the result in Box 2.2 can be set out as follows. First, a developing country would need to grow faster than a rich country in order to catch up. Second, this means growing faster than the steady-state growth rate along a balanced path, which can be taken to approximate the growth rate of a rich (technologically advanced) country in the neoclassical framework. Third, given growth arithmetic, this means the growth rate of the capital stock in the developing country must exceed its target growth rate of output (GDP). Fourth, given diminishing marginal returns to capital, a continual rise in the savings rate is needed. Fifth—a crucial point—an effective way of raising the steady-state growth rate in the developing country is by adopting policies to speed up TFP growth *beyond* that in rich countries. There should be ample scope for this considering how far developing countries are from the technological frontier, an innovative idea addressed in a 1992 paper by Philippe Aghion and Peter Howitt. In a practical sense, Aghion and Howitt reconcile neoclassical and self-sustaining, endogenous growth. Diminishing returns may apply to the frontier, but not to developing countries *within* it, creating a robust platform for sustained growth. Why is speeding up TFP growth important? Because it will bring the steady-state growth rate closer to the target growth rate and lower the required growth rate in the capital stock. In so doing, it will relieve—but not eliminate—the pressure for raising the savings rate, and becomes a fundamental plank in the pursuit of faster growth in developing countries. I shall build on this concept in Chapter 3.

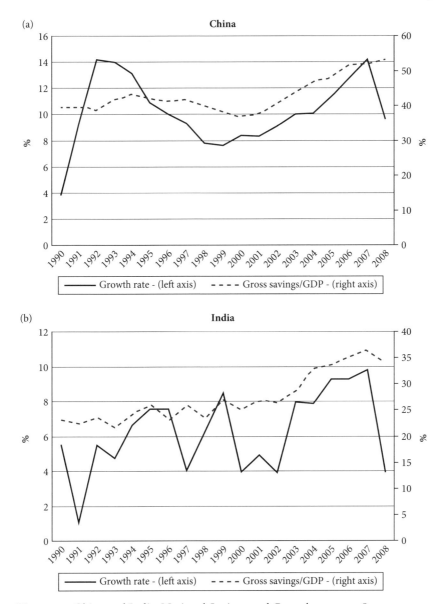

**Figure 2.1** China and India: National Savings and Growth 1990–2008
*Source:* World Bank WDI data.

## A Pragmatic Approach

There are two discouraging takeaways from the preceding survey of the growth literature. The first, from Mankiw, Romer, and Weil, and Alwyn

**Box 2.2** The Savings Rate for a Given Growth Target[a]

Let output, $Y$, be given by: $Y = AK^{\alpha}(\theta E)^{1-\alpha}$, where $A$ is TFP, $K$ is the stock of physical capital, $E$ is the working-age population ("number of workers") augmented by the human capital variable, $\theta$, to obtain effective labor input, and $0 < \alpha < 1$ is the elasticity of output with respect to capital (recall that $a$ being less than 1 implies diminishing marginal returns to capital). This yields the growth equation:

$$g \equiv \hat{Y} = \alpha\hat{K} + \left[\hat{A} + (1-\alpha)\left(\hat{\theta} + \hat{\varepsilon} + \lambda\right)\right], \qquad (i)$$

where a "^" refers to the growth rate of a variable: $\hat{Y} = dY/Y$ is the growth rate of output, $\hat{K}$ is the growth rate of the capital stock, $\hat{A}$ is TFP growth, and $\hat{\theta}$ is the growth rate of human capital. We can write $E = (E/N).N$. If $\varepsilon$ denotes the ratio of working-age population, $E$, to total population, $N$, this gives $\hat{E} = \hat{\varepsilon} + \lambda$, where $\lambda$ is the population growth rate, completing equation (i). I shall refer to the exogenously determined expression on the right-hand side of equation (i), shown in square brackets, as $z$.

It follows from (i), for a given $z$ and target growth rate $g^*$, that $\hat{K}$ must satisfy:

$$\hat{K} = \frac{g^* - z}{\alpha}. \qquad (ii)$$

The capital stock must grow at the constant rate given by (ii) in order to meet the growth target. In a closed economy, $\hat{K} = [sY - \delta K]/K$, where $s$ is the national savings rate and $\delta$ is the rate of depreciation of capital. This can be rewritten as:

$$\hat{K} = s\left(\frac{Y}{K}\right) - \delta. \qquad (iii)$$

From (i), we see that the growth rate along a steady-state balanced growth path equals $\frac{z}{1-\alpha}$. It is easy to show that as long as $g^* > \frac{z}{1-\alpha}$, then $\hat{K} > \hat{Y}$. In this case, we see from (iii) that $s$ must keep on rising to keep $\hat{K}$ at the constant level required by (ii) in order to meet the growth target $g^*$. That is, $s$ must rise continuously on account of diminishing returns to capital as long as the target growth rate exceeds the steady-state growth rate.

**An Example:** Following the cessation of its internal conflict in May 2009, the government of Sri Lanka announced a medium-run growth target of 8 percent. That might have sounded easy, since the country grew at 5 percent throughout the decades-long conflict. But simulations showed that, even assuming a TFP growth rate of 1.75 percent compared to the country's long-run average of about 1 percent, the savings rate would need to rise quickly to 40 percent from prevailing levels of around 25 percent. The estimate of $z$, given human capital and demographic trends, was around 2.67 percent, suggesting from (ii) that the capital stock would need to grow at around 15 percent with $g^* = 8$ percent and $a$ put at 0.35. With initial $K/Y$ estimated at 1.30 and a depreciation rate, $\delta$, of 7 percent, equation (iii) can be used to show that the required savings rate rises in a few years to 40 percent. Furthermore, maintaining $s$ at 40 percent will, over time, lead to a declining growth rate, until the balanced path growth rate of 4.1 percent, given by 2.67/(1-0.35), is reached.

*NB:* As Mankiw, Romer, and Weil (1992, p. 431) note, $K/Y$ ratios vary from around 1 in developing countries ("low saving") to around 3 in advanced economies ("high saving"), which might be considered closer to the steady state.

_____

[a] Based on Box 5 in Fonseka et al. (2012) and Hevia and Loayza (2013).

---

Young, is that income convergence is going to be exceedingly slow, with any significant step-up in target growth rates demanding a large increase in accumulation and savings. Developing countries should not bank on miracles in the form of phenomenal TFP growth rates. The second, from Paul Romer and Robert Lucas, is that bridging the differences between developing and advanced economies in technology and human capital is the central challenge. Income convergence may never occur because of endogenous growth. An implication is that opening up the capital account will help only if it contrives to import superior technology, but there is no obvious mechanism for this to happen apart from bringing in foreign direct investors, who may be deterred for a variety of reasons, from bad governance and macroeconomic instability to poor infrastructure.

The good news is that these impediments, while formidable, are not insurmountable. A pragmatic growth strategy would require developing countries to borrow elements from both neoclassical and endogenous growth. For example, raising the public savings rate or lowering political risk will lead only to a one-shot rise in steady-state income levels in the neoclassical model via more investment or a lower cost of capital as risk premia fall. But combining such actions with the micropolicy trio of hard budgets, import competition, and competitive real exchange rates could push firms to become more innovative and raise TFP growth by adopting better technology. This is a central finding from the country stories in Part Two and could propel persistently higher growth over long periods, for which there is considerable potential considering how far developing countries are from the technology frontier defined by advanced countries. The focus thus needs to be both on accumulation (emphasized in the neoclassical framework) *and* faster TFP growth (emphasized in the endogenous growth framework). Persistently faster growth could stimulate a rise in the savings rate if consumption responds only slowly to the increase in income in line with the habit-formation hypothesis of Christopher Carroll, Jody Overland, and David Weil (2000).

A 1992 paper by Bradford DeLong and Lawrence Summers reinforces the idea that productivity and accumulation need to be pursued together, notwithstanding the decisiveness of TFP growth in the long run.[6] They present empirical evidence that investment in equipment has a strong causal impact on growth of a magnitude that cannot be explained simply by high private rates of return to capital because of depreciation, let alone diminishing marginal returns. They attribute this to the idea that rapid TFP growth and high equipment investment go together *even in technologically advanced countries*. It is not enough to have a high savings rate: barriers to the import of machinery as well as its relative price have to be lowered. Accumulation becomes a vehicle for technological advancement which, when combined with learning-by-doing and the sharing of operating information, results in beneficial external effects. They estimate net social returns to investment in machinery and equipment of the order of 20 percent per year, more than half of which comes from increased TFP. The crucial implication is that policies which make it profitable for firms in developing countries to invest in better machinery and equipment that passes the market test will spur rapid growth. This could include reduced political risk, which does not simply induce private investors "to undertake equipment investment projects that had previously failed to meet hurdle rates," as DeLong and Summers note (1992, p. 195), but *lowers the hurdle rate itself* via reduced risk premia. Chapter 5 on Kenya is a case in point.

In short, developing countries can adopt policy packages that would help spur sustainable growth over long periods of time in their quest to bridge the difference in income and TFP levels with richer countries, which is the heart of the growth challenge. Chapter 3 looks deeper into growth policy pack-ages, in which the aforementioned policy trio plays a critical role in spurring innovation and faster TFP growth.

## Notes

1. Bringing in effective labor units alone still leads to a much higher predicted mar-ginal return to capital in poor countries; if it instead equalized such returns, then a production function which is homogeneous of degree one would imply that workers of equal skill would be paid the same in Mexico as in the USA, which is disproved by the number of Mexicans who are lining up to enter the USA. In other words, workers of equal skill are paid more in the USA than Mexico; Lucas invokes positive externalities to human capital to explain this. This in turn raises the return to capital in the USA relative to a poor country.
2. I shall take up this crucial point in more detail in Chapters 8 and 9.
3. This section draws liberally from an excellent set of survey articles in the *Journal of Economic Perspectives* 8(1) (Winter 1994).
4. This amounts to taking the original production function $Y = AK^{\frac{1}{3}}L^{\frac{2}{3}}$ and rewrit-ing it as $Y = AK^{\frac{1}{3}}H^{\frac{1}{3}}L^{\frac{1}{3}}$, where $H$ represents human capital. See Mankiw, Romer, and Weil (1992).
5. Grossman and Helpman (1994, p. 29); material in square brackets added.
6. Easterly and Levine (2001) argue that accumulation is not the main factor explain-ing cross-country differences in income levels and growth rates, but "something else," which we usually call TFP and which needs deeper investigation. They allow (sensibly) that this does not mean that accumulation is unimportant for developing countries at given stages in their development.

# CHAPTER 3

# In Search of a Growth Policy Package

*Mary, Mary, quite contrary / How does your garden grow?*
—Mother Goose Rhyme

A distillation of the policy content from Chapter 2 would emphasize technology, human capital, and higher investment rates in developing countries' growth strategies. But even the most optimistic development practitioner would concede that technology and human capital are not the only obstacles—and possibly not even the most serious ones—to convergence. Political instability, corruption scandals, bad infrastructure, and expropriation risks in developing countries are all wedges that need to be eliminated. Opening up the capital account could lead to flows in the "wrong" direction in line with the Lucas Paradox (Lucas 1990) or to destabilizing hot money flows, as experience indicates. The difficulty in achieving convergence is underlined by a recent study which computes that, out of some 180 developing countries, only 28 succeeded in erasing more than 10 percent of their income gap with the USA between 1950 and 2008.[1]

Against this dismal backdrop, how can developing country policymakers respond to the numerous technological, economic, and political challenges to sustained faster growth? In this chapter, I present an optimistic answer to this perennial question based on what I learned at the World Bank. This learning flowed from iterating between the reality of a particular country's economic context and theory. But the key was always following the evidence, no matter where it led and especially when it conflicted with the conventional wisdom.

The growth policy package I construct is based on a simple observation: that the country stories recounted in Part Two, reinforced by the experience of emerging markets since the 1980s, demonstrate conclusively that policies to spur growth cannot be separated from policies designed to avoid sovereign debt crises. These policies can be visualized in three interconnected levels:

- Ensuring a healthy *government intertemporal budget constraint*
- Implementing the *micropolicy trio* of hard budget constraints, import competition, and competitive real exchange rates.
- *Managing volatility* from both domestic and external sources.

This "macro-micro" growth policy package is canonical in the sense that it represents the minimum countries need to do to create an atmosphere conducive to faster TFP growth while also raising national saving rates. There are no shortcuts. Implementing it successfully calls for good governance, which is expressed first and foremost in the management of the public finances, as well as for credible institutions in contract enforcement and property rights, financial sector supervision and regulation, and social protection. In the rest of this chapter, I shall connect the government intertemporal budget constraint, the micropolicy trio, and managing volatility to the evolving policy debates on growth over the past two decades.

## The Growth Commission

In 2006, the World Bank convened the *Growth Commission*, consisting of two Nobel Laureates in economics and several prominent practitioners (including top developing country policymakers), that "sought to gather the best understanding there was about the policies and strategies that underlay rapid and sustained economic growth and poverty reduction." I shall focus on the final report of the Commission issued in 2008 (Commission on Growth and Development 2008, abbreviated as GC (2008)). The highlight was the "common flavors" or "common characteristics" the Commission extracted from countries which grew rapidly (at 7 percent per year or more for at least 25 years) and showcased in its 2008 report. Only 13 countries have achieved this feat since 1950, the bulk in East Asia, testifying to the enormity of the challenge. The Commission's report then went on to elaborate on the "policy ingredients" for growth strategies flowing from these flavors.

The last time a similarly sweeping assemblage of economic policies was undertaken was in 1990. John Williamson made a list of the various strands of advice that Washington-based institutions (including the World Bank) were offering Latin American countries to address the economic ills manifested in their debt crisis of the 1980s. He innocently called it the "Washington Consensus," a label that has invited unbridled antagonism because of the connotation "that markets can handle everything" (Williamson 2000, p. 252)— not because of its policy content, as we shall presently see. One is naturally tempted to ask what new insights emerged from the work of the Growth Commission. We shall see that there was not a quantum leap forward, although governance and country-specificity were given more prominence.

In Table 3.1, I map the 5 policy ingredients identified by the Growth Commission (GC) into the 10 policy elements of the Washington Consensus. A close correspondence is apparent between the macroeconomic stability, future orientation, good governance and inclusion of the GC with the prescriptions of fiscal discipline, redirection of public expenditure toward high return projects with potential for improved income distribution, and secure property rights (a prerequisite for "future orientation") of the Washington Consensus; openness of the GC with the trade openness and liberalization of foreign direct investment advocated by the Washington Consensus (as a source of knowhow—the Washington Consensus scrupulously refrained from advocating capital account openness); and emphasis on market incentives of the GC with elements 6 to 10 of the Washington Consensus.

Taken as a whole, the table emphasizes savings and factor accumulation, sustainable public finances, public goods in terms of health, education, and infrastructure, strong leadership, trade openness, and a private sector market orientation. In a 2008 article, Dani Rodrik pointed out the similarity between the GC and the Washington Consensus, but noted a difference: while the Washington Consensus was *presumptive*, the "new approach" is *diagnostic*, focusing on the most important constraints to growth and emphasizing policy experimentation and monitoring and evaluation.[2] While responding to Dani Rodrik, John Williamson (2008) also noted the similarity between the GC report and the Washington Consensus. He allows that the GC brings in governance, which he may not have emphasized sufficiently; and admits that the explicit emphasis on country context in the GC is a step forward. The GC's common ingredients for rapid growth could thus be usefully thought

Table 3.1  The GC and the Washington Consensus

| GC's 5 Common Ingredients | Washington Consensus—10 Elements |
| --- | --- |
| 1. *Macroeconomic stability* characterized by modest inflation and sustainable public finances | 1. Fiscal discipline |
| 2. *Future orientation* manifested in high savings and private and public investment rates | 2. Redirection of public expenditure priorities toward fields offering both high economic returns and potential for improved income distribution such as primary health care, primary education, and infrastructure |
| 3. *Strong leadership and governance* characterized by stability in the rules for investment, a focus on *inclusive growth*, and an effective government which is pragmatic and acts in the interest of all its citizens | 3. Secure property rights |
| 4. *Trade openness* in order to import knowledge and leverage global demand | 4. Trade liberalization |
| | 5. Liberalization of inflows of foreign direct investment |
| 5. Emphasis on *market incentives* and decentralization, including resource mobility and rapid urbanization | 6. Tax reform (to lower marginal rates and broaden the base) |
| | 7. Interest rate liberalization |
| | 8. A competitive exchange rate |
| | 9. Privatization |
| | 10. Deregulation (to abolish barriers to entry and exit) |

*Source:* First column of table: Figure 2, p. 22 GC (2008); second column: direct quote with order rearranged Williamson (2000, pp. 252–3).

of as the Washington Consensus's prescription for avoiding debt crises augmented by governance and growth diagnostics.

## The Government Intertemporal Budget Constraint

The similarity between the GC and Washington Consensus prompts a compelling observation. Policies and country characteristics which foster rapid long-run growth (the motivator for the GC) are closely allied with those that prevent disruptive crises and result in well-managed public finances (the prime motivator for the Washington Consensus). Indeed, John Williamson's 1990 paper on the Washington Consensus (Williamson 1990) was an attempt to list a "desirable set of economic policy reforms" that official Washington, including the World Bank and IMF, wanted Latin American countries to pursue in order to exit the 1980s debt crisis and reignite growth. Not surprisingly, the paper starts with the need for reducing fiscal deficits, discussing whether productive public investment should be netted out and contingent liabilities from bailing out financial institutions included when constructing fiscal deficit targets: ideas that resonated during the emerging market crises of 1997–2001. Williamson's paper then considers tax reform, interest rates, and competitive real exchange rates before discussing the other items listed in Table 3.1.

The *government intertemporal budget constraint* provides a natural organizing principle for all these variables. The country stories in Part Two and the emerging market crises of 1997–2001 demonstrate that what matters eventually is not the fiscal deficit in a particular year or a rule of thumb for the government debt-to-GDP ratio (like the Maastricht criterion of 60 percent) but whether or not the market believes the government can muster the future primary surpluses it needs to pay off its debt; in other words, whether the market believes the government intertemporal budget constraint is healthy. If it does not, real interest rates would go up as creditors would demand a risk premium to compensate for the possibility of default. The cost of capital could then exceed levels that the private sector would find acceptable for making profitable investments in a competitive world. This would impact growth prospects and future taxes adversely, imperiling fiscal sustainability and solvency, concepts that are defined in Box 3.1. The soundness of the government intertemporal budget constraint (GIBC) is therefore the bedrock on which strategies for fast growth must be developed, linking the GC and the Washington Consensus.

From an historical perspective, an important insight from Box 3.1 is that the policy concerns surrounding the "external debt overhang" of the 1980s are strikingly similar to those where "public debt sustainability" and "solvency" became issues during the emerging market crises of 1997–2001. In the latter case, investment and growth suffered because of high real interest rates, macroeconomic uncertainty, and uncertainty about future taxation. Governments raised primary surpluses by cutting public investments—even those in infrastructure, which would have been beneficial from a long-run growth and solvency perspective—until they were able to restore creditworthiness. This fueled a debate known as the "fiscal space" controversy, which will be discussed in Chapter 8.

**Box 3.1**  Debt Sustainability, Solvency, and Overhangs in Emerging Markets

The trajectory of the government's debt-to-GDP ratio (its "debt dynamics") depends upon the primary fiscal deficit, real interest rates, and growth rates.[a] In addition, exchange rate movements affect the debt-to-GDP ratio, as some debt is typically denominated in foreign currency. And government indebtedness could go up if it is forced to bail out the private sector.

**Fiscal Solvency:** The government is solvent when the market believes the present value of future primary surpluses, discounted at rates close to the risk-free rate, is sufficient to pay off the outstanding debt; otherwise, the debt will need to be priced at a discount, with yields rising.[b] Solvency problems would thus be manifested in high real interest rates on domestic debt and high international bond spreads relative to a benchmark country like the USA or Germany.

**Public Debt Sustainability:** The debt-to-GDP ratio is said to be sustainable when no drastic change in the prevailing mix of policies is required. Private investors do not demand high-risk premia to buy government debt and the economy moves along without fear of a fiscal or macroeconomic crisis with the debt-to-GDP ratio on an acceptable trajectory to private investors.

**External Debt Overhang:** This concept, developed by Paul Krugman (1988) and Jeffrey Sachs (1989) during the 1980s debt crisis, refers to a situation where the market does not expect a country's sovereign debt to be fully repaid. The debt then trades at a discount reflecting the probability of default and the expected recovery rate (how many cents on the dollar creditors will receive if default occurs). As a result of an overhang:

- The government is unlikely to be able to borrow *even* for public investments where the economic rate of return exceeds the marginal cost of borrowing.
- Firms would be reluctant to invest even in profitable projects for fear that their returns would be taxed away to service the debt, while politicians would balk at implementing difficult reform as the benefits would be captured by the external creditors (Corden 1989).
- A debt write-down would potentially benefit both the country and creditors; but each creditor would prefer to "free ride" on debt reduction by the others, and gain on her/his entire holding of the country's debt as the secondary market price would tend to rise after the reduction. This "free rider" problem formed the rationale for the March 1989 Brady Plan, whereby the US government threw its weight behind a coordinated debt reduction to break the deadlock in resolving the Latin American debt crisis.

---

[a] I shall derive these results very soon in Box 3.2 with more detailed derivations in Annex 2.

[b] The more common way of defining solvency is to say that the present value of the future primary surplus-to-GDP ratios (discounted at a rate equal to the real interest rate minus the real growth rate) exceeds the initial debt-to-GDP ratio. For a complete derivation and technical discussion, see Burnside (2005), or the technical annex in Aizenman and Pinto (2005).

Another interesting parallel is that the *fundamental causes* of the 1980s debt crisis and emerging market crises of 1997–2001 were the same: unsustainable fiscal deficits combined with policy, institutional, and political economy weaknesses that either enriched political elites at the expense of the taxpayer or resulted in massive bailouts of an overextended private sector.[3] There was another noteworthy constant across the debt crises of the 1980s and 1990s: fixed exchange rates, either explicitly or implicitly; and open capital accounts. Not surprisingly, the *corrective measures* for the crises of the 1980s and 1997–2001 were similar. For example, Jeffrey Sachs (1990) pinpointed the following factors as distinguishing countries which exited the 1980s debt crisis quickly from those which got mired in it: (i) how the borrowed money was used;[4] (ii) the long-run growth strategy in terms of fiscal policy and outward orientation, including competitive real exchange rates; and (iii) speed of policy adjustment to the two exogenous shocks of the early 1980s (the sharp decline in the debtor countries' terms of trade following the OPEC oil price hike and the large increase in interest rates in the USA).

These were essentially the same requirements for emerging markets to exit the crises of 1997–2001. But there were two important differences. First, while there were debt defaults in Russia and Argentina, emerging markets by and large managed the aftermath of 1997–2001 crises on their own, without any major official intervention, as we shall see in Chapter 9. In fact, there was a sharp change for the better in economic governance. Second, emerging markets switched en masse to flexible exchange rates and embarked on a path of self-insurance, an important topic pursued in Part Three.

### Binding Constraint: It's Mostly Fiscal![5]

In their 2005 paper on growth diagnostics, Ricardo Hausmann, Dani Rodrik, and Andres Velasco set out to identify *the* binding constraint to growth. They apply their diagnostic framework to Brazil over the period 1998–2004 and conclude that the then binding constraint to growth was national savings. Using their own logic, I shall argue that if there was a binding constraint to growth over that period, it was Brazil's GIBC. Box 3.2 contains a refresher on macroeconomic accounting and government debt dynamics that should come in handy.

**Box 3.2** A Refresher on Macroeconomic Accounting

A useful open economy accounting identity is the following:

$$\text{National Saving} = \text{Investment} + \text{Current Account Surplus.} \qquad (i)$$

It says national saving can either go into investment at home or be lent abroad via the accumulation of current account surpluses, and can be derived from the national income identity:

$$Y = C^{pvt} + I^{pvt} + G + (X - M), \qquad (ii)$$

where $Y$ is gross national income, $C^{pvt}$ and $I^{pvt}$ are private consumption and investment respectively, and $G$ is government spending, which can be written as $G = C^G + I^G$, that is, as a sum of its consumption and investment components. If we define $X$ and $M$ as the exports and imports, respectively, of goods, services, and factor income (profits, dividends, and remittances), subtract taxes $T$ from both sides of equation (ii) and rearrange terms, we can get: $\left(Y - T - C^{pvt}\right) + \left(T - C^G\right) = \left(I^{pvt} + I^G\right) + CAS$, where the two terms in brackets on the left-hand side of the equation are private saving and government saving, respectively, which add up to national saving; and the right-hand side is simply total investment plus the current account surplus, reproducing equation (i).

Now for some fiscal and government debt accounting. The fiscal deficit is simply the excess of government spending over its revenues, denoted $T$:

$\textit{Fiscal deficit} = G - T = C^G + I^G - T = I^G - \left(T - C^G\right) = I^G - S^G$. Thus, the fiscal deficit is also the excess of government investment over its saving, a useful identity.

It is useful to break up government consumption $C^G$ into two components: noninterest current expenditure, $NICE$, and interest payments on government debt, $iD$, where $i$ is the nominal interest rate and $D$ is government debt, and rewrite the fiscal deficit as: $G - T = \left[\left(NICE + I^G\right) - T\right] + iD$. The first term on the right-hand side (RHS) in round brackets is primary expenditure, while the term in square brackets is the primary deficit. Thus, the fiscal deficit is the primary deficit plus interest payments; and two equivalent ways of writing the fiscal deficit are:

$$\text{Fiscal deficit} = \text{Primary deficit} + \text{Interest payments} = \text{Government}$$
$$\text{investment—Government saving.}$$

Now assume the government borrows to finance its deficit. Then the increase in its debt, $\dot{D}$, is given by:

$$\dot{D} = G - T = PD + iD, \qquad (iii)$$

where *PD* stands for "primary deficit"; and if we define *d* as the ratio of debt to GDP, we can use (iii) and simple calculus to show that:

$$\dot{d} = pd + \left(i - g^{N}\right)d, \tag{iv}$$

where $\dot{d}$ is the change in the government debt-to-GDP ratio, *pd* is the ratio of the primary deficit to GDP, and $g^{N}$ is the nominal growth rate of GDP.[a]

This is enough to equip us to go through the rest of this chapter. Annex 2 and Chapters 5 and 7 on Kenya and Russia build on this box to bring in the effects of inflation and exchange rates on government debt dynamics.

---

[a] This is a continuous-time formulation. In practice, a discrete-time version of (iv) is used, of which a derivation may be found in the annex to Aizenman and Pinto (2005).

Hausmann, Rodrik, and Velasco summarize the determinants of the return to capital in a manner that should be familiar after Chapter 2:

$$r = r\left(A, \mu, x\right). \tag{3.1}$$

In equation (3.1), *r* is the return to capital, *A* is the country's TFP level, $\mu$ is an index of externalities, and *x* captures the availability of complementary inputs such as human capital or infrastructure. Including externalities allows for some form of non-diminishing returns and hence self-sustaining "endogenous" growth along the lines found in Romer and Lucas's work. And it is well known that human capital and infrastructure are prime constraints to faster growth in developing countries. Equation (3.1) feeds into a policy checklist, which forms the core of the diagnostics. The diagnostics are carried out by asking a series of questions based on a binary "decision-tree" approach, in order to zero in on the binding constraint through a process of elimination. Hausmann, Rodrik, and Velasco allow for unstable macroeconomics, bad financial intermediation, corruption, property rights, and so on—questions with a bearing on the return to private investment and evocative of the content of Table 3.1.

Hausmann, Rodrik, and Velasco start their growth diagnosis of Brazil by demonstrating, in two steps, that returns to private investment were high over the period under consideration. First, they argue that there was a paucity of savings in Brazil:

with a debt [in 1998] already at 460 percent of exports, the scarcity of savings was reflected in a spread on external bonds of 1226 basis points and in a real ex-post overnight (SELIC) interest rate of over 30 percent. In January 1999 the country was forced to devalue: the real multilateral exchange rate depreciated by 37.4 percent in 1999...In short, the country has been trying to cope with the paucity of domestic savings by both attempting to attract foreign savings and by remunerating domestic savings at very high real rates.

(Hausmann, Rodrik, and Velasco 2005, excerpts from pp. 12–13)

Second, they infer that returns to investment are high from the following fact: "In spite of very high overnight real interests and very high intermediation costs, investment has outstripped domestic savings and the country has used its capacity to borrow abroad from the rest of the world to the hilt" (p. 14).

But most country economists would look at a bond spread of 1226 basis points and real interest rates of 30 percent and think instantly of default and devaluation risks—in other words, about the sustainability of the public finances and the GIBC. In this case, the binding constraint would be not the level of *national saving* but the *creditworthiness* of the government; or, put another way, insufficient primary surpluses relative to the level of public debt in the eyes of market investors (recall Box 3.1).

So convinced are Hausmann, Rodrik, and Velasco that national saving is the binding constraint to growth that they argue against policies to improve the business environment such as "lowering taxes, reducing public sector prices and improving infrastructure and education [because such measures] may in fact lower public savings and thus reduce total savings."[6] *But a big, if not the single biggest, item impeding public saving and hence national saving is missing in Hausmann, Rodrik, and Velasco's list: interest payments on public debt.* If these are high because of unsustainable public finances and the attendant risk premia, reestablishing creditworthiness and lowering interest rates, and hence interest payments on public debt, could be the most effective way of increasing public saving. This indeed appears to have been the situation in Brazil at the time, as we shall see in Chapter 8.

Governments in the situation Brazil found itself in after 1998 are often forced to cut public investment in infrastructure to raise primary surpluses until they have persuaded the market of their creditworthiness. This strategy involves a tradeoff, which constitutes the core of the fiscal space controversy discussed in Chapter 8: raising primary surpluses by cutting infrastructure investment reduces aggregate demand *and* constrains private investment. This could have harmful effects on long-run growth, hurting debt sustainability. But raising primary surpluses could also lower risk premia and have a beneficial impact on public saving—as interest payments on public debt will go down—*and* on the private cost of capital. After their crises of 1997–2001, most emerging markets went down the higher primary surplus route. The Brazilian government had two choices: default and renegotiate its debt, or run higher primary surpluses. It chose the latter with eventually beneficial results, as we shall see in Chapter 8. Turkey did pretty much the same, as Chapter 9 will show.

## The Micropolicy Trio

Let's go back to equation (3.1) on the returns to capital in order to motivate the micropolicy trio of hard budgets, competition, and competitive real exchange rates. The big growth challenge is how to increase the growth rate of the country's TFP, $A$, which is pre-eminent in the neoclassical growth accounting results of Solow and Denison, and serves as the prime explanation for the lack of income convergence in endogenous growth models. The innovative 1992 paper by Philippe Aghion and Peter Howitt, referred to in Chapter 2, tackles this fundamental question in a way that has considerable relevance for emerging markets. The two authors develop a new framework in which TFP growth is generated by quality-improving innovations in intermediate goods. This framework brings Schumpeterian creative destruction into growth theory by having new intermediate inputs displace the "incumbent" input in a multi-sector framework. New innovations build on the entire stock of knowledge (past inputs) while pushing the global technological frontier out. Growth is accompanied by creative destruction in the form of new innovators pushing out old ones.

Countries can grow through two innovation channels: leading edge innovation, which pushes out the global technological frontier; and implementation of existing innovations, or imitation, which improves quality and raises productivity. Growth is determined by the frequency of each type of innovation, leading edge versus imitation, and the respective frequencies are determined endogenously by profit-maximizing innovators. For given frequencies of innovation, countries will grow faster the farther they are from the global technology frontier because this increases the return to imitation based on knowledge spillovers across countries. The Aghion–Howitt model thus allows convergence based on distance from the frontier, the analogue of convergence based on diminishing returns to capital in the Solow model.

Aghion and Steven Durlauf (2007) elaborate on the growth policy implications of the model just described. They make two arguments: first, all countries, irrespective of the state of their development, need to ensure basics such as intellectual property rights, deeper financial sectors, better human capital, and macroeconomic stability. This list has already been encountered in Table 3.1. Second, the efficacy of other policies (most of which also feature in Table 3.1), such as promoting product market competition and free entry, higher education and stock market finance, varies across countries, regions, and sectors depending upon the distance from the frontier. These factors are more effective the shorter the distance to the frontier because they stimulate leading edge innovation, which is more beneficial for growth than imitation in this circumstance. They illustrate the different emphases in policy by contrasting the growth experiences of the USA and the European Union. The latter has fallen behind the USA because, as it caught up with the USA and approached the global technological frontier, it has not focused sufficiently on product market competition, higher education, and R&D.

A literal interpretation of the Aghion–Durlauf model would suggest that product market competition is not that important for emerging markets because of their distance from the frontier. However, the country stories on Poland and Russia bring out the indispensability of such competition in conjunction with hard budgets and competitive real exchange rates—the micropolicy trio—for placing developing countries on faster growth trajectories. This finding is not confined to transition countries in Europe. The stories on Kenya and India also single out import competition as a vital force for growth. In addition, neither country has had soft budgets for the private sector. This trio, as a complement to lowering legal and regulatory barriers to entry and exit, would put pressure on incumbent firms to innovate and facilitate Schumpeterian creative destruction. Box 3.3 contains the famous Hungarian economist János Kornai's articulation of the hard budget constraint. We shall see from the stories on Poland and Russia that the process

---

**Box 3.3** János Kornai's Hard Budget Constraint[a]

A hard budget refers to financial discipline: a firm should pay its bills and taxes on time; if it does not, its suppliers are free to stop doing business with it. The government should prosecute for nonpayment of taxes, banks should not be compelled to lend to unprofitable firms, and so on. But, ultimately, a hard budget is a political signal that unviable firms will not be bailed out. As Kornai (1986, p. 8) notes: "What is really important is the psychological effect of the constraint.... It reflects in a financial form a deeper socio-economic phenomenon."

On the firm-level impact, Kornai (1986, pp. 10–11) notes: "Schumpeter...emphasized...'constructive destruction': the elimination of old products, technologies, organizations which were surpassed by the more efficient new ones. The soft budget constraint protects the old production line, the inefficient firm against constructive destruction and thus impedes innovation and development." Thus, hard budgets and creative destruction go hand in hand in creating incentives for the adoption of new technologies, higher productivity, and thus faster growth.

What about the social consequences? Kornai (1986, pp. 26–7) notes that "A system based on a perfectly hard budget constraint [...] is a terribly cruel one. [...] Efficiency and security-solidarity are to a large extent conflicting goals."

The Russian stabilization of 1995–8, which was derailed by soft budgets for firms even as workers were not being paid, contradicts this observation of Kornai's, and is discussed in Chapter 7. The solution is for countries to have social insurance and social safety nets for vulnerable individuals and families as a complement to hard budgets for firms and banks. I do not discuss social insurance in this book.

---

[a] Kornai (1986).

---

of both hardening and softening budget constraints is subtle and rife with political economy considerations.

I shall now discuss the importance of the real exchange rate by appealing to the transition from central planning to a market economy in Central and Eastern Europe, which began in 1990. The immediate challenge was how to avoid big output losses and get growth going again—not least to maintain popular support for market-based reform. It quickly dawned that a key factor was going to be the willingness of the government to harden budgets for manufacturing firms and expose them to import competition. For Poland and Russia, this had to be done at the same time as placing public debt on a sustainable trajectory and lowering inflation from high levels. The typical strategy for lowering inflation was to fix the nominal exchange rate—but this almost unavoidably leads to a sharp appreciation of the real exchange rate, leaving little breathing room for enterprises suddenly exposed to hard budgets and competition, making it much harder for them to adjust.

As it turns out, Russia focused on attaining single-digit inflation, ignoring the consequences for the real exchange rate and failing to harden budgets. Poland's approach was diametrically opposed: to harden budgets, increase import competition and let inflation decline gradually in line with fiscal consolidation, with a large nominal devaluation in its second year of transition. Their contrasting transition experiences described in Part Two bring out the efficacy of the micropolicy trio; but this should not convey the impression that the micropolicy trio was relevant only for the transition countries. It was equally important in countries as disparate as India and Kenya, even though the effects were more obvious in the transition economies because of the large, discontinuous changes they had to adapt to.

The challenge, therefore, is twofold: use hard budget constraints and import competition to nudge firms into innovating via the imitation channel of the Aghion–Howitt model, thereby facilitating self-sustaining growth; and keep real exchange rates competitive in order to give firms a reasonable chance against import competition. Box 3.4 sets out the notion of competitive real exchange rates.

## Managing Volatility

While economic volatility has been around forever, it has emerged as a separate branch of macroeconomics only over the last two decades. It has been added to the list of formidable impediments to income convergence because it has strong harmful effects on long-run growth, especially in poor countries.[7] The ability to manage volatility well depends upon governance, institutions, and shock-absorbing wealth cushions. Rich countries have big advantages in all these areas, keeping them ahead—although the lingering consequences of the global financial crisis of 2008–9 and the entrenched sovereign debt-cum-banking crisis in the Eurozone shows even they are not immune to crises and volatility.

From a welfare perspective, we care about the volatility of output and consumption. The natural hope is that the "ups" in these variables will

**Box 3.4** Competitive Real Exchange Rates

At the *macroeconomic* level, a competitive real exchange rate prevents an unsustainable pattern of current account deficits, which would lead to an unsupportable burden of external debt. At the *microeconomic* level, it helps domestic firms to compete with imports. So, while liberalizing trade puts pressure on domestic firms to innovate and become more productive, a competitive real exchange rate enables them to respond without going bust.

How do we know whether the real exchange rate is on an equilibrium path—which is an aspect of its being competitive? This is more art than science. Suppose the real exchange rate is appreciating. You are likely to have as many economists saying it is overvalued as saying the opposite. But real appreciation *by itself* does not mean the real exchange rate has become overvalued. One should look at *macroeconomic* correlates. Suppose real appreciation is accompanied by slowing growth, a rising current account deficit, and falling foreign exchange reserves. These would be red flags warning of an incipient real overvaluation.

But there are also *microeconomic* correlates, which tend to receive less attention. Consider this astute observation by Rudi Dornbusch and Alejandro Werner in a 1994 paper on Mexico (Dornbusch and Werner 1994, p. 270), published a few months before the peso was "attacked" that December: "greater access to world capital markets brings about equilibrium real appreciation. It also improves welfare for workers while rewarding owners of existing capital. Everybody wins, even the government, since the tax base and hence tax revenues expand." It follows that if the tax base is shrinking and workers are not being paid then a real appreciation means the real exchange rate is becoming overvalued *even* if the current account is in balance. That's what happened in Russia in 1998. But if real appreciation is accompanied by rising productivity which keeps firms in the traded goods sector competitive by preventing unit labor costs from getting out of control, then one could say the real appreciation is fine.

Another important lesson has been learned during the recession that followed the global financial crisis of 2008–9: emerging markets where commercial banks had developed currency mismatches by borrowing overseas in dollars or Swiss francs and on-lending in local currency to individuals for mortgages or firms in the non-traded goods sectors could not allow their currencies to depreciate in order to switch domestic demand toward domestic goods, as this might have led to widespread bankruptcy.[a] This is likely to have worsened their own recessions.

---

[a] NB: Even if banks on-lent in foreign currency for houses there is going to be a problem because their borrowers could go bust if the amount they owe suddenly goes up with a real depreciation.

compensate for the "downs" and outweigh them over time. But downs, if deep enough, impair the ability to benefit from the subsequent ups. This is the core reason why volatility, or the standard deviation of growth, has a negative impact on long-run growth, or growth averaged over long periods: high volatility or a proclivity to big output drops could result in crossing some threshold which triggers negative consequences, like a debt crisis, or a reversal in capital flows. At the family level, bankruptcy or the forced fire sale of a key income-earning asset makes it difficult to benefit fully from the subsequent ups. Thus, harmful consequences accumulate, and contrive over time to lower average growth, especially if adverse shocks are a repeated phenomenon.

Box 3.5 contains themes uncovered by the evolving literature on volatility. These include social conflict, fiscal and debt policy, financial sectors and institutions: areas in which developing countries have had prominent weaknesses.

### External versus Domestic Volatility

A common source of *external* volatility for developing countries is terms-of-trade (ToT) shocks. But the eventual impact is amplified or attenuated by a host of domestic factors revolving around the public finances and the financial system. The 1980s debt crisis is a good example. It was triggered by two external shocks: the decline in the debtor countries' ToT when oil prices rose; and the large increase in interest rates in the USA, which fed through into the interest rates that money center banks were charging Latin American countries on their floating rate debt. This triggered a third external shock: a "sudden stop" in capital inflows as banks became reluctant to roll over their loans, forcing Latin American countries to switch to printing money to finance their deficits, with many rationing foreign exchange, leading to rising black market exchange premia. The factors that Jeffrey Sachs identified as distinguishing countries such as Korea, which exited the crisis quickly, from those which got stuck in it, have been listed in the section "The Government Intertemporal Budget Constraint." These factors ultimately have to do with the quality of governance and institutions and center on the GIBC and the bailout of banks run by well-connected political groups.

Weak governance and institutions are the main channel for *domestic* volatility, while also amplifying external shocks. Claudio Raddatz (2007) found

**Box 3.5**  Prominent Themes in Volatility

**Volatility Matters for Long-Run Growth:** Garey Ramey and Valerie Ramey (1995) were the first to demonstrate the negative relationship between volatility and long-run growth in a study that included both the Organization for Economic Co-operation and Development (OECD) and developing countries.

**Social Conflict and Poor Governance Worsen Growth Shocks:** Dani Rodrik (1999) examined the drop in growth rates for various groups of countries between 1960 and 1975, and 1975 and 1989. While the external shocks were similar in magnitude, East Asian countries were apt to recover faster and do better than countries in Latin America, the Middle East, or Sub-Saharan Africa. The key difference was in responses to the shock via fiscal adjustment and relative price changes and the maintenance of productivity—an ability determined by social cohesion (proxied by measures of ethnolinguistic fragmentation) and the quality of governance and the rule of law. Thus, it was not the size of the external shock per se but how it interacted with domestic social institutions, governance, and the rule of law.

**Voracity and Bad Fiscal Policy Turn Windfalls into a Curse:** Philip Lane and Aaron Tornell (1999) emphasize the capture of fiscal policy by politically powerful groups which compete to corner the gains from positive productivity shocks—which are similar to ToT improvements linked to commodity price windfalls. This could lead to voracity or an increase in consumption today which exceeds the windfall, resulting in lower investment and future growth. This idea extends in a natural way to the experience of oil exporters, where a big debt-financed increase in spending during an oil price boom could lead to a debt overhang and stagnation once oil prices fall, as happened in Venezuela and Nigeria. Such problems are magnified by corruption and bad policy aimed at enriching the political elite at the expense of the next generation.

**Financial Sectors Could Easily Get Out of Hand:** William Easterly, Roumeen Islam, and Joseph Stiglitz (2000) examined the drivers of growth volatility itself and highlighted the financial system as a prime determinant. Up to a point, greater financial depth is associated with lower growth volatility; but as financial depth and leverage grow, the financial sector could itself become a source of vulnerability. Few would quarrel with this idea given the events of the past few years. It is worth adding that the fiscal costs of cleaning up the financial sector could become another drag on growth, should a crisis occur.

**Institutions are Key:** Daron Acemoglu and colleagues (2003) argued that crises are caused by bad macroeconomic policies, which increase volatility and lower growth. And that bad macro policies, in turn, are the product of weak institutions. They developed a method to isolate the "historically determined component of institutions" based on the colonization strategy pursed by European settlers, showing this to be the key determinant of volatility, crises, and growth.

*Source:* Mainly Box 2, Overview Aizenman and Pinto (2005).

that external shocks stemming from the terms of trade, natural disasters, real per capita GDP movements in rich countries, humanitarian disasters, and aid flows affected real per capita GDP in low-income countries but accounted for only 11 percent of the volatility of real GDP in these countries. By inference, shocks stemming from domestic economic management, political instability, and violent conflict are considerably more important. Combining this finding with the results reported in Viktoria Hnatkovska and Norman Loayza (2005) on the negative causal impact of volatility on growth, which is accentuated in poor countries with weak institutions, the conclusion is clear: much of the action needed to lower volatility and promote sustained long-run growth has to be homegrown. We shall encounter this conclusion with a vengeance in Chapter 5, which focuses on Kenya.

## Strengthening Institutions

Their superiority in institutional development relative to developing countries is a major reason why the effects of volatility have tended to be muted in countries with advanced economies. However, the ongoing sovereign debt-cum-banking crisis and the need for restoring economic growth via structural reform in Europe suggest that even in advanced countries, the GIBC and the micropolicy trio are central to the growth agenda. The advantage such countries have is that their institutions are more credible, buying them time to adjust.

An implication of the pioneering study of Daron Acemoglu and colleagues (2003) is that there is no quick fix for institutions. Nigeria's experience indicates how difficult the path is. In 2003, the government took a big step forward in addressing the decades-long devastation flowing from the bad decisions made during the oil boom of the 1970s based on a fundamental improvement in fiscal institutions. A little background on commodity price booms will help set the stage.

In the early 1980s, the emphasis of economists, as a result of booming oil prices, was on Dutch Disease. Traded goods could always be imported, but the only way to satisfy the increased demand for non-traded goods was to let their relative price rise via a real appreciation. This would lure labor and other resources toward non-traded goods production, leading to a decline in manufacturing and agriculture. This sounds like efficient adjustment, but

Sweder van Wijnbergen pointed out in 1984 that if learning-by-doing externalities were present in manufacturing, even a temporary shrinkage would
impair productivity growth and, hence, long-run growth—the *"disease"*
aspect of oil booms. Subsequently, when oil prices fell, the emphasis shifted
to *public finances and debt* (had governments saved or run deficits during the
boom years?), and then, eventually, to *governance and institutions* (had corruption, voracity, and bad policy fueled debt overhangs and impoverishment
that went far beyond the pure economic "disease"?). Motivated by actual
developments in oil-exporting countries, the thinking grew beyond the efficient mechanics of adjusting to a commodity price boom to the management
of the public finances and, eventually, to the quality of governance and fiscal institutions. Box 3.6 tells the story of Nigeria's attempt to overcome its
bad legacy and manage volatility better—something that would have been
unthinkable without a sea change in attitudes at the very top.

## Summing Up

Theory stresses savings and investment (in physical and human capital) and,
ultimately, technology, knowledge spillovers, and learning-by-doing externalities in driving long-run growth. Advanced economies have advantages
in all these areas which developing countries may not find easy to erode,
impeding income convergence. In addition, developing countries, especially
low-income countries, could be hurt by bad governance, conflict, corruption,
scandals, and weak institutions, making it difficult to shield long-run growth
from volatility.

Nonetheless, much is within the control of developing countries. Once the
leadership has decided that it wants faster growth for the benefit of all the
citizens, the natural starting point is the better management of the government intertemporal budget constraint; after all, this is the most visible sign
of good governance, with far-reaching consequences. Private investors will
be helped by the more reasonable interest rates and the longer horizons that
sustainable public finances will foster. Basics like property rights, law and
order, and good fiscal and financial institutions—all of which are taken for
granted in advanced economies—will reinforce a positive climate for private investment by lowering risk. Combining this with hard budgets and
import competition would improve resource allocation *and* generate pressure

**Box 3.6** Nigeria—Managing Volatility Better

Not only was there no public saving in Nigeria during the oil price booms of 1973–4 and 1980–1, fiscal deficits rose to 7–8 percent of GDP, amplifying oil price volatility. By the mid-1980s, when oil prices had collapsed, Nigeria's external debt was $19 billion and it began to experience debt-servicing difficulties. Agriculture, once the mainstay of the economy, and non-oil exports, had been decimated by a combination of Dutch Disease and bad policy. By 1985, the real producer prices for cocoa, cotton, and palm oil were 50 percent of their levels in 1975; and just 30 percent for rubber, groundnuts, and soybeans. This was because of monopolistic official commodity boards and the refusal to let the naira depreciate when oil prices fell. Instead, exchange controls were intensified. By 1985, the black market foreign exchange premium was over 300 percent, penalizing agriculture further as procurement prices were set with reference to the official exchange rate. Besides, not much of the earlier public expenditure boom had been directed to help agriculture via better research and extension or rural infrastructure.

Volatility had interacted with weak governance, voracity, and corruption to produce an eventual debt overhang and economic stagnation: per capita GDP *fell* from $264 in 1970 to $256 in 2001 (constant 1995 US dollars) in spite of receipts of $300 billion from oil over this period. In 2001, per capita electric power consumption was just one-fourth of the low-income country average. In 2003, the infant mortality rate was 101 per 1000 live births compared to 79 in low-income countries.

Against the odds, the Nigerian government secured a historic write-off of $18 billion on the $30 billion it owed the Paris Club in 2005. This would have been unthinkable had the government not taken drastic steps to begin the process of fiscal reform and fight corruption. The centerpiece was the adoption of an oil-price-based fiscal rule in 2004: the budget would be based on a conservative reference price with the surplus saved. Nigeria obtained a BB– sovereign credit rating, and economic growth picked up, from 2 percent during the decade ending in 2002 to 6 percent overall and 9 percent for the non-oil economy.

But the central bank was slow to let the naira depreciate when oil prices started falling as the global financial crisis set in after the collapse of Lehman Brothers. Some $17 billion in reserves were used up before exchange restrictions were phased out later in 2009. Concerns appeared about the accuracy of the financial reporting of commercial banks and their exposure to the stock market on account of margin lending for purchasing stocks. Fortunately, decisive steps were taken by the central bank to avoid a systemic crisis. As of mid-2011, yet another administration has signaled its determination to complete the process of governance and structural reform while addressing the infrastructure deficit and improving service delivery.

**The Lesson:** Manage volatility badly, even for a short period, and end up paying dearly for a long time. Corrective action must focus on the public finances and the banking system, underpinned by good governance and committed leadership from the very top.

*Source:* Okonjo-Iweala (2008, 2012), Pinto (1987), and Budina, Pang, and van Wijnbergen (2007).

for adopting better technology, spurring faster TFP growth, while a healthy GIBC will facilitate both reasonable real interest rates and competitive real exchange rates. All this would place the economy on a more positive path.

While much can be done, long lags are likely to be involved before the change in direction becomes credible and entrenched. This will become apparent in the country stories in Part Two. The much-worn cliché, "staying the course," is of the essence as policymakers put the GIBC on a sound footing, implement the complementary micropolicy trio, and take steps to improve the management of volatility.

## Notes

1. Lin and Rosenblatt (2012, table 2). Ten percent is not a particularly ambitious threshold for a 58-year period.
2. Rodrik does not explicitly equate the GC with the new approach, although he notes that its report "emphasizes that each country must devise its own mix of remedies." His use of the word "diagnostic" evokes the growth diagnostics framework of Hausmann, Rodrik, and Velasco (2005), which I discuss later in this chapter.
3. The 1997–8 crises in East Asia (with the exception of the Philippines) originated in the private sector but constituted a contingent and then actual fiscal liability as the private sector was bailed out.
4. Sachs (1990, p. 13) noted that during 1976–85, "about two-thirds of the increase in gross external debt in Argentina and Mexico went to finance private capital flight…" Capital flight was also a serious concern during Russia's 1998 public debt crisis.
5. There is a quip in Washington circles that "IMF" stands for "It's Mostly Fiscal."
6. Hausmann, Rodrik, and Velasco (2005, p. 19); material in square brackets added. This statement confuses "primary surpluses" and "public saving." All the items in this list have an impact on public saving except for infrastructure; raising public investment in infrastructure will lower the primary surplus but have no effect on public saving.
7. This section draws liberally from the Overview chapter of a 2005 volume on volatility edited by Joshua Aizenman and myself (Aizenman and Pinto 2005).

# PART TWO

## Country Stories

The next four chapters constitute the core of the book in that they illustrate why country economics is different from academic economics. And, not surprisingly, each country is different as well. These country experiences capture live examples of the workings of an economy. In each case, the the prior hypotheses about economic problems in the country and how to redress them using theory and the conventional wisdom were not just mildly, but severely, flawed. Nevertheless, the priors were valuable in defining what data to look for and what analysis to conduct, which served as the catalyst for arriving at the eventual conclusion. The difficulty, as noted in Chapter 1, is that the priors are often hard to argue with because they appear convincing, so the country economist may be tempted to stop right there.

For me, Russia in 1998 during the months before its crisis is a case in point. It was hard to go where the evidence led and say that debt was on an unsustainable course, that growth was unlikely to materialize, and, above all, that the high real interest rates and real appreciation spawned by the stabilization program were a root cause of the problem. Influential economists were convinced otherwise and even the leaders of the G7 took turns issuing proclamations that Russia must not be allowed to fail. I remember asking myself whether economics really worked and then discovering that it did—and with a vengeance.

One caveat: an occupational hazard of working on emerging markets is that economic data are often revised, and sometimes only partially, making it difficult to obtain a consistent time series over a given historical period. This applies especially to Kenya. I have presented my results as obtained in real time but am confident that the policy findings reported here remain robust.

# CHAPTER 4

# Why Poland Beat the Odds

*Most important, Poland must begin a rapid process of privatization of state firms, not only to assure efficient resource use in the future, but to prevent the collapse of the stabilization itself in the medium term.*

—David Lipton and Jeffrey Sachs, Key Advisers to Poland (1990a, p. 127)

In 2009, during the worst of the global financial crisis, Poland's economy was the only one in the European Union (EU) to actually grow.[1] The Finance Minister attributed its success to the "innate structural strengths" of the economy and measures taken to prop up aggregate demand. He also pointed to the slowdown the economy had suffered earlier in 2001, "which wrung out a lot of inefficiencies out of the business sector, leaving companies much better prepared."[2]

About six months later, in a speech at Jagiellonian University in Krakow, Olivier Blanchard, chief economist of the IMF, pointed out that Poland's per capita GDP had grown by an impressive 3.1 percent per year from 1989 to 2009, compared to just 1.8 percent for both Hungary and the Czech Republic.[3] He attributed this to neoclassical income convergence: Poland had been much poorer than the other two countries in 1989. Ultimately, therefore, the individual policies or very different approaches to privatization did not appear to have mattered much. But Blanchard's conclusion still leaves the question open about what specifically the three countries did, since we know from Chapters 2 and 3 that convergence is riddled with pitfalls. Capital frequently flows in the "wrong" direction for the reasons adduced by Robert Lucas in his 1990 paper.

To shed light on what Poland did, we have to go back 25 years to the fall of the Berlin Wall, which heralded the collapse of the Soviet empire and the start of the transition from central planning to a market economy in Central and Eastern Europe. Few countries symbolize this transition better than Poland. Stalin reportedly compared bringing communism to Poland to trying to saddle a cow. Would bringing capitalism back, therefore, be easy? Part of the agenda, such as achieving macroeconomic stabilization, or privatizing state-owned enterprises (SOEs), had been encountered in other countries. Other areas, such as reestablishing the institutions of a market economy to protect property rights, and ensuring a functioning and well-supervised financial sector and an appropriate tax system—all while redefining the roles of the state and the private sector—represented a far bigger challenge. On the institutional agenda, Poland would be imitating the USA and Western Europe. *But there was no tried and tested blueprint for implementing all these changes at the same time and on such a large scale.* This ignited debates about speed and comprehensiveness in implementation, about "big bang" versus "gradual" strategies and in what sequence to implement change. In the words of Poland's own architect of reform, Leszek Balcerowicz, the country was embarking on an *Economic Transformation Program*, not simply tweaking polices or implementing marginal change.

Blanchard's clinical 2010 assessment was thus a far cry from 1990, when the transition began in Central and Eastern Europe amidst considerable uncertainty and even fear about how it would play out. Much of the attention then focused on Poland—not only because it was the largest country embarking on a program of radical reform, but also because failure would have been catastrophic. Poland was a test case for the contest between the collapsing centrally planned system of communism and the "triumphant" free market system of Western capitalism. The ideological stakes were high.

As it turns out, Poland's immediate economic challenges were all macroeconomic in nature. In addition to a thriving black market for dollars and a heavy external debt, inflation rose to hyperinflationary levels in the latter half of 1989 as worker-controlled SOEs sought to preemptively raise their wages in anticipation of the switch to a market economy. This was a formidable combination of problems, described in Lipton and Sachs' (1990a) work. But at least one had an inkling about how to deal with them as there were other countries' experiences to draw upon, most of them in Latin America. The microeconomic challenges would prove more daunting.

Once the first noncommunist government since World War II was installed in September 1989, Poland cut its fiscal deficit substantially by slashing subsidies and public investment spending. It also devalued the zloty to bridge the gap with the black market exchange rate, tightened credit policy and reduced real wages by partial indexation of nominal wages to inflation. As a result, the zloty actually *appreciated* in the black market, from about 10,000 zloty per dollar in September 1989 to around 7000 by early December—a remarkable feat given the usually explosive and unstable dynamics associated with black markets for foreign exchange. The official exchange rate reached 6500 by the end of December and, eventually, was devalued by another 45 percent and fixed as a nominal anchor for price stabilization at 9500 zloty to the dollar on January 1, 1990. It was also made convertible for the current account and internal portfolio transactions. It was devalued *beyond* the then black market rate, resulting in a substantial real depreciation and giving the manufacturing sector, dominated by large SOEs, considerable breathing room as trade was liberalized and import competition increased.

## Would Macroeconomic Stringency Be Enough?

So here we are at the start of 1990 with the government's commitment to macroeconomic stringency demonstrated unequivocally during the last few months of 1989. The "big bang" crafted by the architect of Poland's economic reforms, Leszek Balcerowicz, sought at one stroke on January 1, 1990, to establish a market economy by instantly liberalizing prices and foreign trade and signaling that tight fiscal and monetary policies would be pursued. The IMF helped with a large standby loan, while a group of Western countries contributed to a 1 billion US dollar exchange rate stabilization fund—a huge sum in 1990. The central bank, National Bank of Poland, raised the interest rate it charged commercial banks to a *monthly* rate of 36 percent in January 1990, subsequently cutting it to 20 percent in February and then 10 percent in March.

The big bang was a leap into the unknown and fraught with risk. The initial macroeconomic results were, therefore, a huge relief: in a few months, the fiscal accounts were in surplus and foreign exchange reserves were burgeoning. But manufacturing output collapsed, and the Mass Privatization Program aimed at privatizing the large SOEs got mired in political and legal wrangling.[4]

In late 1990, with privatization in limbo, it became evident that the success of Poland's transition hinged on the ability of large SOEs to adapt to the market. If the government's macroeconomic stringency failed to elicit the desired response from the large SOEs, it might be forced to relax credit and reinstate subsidies and import protection, sabotaging the macroeconomic program, as the opening quote from David Lipton and Jeffrey Sachs warned. The reason was size: the state manufacturing sector accounted for 30 percent of GDP, 19 percent of employment, 85 percent of exports, and 60 percent of fiscal revenues.

Ronald McKinnon (1993) had argued that SOEs were value-subtractors and would be wiped out by immediate exposure to unfettered import competition.[5] Even if enterprise assets had intrinsic economic value, another prevalent view based on the principal-agent literature was that, with the government unable or unwilling to exercise its control as equity holder, SOEs would be rapidly decapitalized. Managers and workers would collude to pay out surpluses as wages, run up interfirm arrears, and precipitate a systemic crisis that would force the government to backtrack. The only solution was to privatize rapidly and bring in new shareholders—but this had run into political roadblocks. In anticipation of delays in privatization, SOEs were subjected to two additional taxes: a compulsory dividend in the form of a minimum asset tax levied on the share of the company's equity belonging to the government; and a punishing excess wage tax on increases in the firm-level nominal wage bill above a norm determined by partial indexation to consumer price index (CPI) inflation, known by its Polish acronym, PPWW.

The attempts to enforce SOE discipline notwithstanding, early empirical evidence appeared to confirm the negative priors about SOE behavior. Based on results for the first seven months of 1990, Roman Frydman and Stanislaw Wellisz (1991) found the PPWW seemed not to have restrained wages, except possibly during the very first few months of the transition; and that the easing of credit policy in July 1990 coincided with wages exceeding the norm and a substantial rise in PPWW payments. They concluded that relaxing macroeconomic stringency would simply lead to higher wages and inflation with little increase in output; while maintaining stringency would not achieve much without new incentives for maximizing the value of the firm. On decapitalization, Frydman and Wellisz inferred this was occurring via asset sales by bankrupt companies in order to enable punctual payment of the dividend: if this tax were not paid for three months, it would trigger bankruptcy proceedings, and bankruptcies were extremely rare. "We conclude that, in order to improve both the macroeconomic and microeconomic responses of the Polish economy, widespread privatization appears to be necessary."[6]

As it turns out, the large Polish SOEs were in the forefront of the economic turnaround which occurred in 1992 *even before they were privatized*. The rest of this chapter sets out why. To give away the punch line, macroeconomic stringency did indeed prove insufficient. The dividend and excess wage tax both played a positive role; but what swung the pendulum was the micropolicy trio of hard budget constraints, import competition, and competitive real exchange rates. Box 4.1 sets out the analytical links to Chapters 2 and 3.

## Studying SOE Behavior

The fear about decapitalization was well founded. SOEs were "self-governing" under the direction of a workers' council empowered to hire and fire the manager, determine managerial compensation, and approve all strategic, and even operating, decisions. With worker-controlled enterprises, there would be no countervailing force to paying out value added and even the proceeds of asset sales (which were permitted under the governance framework) as wages. Such enterprises had no incentive to increase value added through better cost control, product mix changes, or improved marketing, but complete discretion (subject to the PPWW) on how it was disposed of.

Managers served at the pleasure of the workers' council with their compensation packages biased in favor of wage increases. They received between five and seven times the average wage in the firm and were also eligible for a bonus; but with a tenuous link to profits. For example, in 1990, if the firm made $50 million of profits (profits before tax minus PPWW), the manager would get a bonus of $3800 for the year; in a case where the manager's wage was seven times the average wage in the firm, equivalent compensation would be obtained by a one-time rise in monthly wages of $45. Quite

**Box 4.1**  Poland—Analytical Interlude

The goal in 1990 was simply to get Poland's economy off the ground in an environment which was changing abruptly and massively. The challenge was not couched in terms of any particular growth model but more in terms of which combination of policies and reforms, and at what speed and in which sequence, would deliver quick results. If McKinnon's hypothesis about Polish SOEs being "value-subtractors" had been correct, an extreme case of Schumpeterian creative destruction would have ensued. But what would have been created in the wake of the SOEs' destruction? Since there were not any domestic rival firms or entrepreneurs to step into the breach, a massive influx of FDI would have been needed. But FDI was unlikely to be attracted to a country undergoing a huge economic experiment with an external debt overhang to boot; indeed, Poland began receiving FDI in significant volume only in 1996. A social and economic catastrophe would have occurred. As it was, real output contracted by 12 percent in 1990.

A more plausible hypothesis was that SOEs had positive value at market prices but were also well within the global technology frontier of the Aghion and Howitt model discussed in Chapters 2 and 3. Creative destruction could then have taken two forms: reallocation of assets via sales by SOEs; and imitation, or implementation of existing innovations, as SOEs began to compete for market share. Both would have contributed to recovery, and resulted in technological upgrading. But SOEs were crippled by bad incentives, as discussed in this chapter. And privatization had fallen victim to politics. Yet SOEs were in the forefront of the economic recovery that began in late 1991.

Attempting to understand SOE behavior through a firm-level study with an open mind and an admission that we were clueless led to the factors that underpinned the early Polish transition's version of creative destruction: hard budget constraints, product market competition, and competitive real exchange rates, or the *micropolicy trio*. In addition to the Aghion–Hewitt argument, the links to Chapters 2 and 3 include:

- Hard budget constraints (Box 3.3). But note that the political economy and process of hardening budgets is going to vary from country to country. The process is neither instantaneous nor permanent, that is, setbacks are eminently possible.
- Competitive real exchange rates (Box 3.4). Poland was one of the few, if not the only, emerging market to avoid clinging tenaciously to its fixed nominal exchange rate anchor once inflation was reduced. The consequences for countries such as Argentina later in the 1990s were nothing short of disastrous, as eloquently laid out in Michael Mussa's 2002 postmortem.
- Product market competition. For many developing countries, liberalizing imports is the quickest way to introduce such competition and signal to incumbent firms that they need to innovate. This was an integral factor of Poland's successful turnaround in 1992 but no less important in Kenya and India, as we shall see in Chapters 5 and 6.

apart from these incentives was the question of ability: up to January 1, 1990, managers' talents consisted of skillful bargaining with the central authorities about subsidies, special allocations of raw materials, and a bigger share of centrally financed investments. Overnight, they awoke to a frightening new world emphasizing macroeconomic stringency, and price and trade liberalization. Ultimately, they would have needed to decide whether it was worthwhile making a wholesale adaptation to the market's rules, or strip assets and run. This was the pivotal issue, rendered even more crucial by the slowdown in privatization.

On January 1, 1991, the Council of Mutual Economic Assistance (CMEA: the preferential trade between the former Soviet Union and its satellite states) was dismantled, much sooner than expected. Poland had benefited significantly in the form of heavily subsidized oil and gas imports from the former Soviet Union and a more-or-less captive market for many of its uncompetitive exports. The size of the shock was large, estimated by Leszek Balcerowicz at between 3.5 and 5 percent of Poland's 1991 GDP. The enterprise sector slid into recession and Poland seemed headed for a high-inflation collapse as the fiscal deficit unexpectedly widened. This was in sharp contrast to 1990, when the big surprise was that no SOEs went bankrupt. Remember the big devaluation on January 1, 1990? This had helped by shutting down import competition, as did the input subsidies and market access associated with CMEA trade. By early 1991, though, the slack in the exchange rate had vanished, intensifying import competition and coinciding with the shock from the dissolution of CMEA trade. Disappointed with the SOE response, the government devalued the zloty on May 17, 1991 by a sizable 17 percent against the US dollar. This would prove to be a crucial step, as we shall see later in this chapter.

The only way of forming a clear picture about whether SOEs were going to deliver or fail utterly was to visit them and talk to their managers. As the Bank's country economist in Warsaw, I was charged with this task, along with two professors from Lodz University, Marek Belka and Stefan Krajewski. It would take us nine months, distributed over two years, to uncover the insights presented here. We decided to focus on large SOEs because if they could be shown to be responding positively to market forces, it would be reasonable to assume that smaller firms, with their more limited political clout and greater agility, would be doing the same. The sample was restricted to

75 SOEs, the 15 largest in 5 different manufacturing sectors based on 1989 sales: metallurgy, electromachinery, chemicals, light manufacturing (such as textiles and leather), and food processing. While this was a nonrandom sample, it embodied a considerable amount of geographical and product variance. These enterprises were part of Poland's Lista 500, its version of the Fortune 500. But we deliberately excluded the biggest shipyards and steel mills because these would dominate the calculations.[7]

Data were collected directly from the enterprises by us, which was a big advantage over getting data from the Polish Central Statistical Office (GUS) because we could more easily verify any numbers that looked out of line and also obtain data on new variables such as the PPWW and dividend payments, which might not necessarily be reported to GUS. Besides, GUS was constrained in its ability to share firm-level information on confidentiality grounds. Equally importantly, we were able to interview the managers and correlate their qualitative answers on questions such as, "How easy is it to get bank loans?" with quantitative results such as profitability. We visited the sample SOEs between mid-May and end July 1991, and in addition to interviewing the managers, obtained monthly data on all key variables feeding into the profit and loss account and balance sheet between June 1989 and March 1991. We got a good response because SOE managers were fed up of the bad press they were getting (imbued with the stereotype that they were unresponsive and destroying their enterprises) and anxious to tell their side of the story. There was good news, but our overall assessment was discouraging.

## SOE Visits: May to July 1991

The first burning question was: Were SOEs the "value-subtractors" they had been branded? We had obtained monthly, firm-level data for the period June 1989 to March 1991—6 months before the big bang and 15 months after it— which would enable us to examine trends in enterprise profitability, a natural yardstick of efficiency and a guide to investment decisions in a market economy. But profitability measures had to be purged of factors that may have artificially inflated them, such as devaluation gains on inherited dollar accounts as well as government subsidies and income from the sale and leasing of enterprise assets, to obtain underlying profitability. The results are

**Table 4.1** Quarterly Trends in Underlying Profitability (Underlying profits/net sales %)

| Sector | 1989.4 | 1990.1 | 1990.2 | 1990.3 | 1990.4 | 1991.1 |
|---|---|---|---|---|---|---|
| Metallurgy | 38 | 36 | 29 | 20 | 13 | 17 |
| Electromachinery | 35 | 21 | 19 | 23 | 18 | 2 |
| Chemical | 31 | 19 | 17 | 13 | 19 | 9 |
| Light | 37 | 20 | 9 | 7 | 4 | -2 |
| Food | 18 | 16 | 22 | 23 | 22 | 18 |

*Source:* Table 1 in Pinto, Belka, and Krajewski (1992).

shown in Table 4.1 from the fourth quarter of 1989, 1989.4, to the first quarter of 1991, 1991.1.

With the exception of the food processing sector, the declining trend in profit margin (measured by the ratio of underlying profitability to net sales) demonstrated that the latitude of firms to apply cost-plus pricing was diminishing over time as a result of import competition and the fixed exchange rate. It might also have captured the evaporating inflationary gains on inventories carried over from 1989, which we were unable to correct for. Electromachinery, which was heavily dependent upon the CMEA market, suffered a precipitous decline during the first quarter of 1991. This sector alone supplied 15 percent of fiscal revenues! The chemical sector companies experienced a similar drop—these companies were exceptionally large beneficiaries of CMEA subsidies on energy. The light manufacturing sector companies' collapse came much earlier, in 1990.2. This sector was subject to price competition almost immediately from South East Asian and private, unrecorded imports of leather goods and textiles. The two sectors which appeared most vulnerable were thus electromachinery and light manufacturing, but there was no compelling evidence on widespread "value subtraction."

The second crucial question was whether there was any evidence of decapitalization in view of the well-known deficiencies in SOE governance. We found that asset sales were the highest in sectors such as electromachinery and light industry.[8] But these were the sectors with the lowest underlying profitability! Hence, the Frydman–Wellisz concern about enterprises selling assets in order to pay wages had a good side to it, in that less profitable firms were downsizing. Additionally, we found little evidence of decapitalization via wage maximization. Had managers and workers been hell-bent on paying out SOE surpluses as higher wages, this would have shown up in the reckless incurrence of PPWW payments. But a simple measure we developed—the ratio of PPWW to disposable cash—was small in 1990, averaging no more than 11 percent. Interestingly, light industry firms incurred virtually no PPWW either in 1990 or the first quarter of 1991; but by the end of the sample period, the fixed dividend tax was a whopping 260 percent of their shrinking profits after income tax. Besides, except for the beleaguered light industry, new investments comfortably exceeded depreciation, suggesting an augmentation of plant and equipment.

The third important question was whether there was any evidence of resources being reallocated in line with the new, market-based relative prices and profitability. The earlier finding on asset sales by less profitable firms had its parallel in employment. Employment reduction during 1990 ranged from a high of 17 percent among the least profitable light industry firms to 7–9 percent in metallurgy, chemicals, and electromachinery, and close to zero in food processing. Electromachinery firms led with a further 5 percent reduction in their workforce during the first quarter of 1991 as a result of the collapse of CMEA trade.

This was not all: were banks doing their bit in improved resource allocation by lending to profitable firms? The sample evidence indicated that, in spite of sharply higher real interest rates, bank loans were more likely to be going to firms where unsold finished goods were piling up than to profitable firms. This suggested an important "softness" in the budget constraint for SOEs. The government had slashed subsidies, but bank lending was slanted toward the weaker firms. Besides, the more profitable and liquid firms might have felt obliged to help out their fellow SOEs by turning a blind eye to inter-firm payment arrears. In other words, while import competition had put a lid on price increases by SOEs, their budget constraints had not fully hardened, in that easy bank loans and interfirm credit served as safety valves.

The fourth important question was whether there was any change in the way SOEs were being run, notwithstanding the slow pace of privatization. We came away impressed by SOE managers, who were de facto acquiring control. Attitudes and organization structures were shifting toward profits and marketing, with the number two position in the firm going to the deputy in charge of finance or sales as opposed to production and technology, as in the old days; but there was undeniably a serious principal-agent problem with managers serving at the pleasure of the workers' council. Besides, looking ahead, decapitalization could not be ruled out. Workers were bound to get restive and demand higher wage awards irrespective of the consequences for the long-run health of the firm, pointing to the urgent need for formally empowering managers and rectifying their compensation structure. We concluded, like Frydman and Wellisz, that macroeconomic stringency was insufficient to engineer firm-level change.

## SOE Visits: August–September 1992

Against all odds, the first signs of an economic upturn began appearing toward the end of 1991. By the first quarter of 1992, aggregate statistical data showed growing enterprise sector profits and sales. We decided another round of visits was needed to see if we could find concrete evidence of a turnaround at the firm level, and conducted these in August and September 1992. The managers were happy to see us because we had sent each of them a ten-page Polish summary of our main findings from the first round of visits: this was important because they had the final say in sharing profit and loss and balance sheet information with us! In Box 4.2, I describe our encounter with the director of a large meat-processing plant.

In contrast to the first round of visits, which had been akin to setting off on the high seas without a compass, we had a better idea of what to look for this time: namely, were there definite signs of positive change in enterprise and bank behavior that would contribute to solid micro-foundations for growth? We were able to extend our data to the end of June 1992 and thus now had three years of monthly information on the performance of our sample SOEs. By the tail end of the sample period, the ephemeral factors that had supported profitability in 1990 and 1991 had vanished. Therefore, instead of by their *industrial sector*, as in the first round, we decided to classify the SOEs according to their *financial performance* over the last six months of the sample period, January to June 1992: AAA connoting positive retained earnings after paying all taxes; AA connoting positive pre-income tax profit but negative retained earnings; and A connoting negative pre-income tax profit, that is, loss-making enterprises. Of the 64 firms responding to the repeat survey, there turned out to be 31 AAA firms, 8 AA firms, and 25 A firms. This finding in itself indicated that SOEs were not a complete write-off. I focus on the

---

**Box 4.2**   The Importance of Being Earnest

The ten-page Polish summary of our findings from the first round of visits that we had sent to all the participating SOEs proved a lifesaver. A colleague from the Warsaw office of the World Bank and I had kicked off the second round of visits with a meeting at a large meat-processing factory located in Bydgoszcz. It was an uncharacteristically hot August afternoon. When we got to the office of the General Director, which was located on the top floor, the windows were open and a warm breeze wafted in. He was smoking a cigarette and in a bad mood, not making the slightest attempt to conceal his ill temper. From the open windows, you could see smoke billowing from the factory chimneys, which left me with this uncomfortable vision of inhaling millions of microscopic fragments of processed meat.

"What do you want?" he demanded gruffly.

"You see, the economy is turning around and we don't think this would be possible unless the large state enterprises were turning around as well. We would be very interested in your views on this, and also need your permission to extend our data set." We had sent the spreadsheet of each firm out in advance with a request for the data since our visit a year ago.

"I have had so many visits from so-called researchers, but most didn't bother to give us any feedback in spite of promising to do so. Some of them did, but to tell you the truth, their reports were terrible. *Completely* unscientific. There was only one decently documented report I can recall."

"Which one was it?" I nervously asked.

He scowled, shuffled unenthusiastically through the piles of papers on his desk, and then pulled each drawer of his desk open in turn. But his search drew a blank, only heightening his irritation. Fortunately, we had brought spare copies of our summary along. I thrust one before him and asked: "Does this one ring a bell?" He leafed through it quickly while we held our breath. Finally, he said with a smile: "Yes, this is the one." It was a love fest after that, to be repeated with many more enterprise directors in many more cities.

---

two extreme groups, AAA and A, to tease out the implications for SOE and bank behavior.

We found that real sales in AAA firms hit rock bottom in April 1991 but rebounded after the May 1991 devaluation, the first relaxation of the nominal anchor since the big bang. Interestingly, this devaluation was a tacit admission that the enterprise sector needed relief following the disruption caused by the demise of CMEA trade and the attendant sharp decline in Poland's terms of trade. But the data showed, most noticeably for AAA firms, an impressive reduction in the ratio of materials and energy costs to sales after a spike resulting from the disappearance of CMEA-related subsidies. When asked to rate the importance of product mix changes as a factor stimulating increased sales on a zero-to-five scale, AAA firms averaged 3.2 compared to 1.5 for A firms. This demonstrated that SOEs were taking steps to cut costs and cater to market needs and were not waiting passively to be helped out by another devaluation that would keep import competition at bay.

On employment and wages, the data showed that for the sample as a whole, labor was reduced by 27 percent between December 1989 and June 1992. The least profitable A firms shed the most labor. Although employment reduction in the sample firms had lagged behind output reduction up to March 1991, as one might expect from worker-controlled SOEs, the reduction continued steadily after that, even though sales had stabilized. The evidence on wage restraint was also encouraging, with more profitable firms paying significantly more by the end of the sample period. After rising in 1991, the share of the PPWW in disposable cash dropped significantly during the first six months of 1992. Thus, the fears after the first round that wage increases might be on an explosive upward path appeared not to have materialized. Besides, PPWW payments were incurred largely by profitable firms.

## Hardening of the Budget Constraint

The findings in the "SOE Visits: August–September 1992" section were similar to those from the first round, with the added confidence that now genuinely profitable SOEs were emerging. Further, these SOEs were taking the initiative to implement market-oriented management instead of simply waiting for the government to do something. But what about the banks, which in any market economy, play a vital role in resource allocation? Had their behavior changed? The short answer is yes, but not before a significant strengthening of their governance. The main commercial banks then consisted of nine banks spun off from the National Bank of Poland in 1989. These were the erstwhile regional offices of the communist-era monobank, used to dealing with SOEs. There were issues, therefore, both of banking expertise and established relationships that were bound to influence lending decisions.

Indeed, our first round of visits indicated that banks had softened the enterprise budget constraint at least up to March 1991. The collapse of

CMEA trade led to a sharp deterioration in bank portfolios. The government decided to take an extremely important step: it commercialized the nine state banks, established supervisory boards, and brought them under the direct control of the Ministry of Finance (MOF) during the fourth quarter of 1991. That October, the MOF forbade lending to some 2000 firms in trouble, many of which were private.

To check whether the strengthened control over the banks had made any difference, the sample period was split into two: the nine quarters 89.3–91.3 and the three quarters 91.4–92.2. Regressions were run to answer the question of whether lending was demand driven in response to enterprise losses or whether banks had prospective profitability in mind in new loan decisions. The first would be a clear signal that banks did not exercise governance; the second would signal to loss-making firms that reform was necessary if access to loans was to be maintained. In a nutshell, the regression results showed a dramatic change starting in 1991.4, with banks beginning to lend based on profitability of SOEs.[9]

These quantitative findings were very much in line with responses to direct survey questions. Managers unanimously reported changed bank behavior. As they described it, in 1990 banks acted like "cashiers," eager to dole out money. By 1992, banks were behaving like "partners" with an equity stake in the company, and had become highly quality conscious. Managers also indicated that, as a result of rising competition among banks for the limited number of sound clients, good firms were bargaining for lower interest rates. Based on numerical ratings by SOE managers, AAA firms experienced the same ease in getting loans as in 1990, while there was a sharp diminution for A firms in 1992. Impressively, both types of firms reported increased bank involvement. When asked why bank behavior was changing, SOE managers' most frequent reply was that such change was being forced by the banks' own vanishing net worth and deteriorating portfolios. And banks, like enterprises, were learning. Although the SOE managers never alluded to it, there was a remarkable coincidence between their perceptions of tighter bank behavior and the change in the governance in late 1991 of the nine commercial banks spun off from the National Bank of Poland.

Reinforcing the positive change in bank lending, better-off SOEs had become more circumspect about interfirm arrears, realizing the government was not going to compensate them or orchestrate netting-out exercises. This left the government. Subsidies had been slashed but tax arrears remained, especially for A firms; AAA firms were virtually current on tax payments. Tax arrears were thus correlated with collapsing profits; but this could do only limited damage because tax arrears cannot exceed tax liabilities, unlike with an open-ended subsidy. Besides, the government more than compensated by slashing budgetary subsidies and changing the governance of the nine commercial banks spun off from the central bank.

## Why Did Managers Restructure?

A last mystery remains. Why did SOE managers start serious restructuring? The hardening of budgets and the compression of profit margins as a result of import competition could simply have prompted them to cut and run, since their compensation was not linked to the long-run value of the firm. Our survey evidence showed that managers believed that the reforms were permanent and that the hard budget constraint was going to last. But it also indicated something more subtle: managers believed privatization was inevitable. Only 8 out of 59 responding managers felt they would remain SOEs in the near future: 43 expected privatization soon, 5 expected managerial contracts for restructuring, and 3 had already been privatized.[10] When asked why they had focused on the long-run solvency of the companies, managers would mention emotional reasons, patriotism, and the like; but when pressed, they indicated that they expected financial rewards at the time of privatization, in the form of stock options as well as retaining their jobs as the new CEOs. They were trying to establish reputations as capable managers.

We sought more information on the reputation effect by circulating a new questionnaire to the same firms that had participated in the earlier survey.[11] The managers of the sample SOEs were asked to write a few sentences explaining why they had initiated restructuring; the predominant answer was that they had no choice. To save the jobs of workers and their own, they had to respond to the new economic forces. They were also asked to rank the importance of nine different factors on their behavior on a zero (unimportant) to five (extremely important) scale; and to pick the three most important factors. Thirty-six replies were received. Table 4.2 shows the average response, on a zero-to-five point scale, to each factor.

**Table 4.2** Managers' Responses to Questions on Motives for Restructuring

| Factor | Average Rating | Times Selected in the Top 3 |
|---|---|---|
| A. Pressure from government | 1.31 | 1 |
| B. Increase chances of keeping job | 1.94 | 1 |
| C. Patriotism | 2.75 | 6 |
| D. No subsidies | 3.69 | 18 |
| E. Demonstrate ability and increase mobility | 4.03 | 14 |
| F. Pressure from banks | 2.86 | 9 |
| G. Fear of losing job | 1.31 | 0 |
| H. Market pressure | 4.86 | 34 |
| I. Import competition | 4.36 | 25 |

*Source:* Table 16, Pinto and van Wijnbergen (1995).

The prominence of competition and hard budgets and competition is obvious from the ratings given to market pressure (H), import competition (I), and elimination of subsidies (D). Demonstrating ability through restructuring and thereby increasing mobility (E) received the third-highest rating overall. Not surprisingly, in view of the ease of securing bank loans until late 1991, the pressure from banks, while important (F), was not primary. Managers did not appear particularly concerned about job security (B), and this was confirmed by the low rating given to the fear of losing job (G); B made the list of the top three factors only once, and G, never.

## Kornai and Schumpeter

Notwithstanding the unexpectedly positive response of SOEs to the Polish reforms, it was expected that growth would eventually come from privatized and *de novo* private firms. However, as modeled by Philippe Aghion, Olivier Blanchard, and Robin Burgess (1994), and Philippe Aghion and Olivier Blanchard (1994), there were bound to be links between the shrinking state-owned sector and a growing private sector as part of efficient adjustment. Our firm-level data on fixed asset sales and labor shedding showed that this process began early on. Further, the least profitable firms had released a bigger share of both assets and labor, consonant with efficient adjustment. A survey in late 1993 of 200 *de novo* private, privatized, and state-owned firms by Marek Belka and colleagues (1995) found that no less than 33 percent of the assets of the *de novo* private firms was over five years old, suggesting acquisition from downsizing state firms. In other words, Kornai's hard budget and import competition had stimulated the transfer of assets and human resources from inefficient incumbents to efficient new entrants, along Schumpeterian lines. And hard budgets and reputation effects led SOE managers to behave in a manner that was completely opposite to initial predictions, and also more positively than predicted by the then burgeoning transition literature.

## Lessons from Poland

Poland's early transition experience points to five insights. First, the government cannot rely simply on macroeconomic stringency and sit back. Economic governance must nurture the "macro–micro linkages" referred to in Chapters 1–3. Second, it offers a crystal-clear glimpse into exactly what needs to be done at the micro level, in the form of the micropolicy trio of hard budgets, competition, and competitive real exchange rates. The cogent nature of this trio and how it feeds back into macro fiscal and debt sustainability will be reinforced by Russia's diametrically opposed experience. As luck would have it, the pivotal nature of the micropolicy trio was isolated by chance: by an inquiry into how Polish SOEs were behaving only because privatization had stalled. This brings us to the third insight, on privatization itself.

Suppose Poland had indeed been able to privatize its large SOEs as rapidly as envisaged in its big bang strategy. There is no guarantee that this would have instantly improved corporate governance. David Lipton and Jeffrey Sachs were aware of this (1990b, p. 295): "Even though we favor rapid privatization, we doubt that privatization will produce immediate, large increases in productivity or managerial efficiency. The real gains from private ownership will take years to manifest themselves …" The urgency about privatization was thus not to generate a quick upside as to thwart what most believed would be a sure and costly downside had SOEs stayed under the control of workers' councils: namely, falling output and enterprise profitability and a wage explosion. These bad microeconomic outcomes would, in turn, eventually subvert macroeconomic stabilization because of falling output and taxes. But a nasty surprise was in store for everyone. Countries like Czech Republic and Russia, which succeeded in mass privatizing much faster than Poland, discovered this was no prophylactic against asset stripping and even fraud. The reasons varied. In Czech Republic, voucher-based mass privatization led to the creation of privatization funds, which themselves defrauded their minority shareholders. Such privatization funds were frequently operated by banks, which created conflicts between banks as creditors and voucher fund managers.[12] In Russia, privatization was accompanied by a punishing macroeconomic environment and the rise of barter and arrears, which fueled asset stripping and the defrauding of minority investors instead of producing more efficient enterprises. Combining these experiences with Poland's leads to *the* essential lesson on privatization: it will deliver only if combined with the micropolicy trio of hard budgets, competition, and competitive real exchange rates. Otherwise, there are no guarantees of higher enterprise efficiency and profitability. Privatization must be part of a bigger package, and is unlikely to improve governance, raise efficiency, and promote competition without the micropolicy trio.

The fourth insight has to do with the nature of economic transformation itself and how budgets get hardened. It takes time to change behavior and become credible *even* when reforms are implemented with a "big bang" as in Poland. In particular, the process of hardening budget constraints is far from instantaneous, with nuances that are likely to vary from country to country. In the Polish case, the government was quick to slash budgetary subsidies but bank loans continued to soften the SOE budget constraint until the governance for banks was strengthened in the fourth quarter of 1991. The final step was when better-off SOEs began paying attention to their accounts receivable and realized the government was not going to compensate them for interfirm arrears. Thus, it took a good two years for budget constraints to harden and become credible, pointing to the importance of tracking the dynamics of this process and exercising the needed policy vigilance.

Fifth, Poland's experience underlines the need for pragmatism in exchange rate management, illustrated eloquently by the devaluation of the zloty in May 1991 following the collapse of CMEA trade and the related terms-of-trade shock. To have hung on tenaciously and indefinitely to the fixed peg to the dollar established on January 1, 1990 might well have led to disastrous outcomes, as indeed happened in Russia in 1998 (discussed in chapter 7) and especially Argentina in 2001.

To conclude, the serendipitous SOE study conducted over 1991 and 1992 highlighted three elements as having been critical in strengthening the microeconomic foundations for growth and thereby bolstering macroeconomic stabilization: (i) hard budget constraints; (ii) import competition; and (iii) competitive real exchange rates. A fourth more subtle, but no less critical, factor was managers' concerns about their own reputations.

## Epilogue

When Marek Belka, Stefan Krajewski, and I set out to understand how the large Polish SOEs were responding to the big bang, we were simply on a fact-finding mission. Given the unprecedented nature of Poland's transition, there was no established conceptual framework to turn to. We invented it as we went along, especially during the first round of SOE visits. Chance played a big role in that, had privatization been implemented rapidly, there would have been little appetite for such research. And had we decided to investigate the behavior of privatized SOEs, it is quite likely that the positive findings would have been attributed to privatization rather than the micropolicy trio of hard budgets, import competition, and competitive real exchange rates. At a minimum, privatization would have obscured the efficacy of this policy trio.

Alternatively, mass privatization might have been a flop, as in the Czech Republic and Russia. As it turns out, there was considerable concern that our findings on the positive adaptation of Polish SOEs would be used as an argument *against* privatization. In this, our discussions with SOE managers proved decisive. They were anticipating privatization and this, together with hard budgets and import competition, pushed them to restructure in order to demonstrate their abilities. No less a bastion of private ownership than the *Wall Street Journal* picked up this subtlety after our findings were published in the *Brookings Papers on Economic Activity*. The story line said it all: "In Poland, Privatization's Benefits Precede It."[13]

Poland ended up growing faster than any other large country in Europe in 1993 and 1994. Much of the growth was export based, linked to the economic turnaround in Western Europe. SOEs had been instrumental in exports right from the start, and successfully sought new export markets after the collapse in internal demand in 1990 and the demise of CMEA trade in 1991.

Industrial production, almost 70 percent of which came from SOEs, grew at 4 percent in 1992, 5.6 percent in 1993, and 13 percent in 1994. Our findings, based on a relatively small sample of politically sensitive large SOEs, turned out to have staying power.[14] So did the hard budget constraints and competition put in place by Leszek Balcerowicz, as illustrated in Box 4.3 by a conversation with an SOE manager during the second round of visits.

A last point. It might appear a serious omission not to have mentioned Poland's external debt problem and how it was resolved. First, the numbers. At the end of 1989, Poland owed $28 billion to Paris Club creditors, $9 billion to commercial banks, and $2 billion to CMEA countries, which in total exceeded 80 percent of GDP.[15] Second, this is what happened. All principal

---

**Box 4.3** The Virtue of Policy Consistency

After we had run through the questionnaire with the general director of a heavy engineering company in Piotrków Trybunalski that made lifting equipment for mines, he walked to the window and began waxing philosophical. "You know," he went on as he stared toward infinity, "things have changed since we last met. We are now finally getting free from the old thinking and are willing to take more risk. Let me tell you a story. A few days ago, I was driving along the highway and all the cars were well above the speed limit, something inconceivable even a few months ago. Suddenly, a police car appeared and we all fell obediently in line behind it. Problem is, it was going so damn slow so we were all hoping it would leave the highway at the next exit, but it did not. Finally, the driver in the first car behind it plucked up the courage to turn on its blinker and pass the police car. We were all expectantly waiting to see what would happen. Nothing did, so one by one, all the cars sped by the police car."

"So what do you think now of the Balcerowicz Plan?" I asked. This was hardly an innocent question. Leszek Balcerowicz's "shock therapy," epitomized by the "big bang" on January 1, 1990 had left SOE managers with a stark choice: make it on their own or go bust. Even icons of the Polish Solidarity Movement, instrumental in the demise of communism in Poland, such as the Ursus Tractor Factory and the Gdansk Shipyard, where Lech Wałęsa once worked, were not spared. It was the ultimate hard budget constraint, Darwinian in its ruthlessness.

"Let me be frank," he retorted. "I used to hate Balcerowicz, but then I began to admire him."

"What accounted for this change of heart?"

"Simple. Every time I went to the Ministry of Industry I was given a different answer about how they were going to help us, depending upon whom I spoke to. But from the Ministry of Finance, there was always the same answer: 'Sorry, we can't help you. Either you make it on your own, or you go bankrupt.'"

and interest payments on Paris Club debt falling due between January 1990 and March 1991 were rescheduled, resulting in significant cash flow relief. Subsequently, in April 1991, Paris Club creditors agreed to reduce their claims by 50 percent in present value terms in two steps: 30 percent immediately and 20 percent in April 1994, conditional upon successful adherence to an IMF program. The second step would also depend upon an equal debt reduction agreement of 50 percent with Poland's commercial bank creditors under the auspices of the London Club. Both the Paris and London Club deals were completed successfully, reducing Poland's external debt to GDP ratio to 46 percent by the end of 1994.

The debt agreement was clearly important in helping Poland achieve its fiscal deficit reduction and inflation targets, as the analysis in Sweder van Wijnbergen and Nina Budina's 2001 paper shows. But was it the crucial factor? Had Poland's SOEs not begun adjusting under the pressure of hard budgets and import competition, and with the assistance of a pragmatic exchange rate policy, my guess is that it would all have come to naught, because achieving the fiscal and inflation targets under the IMF program would have been impossible. Debt relief was important, but the pivotal factor was the positive response of the SOEs under the influence of the micropolicy trio.

## Notes

1. This chapter draws liberally on joint work with Marek Belka and Stefan Krajewski (Pinto, Belka, and Krajewski 1992, 1993) and Sweder van Wijnbergen (Pinto and van Wijnbergen 1995).
2. "Jacek Rostowski: Proud of Success in Recession." Jan Cienski, *Financial Times*, November 17, 2009.
3. Blanchard (2010).
4. For Leszek Balcerowicz's own assessment and the importance he attached to big bang stabilization and liberalization, see Balcerowicz (1994).
5. McKinnon (1993, ch. 12). McKinnon's thesis was first presented in 1991 in an Economics Focus article, "The Value-Subtractors of Eastern Europe," *The Economist*, 5 January 1991.
6. Frydman and Wellisz (1991).
7. For a detailed description of the sample, see Pinto, Belka, and Krajewski (1993, Appendix A).
8. See Table 2 in Pinto, Belka, and Krajewski (1992).
9. For details, see Pinto and van Wijnbergen (1995).

10. Remember, this was in mid-1992. The Mass Privatization Program for large SOEs took until 1995 to be implemented.
11. See Pinto and van Wijnbergen (1995, Annex C).
12. Richter (2011) contains a damning account of the Czech Republic's voucher privatization. A note on the word "tunneling" in the title of his paper: this word was coined specifically to describe the "nation's collective desperation over the corporate asset-stripping scandals that followed in the wake of the country's voucher privatization program in the early 1990s...." (p. 24). Chapter 7, on Russia, will illustrate the costly consequences of privatization with rampant soft budgets.
13. Lindley H. Clark Jr. "In Poland, Privatization's Benefits Precede It." *Wall Street Journal*, August 27, 1993.
14. The main results we obtained were confirmed subsequently by a 3300-firm survey conducted by Carlin, et al. (2001). See also chapter 7 of EBRD (1999).
15. Numbers from Lipton and Sachs (1990a, p. 119) and debt ratio from van Wijnbergen and Budina (2001, p. 307).

# CHAPTER 5

# Kenya's Achilles Heel

*It feels good to make history for Kenya and win the gold.*

—Samuel Kamau Wanjiru, winner of the 2008 Olympics Marathon

*Kenyans are Kenyan only once every four years, during the Olympics. The rest of the time, tribal loyalties rule.*

—Former senior government official, informal conversation, early 2007

In February 2006, BBC News ran a story that the World Bank was suspending loans worth $250 million to Kenya "which is embroiled in a high-level scandal."[1] Though unusual, this move was consonant with the perceived deterioration in Kenya's governance and its proclivity for corruption scandals. But was it the right move? One could reasonably have concluded from the subsequent December 2007 presidential elections that it was. Not only were those elections marred by fraud, up to 800 people were killed in the tribal violence that followed and another 600,000 people were displaced. But the situation was not so simple, as we shall see.

Kenya was on the verge of acquiring emerging market status by issuing a Eurobond when the botched presidential election of December 2007 intervened. It had lowered government indebtedness substantially over the previous decade. This was accomplished the old-fashioned way: by increasing primary fiscal surpluses during the early 1990s, when Daniel arap Moi "ruled Kenya using a strategic mixture of ethnic favouritism, state repression and marginalisation of opposition forces, utilising violence, detention and torture."² This was paradoxical because one does not expect sensible economic policy from a repressive regime. After the peaceful presidential elections of December 2002, when Mwai Kibaki took over, the reduction in the government's debt-to-GDP ratio sped up as a result of a growth acceleration and lower interest rates—in contrast to the easier debt write-offs its neighbors, Tanzania and Uganda, received under the HIPC–MDRI program referred to in Chapter 1. In October 2006, Kenya obtained its first-ever sovereign credit rating from Standard & Poor's, and a September 2007 Reuters' story (cited in an internal World Bank market tracking report) noted its plan to issue a $150-million Eurobond in 2008. But this was scuttled by the chaotic and violent aftermath of the December 2007 presidential elections.

The manner in which Kenya lowered government indebtedness should have given pause to those anxious to dismiss it as a governance basket case, a label that persisted even after the 2002 elections. Kenya could have opted to slash the government debt-to-GDP ratio through default or hyperinflation—but instead did so through better economic policy. Where did the spur for this better policy come from? Kenya suffered a sudden stop—not in private capital inflows, the scourge of emerging markets—but in official capital inflows in the early 1990s when donors froze aid on governance grounds.³ Notwithstanding his repressive rule of Kenya, arap Moi was staunchly anti-communist, which endeared him to the Western powers, and indeed the US Navy had access to Mombasa port during the Cold War era. But arap Moi lost this geopolitical bargaining chip when the Berlin Wall came down and the thaw set in. In 1991, the emphasis among donors switched to governance and aid was frozen. Official net foreign financing to the government became negative in 1994/5 and stayed negative right up to 2006 (the year the analysis reported here began), except for two years in between when there was debt rescheduling. During the period covered here, the Kenyan government financed itself on net by issuing debt domestically at market interest rates.

Two positives flowed out of the 1991 aid freeze: multiparty democracy was adopted in 1992 with a two-term presidential limit, marking the beginning of the end of the arap Moi regime; and far-reaching economic reforms were implemented—but not before the Goldenberg scandal erupted (which I shall discuss in the next section). Indeed, with the smooth presidential transition of 2002, Kenya appeared to have crossed a threshold. But, sadly, it was unable to maintain the positive momentum, as the December 2007 elections

> **Box 5.1** Kenya—Analytical Interlude
>
> Kenya's story from the early 1990s to the December 2007 presidential elections captures the following results from Chapters 2 and 3:
>
> First is the importance of hard budget constraints. In this case, however, the application is to the government itself. Once Kenya faced a cutoff in aid on governance grounds in the early 1990s, the government went ahead with political and economic reform, taking steps to raise revenues while also liberalizing trade and the foreign exchange market.
>
> Second, the private sector stressed the importance of import liberalization started during the early 1990s as a major factor in spurring firms to become more efficient. We saw in Chapter 4 that competition from imports was crucial in Poland's growth story and we shall see that it was equally so in India's growth takeoff in the early 2000s.
>
> Third, Kenya's experience captures the pivotal importance of managing domestic volatility, especially from political and social sources. *The failure to do so will trump good economic policy* and produce a boom–bust pattern that will condemn the economy to slow long-run growth, a fundamental result discussed in the section on economic volatility in Chapter 3. Higher political risk will raise interest rates at the macro level, while shortening investment horizons and raising the cost of capital at the micro level, leading to adverse micro–macro linkages that will eventually reverse any improvement in government debt dynamics. This is by far the most important lesson from Kenya's experience.

showed. In common with many low-income countries, Kenya suffers from political uncertainty driven by social fragmentation—an impediment it has so far been unable to surmount. Its experience illustrates the challenges low-income countries, especially those in Africa, are going to encounter in joining the ranks of emerging markets; while the remarkable economic results achieved between 2003 and 2007 underlines the importance of lowering political risk and healing social divisions permanently. Box 5.1 sets out the analytical links between the Kenyan experience and Chapters 2 and 3.

## A Kenyan Conundrum

In the summer of 2006, I was invited by my colleagues in the Africa region of the World Bank to analyze Kenya's macro-fiscal policy from the perspective of accelerating economic growth. Never having visited or worked on the country before, I devoured reports on Kenya from the World Bank, the

IMF, and the Economist Intelligence Unit (EIU). Typical were the following quotes from the May 2006 EIU report, "Kenya at a glance 2006–07":

> The president...will struggle to see out the remainder of his term because of the damage to his authority and credibility caused by the "no" vote in the constitutional referendum and corruption scandals that have led to the resignation of three senior ministers.
>
> The Government of National Unity continues to confront serious divisions...

Reinforcing this negative assessment was a 2004 IMF study of Kenya (IMF 2004, p. 5) which noted: "The low TFP growth over the past two decades has been significantly associated with poor governance and high inflation."

The picture that emerged was of a corrupt, politically unstable country. I therefore expected to find stagnant growth, high real interest rates on domestic debt (interest rates on external debt were set officially at concessional levels), and badly managed public finances manifested in unstable government debt dynamics. But growth had accelerated starting in 2003, government indebtedness had been slashed, and simple calculations revealed something remarkable: the real interest rate paid by the government on its domestic debt had dropped from a range of 15–20 percent over the 1998–2002 period to below 5 percent after 2003 and stayed there up to 2006. At the margin, real interest rates on Kenyan shilling 91-day T-bills had fallen to the 1–3 percent range. Government indebtedness had been slashed without debt relief and economic growth had picked up substantially. As Table 5.1 shows, the evidence did not stack up in favor of the priors.

**Table 5.1** A Pleasant Kenyan Surprise

| Priors | Evidence |
| --- | --- |
| • Badly managed public finances, unstable debt dynamics | • Government debt lowered from 73% of GDP in 1995/6 to 45% in 2006/7 |
| • High real interest rates | • Real interest rates on domestic debt exceptionally low 2003–6 |
| • Stagnation | • Real GDP from stagnation during 1991–2002 to 5.5% average annual growth during the four years 2003/4 to 2006/7 |

I was convinced interest rates were being manipulated, a position I clung to until I reached Nairobi that July of 2006 and discovered that the Kenyan shilling is fully convertible. This means that the central bank could choose either the path of the exchange rate or the interest rate, but not both, in line with the macroeconomic policy trilemma. If it tried to keep domestic interest rates artificially low, the shilling would tend to depreciate against the dollar as investors moved out of shilling assets. But, once again, the evidence did not cooperate: the Kenyan shilling was actually *appreciating* against the US dollar between 2004 and 2006 in nominal terms! Having ruled out manipulation (it is a bit of a letdown when things do not conform to your priors) I decided to ask officials in the Ministry of Finance and private sector investors why interest rates had fallen so low. And the answer invariably was: "Because the government's borrowing requirements have come down." This made perfect sense; but one should always be suspicious of answers which make perfect sense. So I asked myself: when do the government's borrowing requirements come down?

Borrowing requirements come down when one or more of the following happen: (a) the government makes the central bank finance its fiscal deficit, that is, it prints money; (b) the government uses privatization proceeds to finance its fiscal deficit instead of borrowing; and (c) the government reduces its fiscal deficit. Option (a) is easy to rule out for Kenya: if it works, it will do so only briefly because much of government's domestic debt is short-term and investors will soon demand higher nominal interest rates to compensate for what they see as the risk of rising inflation. In fact, Kenya eschewed inflationary finance after 2003. Option (b) did not apply: privatization proceeds were not a major factor during the period under consideration. This left option (c). Keeping in mind that the fiscal deficit is the sum of the primary deficit and interest payments, Figure 5.1 plots both as shares of GDP between 1992 and 2008.

Kenya was running primary surpluses (or negative primary deficits) throughout this period except for the last three years, 2006 to 2008. These surpluses were sizable, especially over the period 1994–6, as the government sought to restore credibility in the wake of the Goldenberg scandal. Here's what happened. Desperate for foreign exchange after the freezing of foreign aid in 1991, the Kenyan central bank attempted to encourage exports by offering a special foreign exchange premium, of which a company called

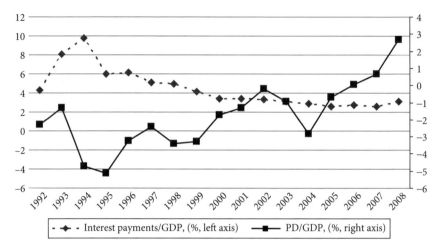

**Figure 5.1**  Kenya: Primary Deficit and Interest Payments 1992–2008
*Source:* Calculations based on World Bank data.

Goldenberg fraudulently took advantage. It set up a round-tripping scheme (buying dollars from the market, repackaging these as the proceeds from gold and diamond exports, and selling these to the central bank at the offered premium and then repeating the process) which is estimated to have cost between $600 million and $1 billion, or a sizable 9–16 percent of 1994 GDP.[4] Banks connected to Goldenberg collapsed and, with its credibility in tatters, the government was forced to ramp-up primary fiscal surpluses while also shifting to the domestic debt market to pay off maturing external debt, even as interest rates spiked. Interest payments on government debt were 8 percent of GDP in 1993, peaked at close to 10 percent of GDP in 1994, and then declined steadily after that, even before the 2002 elections (Figure 5.1). This indicated that the hike in the primary surplus had almost immediate positive consequences. In addition, economic liberalization was pursued. By the end of 1994, prices, interest rates, and the exchange rate were all liberalized.

The fiscal deficit (primary deficit plus interest payments) dropped from the 5–7 percent GDP range in the early 1990s to the 1–3 percent range after 1995 right up to 2006, lending credence to the answer that real interest rates on domestic debt were indeed falling because borrowing requirements were going down as averred by Finance Ministry officials and private firms.[5] But the crucial point is that, after 1995, the fiscal deficit, and hence borrowing requirements, came down *because* interest payments were coming down; the primary surplus was on a *decreasing* trajectory. Emerging markets like Brazil and Turkey were having a hard time lowering their real interest rates after the crises of 1997–2001 in spite of large, sustained *increases* in their primary fiscal surpluses, as we shall see in Chapter 8. Obviously, reforms during the arap Moi era helped Kenya. But I shall argue later in this chapter that the 2002 elections were a threshold event in lowering political risk, lengthening private sector investment horizons, and putting growth on a much more positive path, as is apparent from Table 5.1. Some background is in order before I present the evidence based on the underlying improvement in the government's debt dynamics, and ultimately on what the private sector said and did.

## Political Risk, Cost of Capital, and Private Investment

Reduced political risk can lower the interest rates the government pays on its debt, thereby lowering fiscal deficits and improving debt dynamics. Since the government is the best credit in most countries, lower interest rates for it translate into a lower cost of capital for the private sector, which could spark more investment and faster growth.

Let's start with the government. If capital is freely mobile, the nominal rate of interest the Kenyan government pays on its one-year T-bill, $i$, will be linked to the interest rate in a benchmark country like the USA via an equation like:

$$i = i^{US} + \hat{e} + (\pi + \theta), \tag{5.1}$$

where $i^{US}$ is the nominal interest rate on one-year US T-bills and $\hat{e}$ is the target rate of depreciation of the Kenyan shilling/dollar exchange rate. As an example, suppose the interest rate on one-year US T-bills, $i^{US}$, is 3 percent and the Kenyan central bank announces a target rate of depreciation, $\hat{e}$, of 5 percent. Then investors would demand at least 8 percent on Kenyan T-bills: this is standard interest rate parity. But we would expect that the higher the political risk, the higher the chances that the government might inflate away its debt or renege on its debt contracts, raising devaluation and default risks, and hence the interest rate investors demand for buying government debt. In equation (5.1), $\pi$ is the devaluation risk premium, that is, compensation for a situation where the depreciation of the currency exceeds its official target; and $\theta$ is the default risk premium, that is, compensation for the risk of default relative to a benchmark country like the USA.[6]

Underlying equation (5.1) is a simple point: devaluation and default are both ways of restoring balance to the government intertemporal budget constraint by lowering the debt-to-GDP ratio. The alternative is to increase primary surpluses and/or implement structural reforms to enable faster growth. Since the market is presumably aware of these more palatable alternatives, high devaluation and default risk premia imply it does not attach much credence to their success.

While devaluation and default risks are readily understandable for emerging markets, what is their relevance for low-income countries like Kenya, which borrow from official sources? The answer is that most low-income countries borrow significantly at the margin from their domestic capital markets by issuing Treasury bills at market interest rates. These rates are driven by an equation similar to (5.1), considering that capital accounts tend to be open and foreign portfolio investors often participate in these markets.

Turning to the private sector, apart from raising its cost of capital, political risk has a profound effect through its impact on investment horizons. When political risk is high and governance weak, property rights are likely to be shaky and expropriation risks high, leading to short horizons. Horizons would also shorten if there is a danger that the rules for business might change abruptly with a new political leader. An example illustrates how damaging short horizons can be.

A private firm is considering whether to invest the equivalent of $100 in a given project. Its opportunity cost would be the $i$ of equation (5.1), as it could simply put the money in Kenyan T-bills. Assume that $i$ is 10 percent and that the project involves buying a machine which lasts for 20 years; it depreciates at 5 percent per year. In this case, the firm would require a minimum return of 15 percent in order to invest in the machine. Thus, the minimum or hurdle rate of return is $i$ plus the rate of depreciation of the machinery, which would just about make the firm indifferent between putting its money in T-bills and investing in the project. However, in an uncertain political environment, the firm may have to exit the business before the 20 years are up. For the sake of argument, assume elections are going to be held in a year's time and if the outcome is bad, the machine will have to be hastily disposed of in a fire sale to politically well-connected firms for $70. In this case, the hurdle rate of return will shoot up to 40 percent and the investment, although profitable in a normal environment, may never take place. Thus, short horizons raise the hurdle rate of return and, if this becomes excessively high, little investment will take place, leading to stagnation.

## Competing Explanations for the Economic Improvement

Two potential candidates vied with reduced political risk as an explanation for the acceleration in growth and the accompanying drop in real interest rates after 2003 even as primary surpluses shrank. The first was the lagged benefits from reform that had been carried out during the arap Moi era. Pushed first by the aid freeze and then by the need to counteract the Goldenberg scandal, the government ramped-up primary surpluses and liberalized prices, and the trade and exchange system. Later, it cut marginal tax rates sharply for income tax and the value-added tax (VAT) which had been raised to enable the large primary surpluses needed after Goldenberg.

These were remarkably positive steps for any country, leave alone one considered to be badly run and politically unstable; the arap Moi regime chose not to repudiate Kenya's debt, although this would have been in keeping with its perceived character. By the early 2000s, Kenya was collecting 21–23 percent of GDP in revenues, several percentage points higher than its neighbors, Tanzania and Uganda. Equally impressive was its reliance on broad-based taxes like VAT and the income tax, symptomatic of good fiscal management, instead of printing money and taxing imports—the easy ways out for a society torn by conflict.

The second competing explanation is that all developing countries were benefiting from the benign global environment which set in after September 11, 2001 and persisted until the subprime mortgage crisis reared its head in the summer of 2006 in the USA. The lagged effects of the arap Moi era reforms, plus the historically low global interest rates between 2001 and 2006, could have lowered Kenyan interest rates after 2003. The latter would have worked by lowering $i^{US}$ in equation (5.1). Indeed, interest rates on 91-day US T-bills fell from 3.5 percent in 2001 to 1 percent in 2003; but the rate on the 91-day Kenyan T-bill fell by much more, from 12.7 percent in 2001 to

3.7 percent in 2003, even through inflation rose slightly. So there was clearly a Kenya-specific effect increasing the attractiveness of Kenyan shilling assets.

Thus, good things happened during the arap Moi era following the aid freeze, and the benign global economic environment helped. Let us now examine the government's debt dynamics and see what light this sheds on the December 2002 elections as a positive turning point.

## Government Debt Dynamics

This section identifies the main factors driving the reduction in government debt from 73 percent of GDP in 1995/6 to 45 percent in 2006/7, and demonstrates a discernible improvement after 2003, following the successful presidential transition of December 2002. A good starting point is equation (iv) in Box 3.2, which I shall rewrite as:

$$\dot{d} = pd + (r - g)d \qquad (5.2)$$

where $d$ is the public debt-to-GDP ratio, $\dot{d}$ its change over time, $pd$ the ratio of the primary fiscal deficit to GDP, $r$ the real interest rate, and $g$ the real growth rate of GDP.[7] Since the government can borrow either in local or foreign currency, the effective real interest rate would reflect movements in nominal exchange rates as well the difference in inflation rates between Kenya and the USA, assuming for simplicity that all foreign borrowing is in dollars. All this can be combined to get the following expression for $r$ (derived in Annex 2 as part of equation (A10')):

$$r = wr_d + (1 - w)(r_\$ - \rho). \qquad (5.3)$$

In equation (5.3), $w$ and $(1-w)$ are the shares of local currency (Kenyan shilling) and dollar-denominated debt in total government debt respectively, and $r_d$ the real interest on Kenyan shilling debt (the nominal interest rate adjusted for inflation). The real interest rate paid on dollar debt, $r_\$$, is the nominal dollar interest rate paid by the Kenyan government on its dollar borrowings adjusted for US inflation—for example, if Kenya pays 3 percent on its (concessional) dollar loans and US inflation is 2 percent, $r_\$$ would be 1 percent; while $\rho$ is the real appreciation of the dollar/Kenyan shilling exchange rate (defined so that $\rho$ is positive when the bilateral real exchange rate with

**Box 5.2** Decomposing Debt Buildups or Reductions

Suppose the government is running a primary fiscal surplus of 3 percent of GDP every year (that is, *pd* equals –0.03 in equation (5.2)). This by itself would act to lower the debt-to-GDP ratio by 3 percentage points *every year*. So if it started at 73 percent of GDP it would end up at 70 percent by the end of the year. On the other hand, a primary fiscal deficit of 3 percent to GDP would raise the debt-to-GDP ratio to 76 percent by the end of the year.

   Now suppose the economy were growing by 6 percent per year. This would lower the debt-to-GDP ratio by approximately 4.4 percentage points of GDP in a year, starting with a 73 percent debt-to-GDP ratio; looking at equation (5.2), this is simply $-gd$, where $g$ is 6 percent and $d$ is 0.73.

   Since some of the debt is in dollars, the debt-to-GDP ratio will fall if the Kenyan shilling appreciates against the dollar and rise if it depreciates instead. Looking at equation (5.3), the impact will be higher the larger the share of dollar-denominated debt in total government debt and the bigger the real appreciation of the Kenyan shilling; $(1-w)$ was 60 percent in 2002/03.

   Equation (5.3) can be used to isolate the effect of movements in the real exchange rate on the debt-to-GDP ratio. This can be done by rewriting equation (5.3) as follows: $r = \tilde{r} - (1 - w)\rho$; by comparison with equation (5.3), it follows that $\tilde{r} = wr_d + (1 - w)r_\$$, while the rest is the impact of the real appreciation/depreciation.[a] The so-called debt decomposition results presented in Table 5.2 rely on the discrete-time equivalent of such an equation; a derivation of the latter is presented in Aizenman and Pinto (2005, p. 554).

---

[a] We shall make use of this result in Chapter 7 on Russia as well.

the dollar appreciates), so that $r_\$ - \rho$ is simply the real interest rate paid on dollar-denominated debt translated into Kenyan shilling terms. Equation (5.3) can be used to isolate the impact of real exchange rate movements on the debt-to-GDP ratio. Box 5.2 contains some numerical examples to illustrate how equations (5.2) and (5.3) can help.

   Table 5.2 presents the results we are interested in, with the 11-year period divided into two subperiods: the first 7 years 1996/7 to 2002/3; and the last 4 years 2003/4 to 2006/7, in order to see if there was any change after 2003.[8]

   The numbers shown in the last three columns of the table are the average *annual* changes induced in the debt-to-GDP ratio by the factors shown in the first column. The effect of the primary fiscal balance is shown in row 1. Over the first seven years, primary surpluses acted to *lower* the government's debt by 1.7 percentage points of GDP per year; but over the next four years, the

**Table 5.2** Factors Explaining Falling Indebtedness 1996/7–2006/7
(% points of GDP, annual average)

|  | 1996/7 –2002/3 | 2003/4 –2006/7 | 1996/7 –2006/7 |
|---|---|---|---|
| Change in public sector debt | −1.4 | −4.5 | −2.5 |
| *Contribution from* | | | |
| 1. Primary deficit | −1.7 | 0.4 | −0.9 |
| 2. Real GDP growth | −1.5 | −3.3 | −2.1 |
| 3. Real interest rate | 2.2 | 0.4 | 1.5 |
| 4. Real exchange rate | 0.8 | −2.2 | −0.3 |
| 5. Other factors | −1.2 | 0.2 | −0.7 |

*Source:* Bandiera, Kumar, and Pinto (2008), based on Statistical Bulletins of the
Ministry of Finance of Kenya and the 2009 Debt Sustainability Analysis.

primary balance went into deficit and *raised* debt by an average of 0.4 percentage points per year. The effect of the switch in the primary fiscal balance was, therefore, to raise the debt-to-GDP ratio by 2 percentage points per year. Here are the highlights from the table:

- The pace of debt reduction accelerated by 3 percentage points of GDP after 2003 from 1.4 to 4.5, even though the average primary surplus fell by 2 percentage points.

- Growth acceleration helped (row 2).

- But the biggest impact came from the joint effect of the drop in the real interest rate and real appreciation of the Kenyan shilling (row 3 plus 4). This switched from *raising* debt by 3 percentage points per year to *lowering* it by 1.8 percentage points after 2003, a swing of close to 5 percentage points of GDP *per year*!

Essentially, Kenyan shilling-denominated assets became more attractive as a result of lower political risk, leading to falling interest rates and an appreciation of the currency, both of which dramatically improved debt dynamics.

## Polling the Private Sector

It was finally time to ask the private sector. The December 2002 presidential election had resulted in a smooth transition from the much-reviled, long-time incumbent Daniel arap Moi to Mwai Kibaki, who had a reputation for being pro-business. Could this have lowered political risk in the eyes of investors, leading to a fall in real interest rates by reducing devaluation and default risk? From informal polls, it quickly became apparent that the private sector regarded the election as a watershed. "You no longer need political connections to do business," was a common reply to the question of whether the December 2002 presidential succession had lowered political risk, with firms more apt to reinvest their profits than before 2003.

Further confirmation of the crucial nature of lower political risk was obtained when the World Bank's 2007 Investment Climate Assessment (ICA) survey results were compared with those from 2003. Based on a panel of 169 manufacturing firms that participated in both surveys, the fraction of manufacturing firms which perceived political instability or uncertainty as a "major-to-severe" constraint dropped sharply from 47 percent in 2003 to 18 percent in June 2007, as shown in Table 5.3; while the fraction considering macroeconomic stability to be a major constraint dropped equally sharply from 50 percent in 2003 to 28 percent in 2007. Interestingly, electricity and

**Table 5.3** Firm Perceptions of Major or Severe Constraints to Business (% reporting issue as constraint)

| Issue | 2003 | 2007 |
|---|---|---|
| Crime, Theft and Disorder | 69 | 59 |
| Tax Rates | 69 | 56 |
| Electricity | 47 | 55 |
| Corruption | 73 | 54 |
| Transportation | 36 | 53 |
| Practices of Competitors in Informal Sector | 64 | 50 |
| Tax Administration | 52 | 50 |
| Customs and Trade Regulations | 40 | 42 |
| Telecommunications | 45 | 28 |
| Business Licensing and Permits | 13 | 28 |
| Macroeconomic Instability | 50 | 28 |
| Access to Finance | 71 | 26 |
| Political Instability | 47 | 18 |
| Access to Land | 23 | 16 |
| Labor Regulations | 22 | 16 |
| Inadequately Educated Labor Force | 31 | 11 |

*Source:* World Bank (2003b and 2007), reported in Bandiera, Kumar, and Pinto (2008).

transportation were viewed as bigger constraints in 2007 than 2003, which fits with the idea that investment was picking up and the lack of infrastructure was beginning to bite. Another worthwhile observation is that the fraction of respondents labeling access to finance as a constraint dropped dramatically from 71 to 26 percent, explicable by the "reduced borrowing requirements of the government," with its beneficial impacts on the private sector's cost of capital. The 2007 Investment Climate Assessment reported that a bigger percentage of surveyed manufacturing firms were preparing multiyear business plans in 2007 (58 percent) than five years before (49 percent).

There was a coincident impressive takeoff in machinery and industrial transport equipment imports starting in 2003. These imports averaged 5.6 percent of gross domestic expenditure (GDE, defined as consumption plus investment plus government spending) over the 1996–2002 period, but rose sharply to an average of 9.3 percent of GDE over 2003–06. This was a positive sign for faster long-run growth and productivity: recall the 1992 study by Bradford DeLong and Lawrence Summers referred to in Chapter 2, in which they argued that there is a strong, possibly causal, link between equipment investment and long-run growth because better equipment and technology would facilitate learning by doing and knowledge spillovers. For a low-income country like Kenya, the increase in machinery imports was a good omen. Indeed, microeconomic evidence from the 2007 Investment Climate Assessment confirms significant growth in total factor productivity during the period 2002–6 after stagnation during the 1990s.[9]

In addition to pointing to lower political risk, private sector firms I informally interviewed in mid-2006 unanimously concurred that the economic reforms set in train by the cutoff of donor funding in the early 1990s had been a major stimulus to higher efficiency and productivity. Box 5.3 highlights the efficacy of import competition in stimulating higher efficiency at the firm level. Combined with the rising imports of machinery and shared learning across firms, a conducive atmosphere for rising productivity was being established.

## Insights from Kenya

The first lesson is about lags and the importance of hard budgets. Events during the arap Moi era shows that even a country with governance problems can

---

**Box 5.3** Vignettes from Interviews with Private Sector Firms, July 2006

- Firm owners said that import tariff reductions had spurred exports because it had lowered their costs.[a] One firm described this as decisive in doubling its capacity in 2003, even more important than the fall in interest rates.
- All firms pointed to falling profit margins as a consequence of greater import competition being instrumental in generating pressure to increase productivity by reducing waste and technological upgrading. Many mentioned adopting Gemba Kaizen techniques to reduce waste, get workers more involved in preventive maintenance, and ensure jobs on the shopfloor were done more productively.[b]
- Kenyan labor force was typically described as well educated and the best in the region.

In short: import competition was forcing firms to become more innovative, while cheaper imports increased the incentive for exports and spurred capacity expansion.

---

[a] The reader will recognize this as Lerner symmetry: a tax on imports is a tax on exports.

[b] Gemba Kaizen in Japanese means change for the better (kaizen) in the workplace (gemba). It was originated by Masaaki Imai, a Japanese management consultant, who established the Kaizen Institute in 1986.

---

achieve significant reform if the government faces hard budget constraints, as Kenya did after aid was frozen in 1991; but there is a risk. Arap Moi could have defaulted and driven his country into the ground, as Mugabe did in Zimbabwe. As it turns out, significant fiscal, monetary, and trade reforms were implemented during his rule. But long lags were involved in reaping the benefits; and the threshold of clean elections in the shape of the December 2002 elections had to be crossed before these materialized.

Second, the positive impact of lower political risk on debt dynamics and the macroeconomic environment was reinforced by complementary microeconomic improvements in the investment climate. The lower cost of capital and the real appreciation, which made imports of machinery cheaper, helped the private sector. Hence, what we were witnessing in 2006 was a virtuous, self-reinforcing cycle of macro–micro linkages (depicted in Figure 5.2) that should have made the Kenyans proud until the disastrous December 2007 elections.

Third, one should be cautious about premature declarations of victory when political risk is grounded in social fragmentation driven by tribal

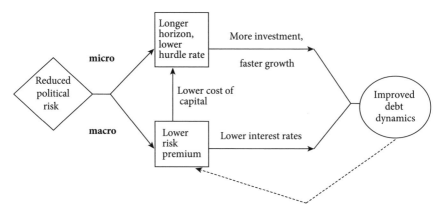

**Figure 5.2** Political Risk, Investment, and Debt Dynamics

rivalry, as in Kenya. With the wisdom of hindsight, there was overconfidence that Kenya had licked the problem of presidential transition based on the successful December 2002 presidential election. Political scientists whom I met in July 2006, and again during a second visit in February 2007, felt that it no longer mattered who the incumbent president was because, as the private sector had noted, political connections were no longer needed for business. It was also argued that elections could no longer be stolen because of cell phones and the Internet: people would text in results as they came in, preventing ballots from being "miscounted" at a later stage. This assessment proved excessively optimistic, as demonstrated by the setback during the December 2007 elections.

Looking forward, much of the action to lower politically and socially driven volatility in Kenya has to be homegrown; it cannot be imposed by donors. This underlines a powerful message: for many low-income countries, creating a foundation for political stability and long-run social cohesion is as important for sustained long-run growth as economic reform. One has to only look at countries like China, India, and Vietnam to realize that Kenya will need political stability and social cohesion for a prolonged period of 15 to 20 years if it hopes to make a breakthrough in terms of its growth trajectory. Otherwise it will remain mired in the discouraging stop-go, volatile pattern of growth so familiar in low-income countries over the past few decades.

## Postscript

In February 2010, I presented my findings on Kenya at Columbia University's Institute of African Studies. It is not often that an economist gets to interact with political scientists. Besides, some of the professors in the audience routinely spent up to six months a year in Kenya and knew it far better than me! The irony is that my Bank colleagues and I had woven political risk into our story completely by accident because it turned out to be the only tenable explanation for the sharp decline in real interest rates on Kenyan shilling T-bills. And yet the importance of lowering political risk proved to be the crucial insight from Kenya.

The key point I took away from the Columbia University seminar was that political risk is a many-splendored thing. Expropriation risks are different from those posed by social fragmentation and potential civil strife. Big and small firms may react differently to political risk depending upon access to political patronage. Besides, the business and political elite could coincide. These nuances are important because they affect private investor behavior differently. As one professor pointed out, the key issue for Kenya was to understand how social cohesion got broken. Simple redistribution might not be enough; there was considerable impunity at local levels clubbed with violence. This meant a deeper analysis of political risk in Kenya was needed. In any event, the experience over the 2003–7 pointed to the following as a minimal agenda to aim for: (a) continue the good management of the public finances; (b) continue to take steps to sever the links between political connections and business; and (c) ensure clean, nonviolent elections.

So was the World Bank right to pull its Kenya loan in February 2006? The economic analysis showed that the public finances were being well managed and that there had been a positive trend in private sector perceptions about falling corruption and political risk after the December 2002 elections. In such circumstances, an alternative to pulling loans is to give credit where credit is due, while at the same time conveying a message which says, "Forget about the 10 percent growth rate target in your Vision 2030 if you can't entrench political stability and social cohesion"; and initiate a public debate on this.[10] This could have a powerful effect and convey that, for countries like Kenya, addressing political risk and social cohesion is as important as economic fundamentals.

## Notes

1. "Wolfowitz 'to target corruption'." BBC News, February 7, 2006. <http://news.bbc.co.uk/2/hi/business/4688022.stm>.
2. From the abstract to Steeves (2006).
3. Much of this is based on a long conversation with Professor Terry Ryan in Nairobi in 2006. He is rightly credited with being the moving force behind the market-based reforms during the arap Moi era.
4. Warutere (2005).
5. The fiscal deficit went above 3 percent of GDP in 2007 and then got close to 6 percent in 2008; but 2008 was marred by the disastrous presidential elections of December 2007 and the global financial crisis.
6. This formulation draws upon Frankel and McCarthy (1988).
7. Essentially, inflation is being subtracted from the nominal interest rate and nominal growth rate in equation (iv), Box 3.2 to get equation (5.2). See also the derivations in Annex 2, equation (A9').
8. The choice of this period was dictated by practicality: we had a consistent, unrevised data series at the time of the study, namely, 2006–07.
9. Soderbom (2004) reported that average firm-level TFP increased by 7 percent (but was not statistically significantly different from zero) over the entire 1999–2002 period. Using a similar methodology, ICA (World Bank 2007) reports a statistically significant TFP increase of 15 percent over 2002–06 in manufacturing firms.
10. This book refers to the October 2007 version of Kenya's Vision 2030, published three months before the fateful December 2007 elections.

# CHAPTER 6

# India's Unanticipated Growth Takeoff

*The growth rate of an entire economy is not an easy thing to move around.*
—Robert E. Lucas Jr. (1988, p. 13)

You might think that if a country's growth rate doubles to 8 percent from less than 4 percent the previous year, and then stays at this higher level, someone might have anticipated it. Especially if that country is India, with over a billion people and home to some 25 percent of all the world's poor. This is what happened in 2003/4. Yet the World Bank, the IMF, all the eminent economists who track India, even the Government of India, missed the takeoff.

Why did no one anticipate it? The growth spurt did not fit with conventional wisdom: a country where the debt of the consolidated government had risen from less than 50 percent of GDP in 1980 to over 80 percent in 2002/3, where the fiscal deficit was in the 9–10 percent of GDP range, and where the real interest rate paid on government debt was rising, with growth slowing after 1997, should have been on the verge of a macroeconomic crisis, not a growth spurt. Prominent economists writing early in the new millennium spoke of fiscal profligacy, a looming crisis, and wasted opportunity—on the very eve of the 2003 growth takeoff. The World Bank itself concluded in its 2003 development policy review that, while a crisis was unlikely, growth was being stifled by the fiscal stance.[1] A fiscal adjustment aimed at raising revenues, reducing wasteful food, fertilizer, and energy subsidies, and improving the composition of public spending was recommended for spurring growth.

There is another explanation why the growth spurt was not anticipated, silly though it may seem. Economists tend to be specialized, and those working on the macro naturally concluded that rising government debt and deficits would lead to a slowdown in private investment through the standard channels of crowding out, uncertainty, and higher interest rates. Private investment became sluggish after 1997, confirming this view. But there was something deeper going on at the microeconomic level, which was missed: a transformation making Indian firms more competitive on the world stage. A striking feature of the growth spurt was that it was driven by the manufacturing sector. Its growth had languished at 2 percent per year for six years before jumping to 7 percent in 2003/4 and then to 8 and then 9 percent in the two years which followed. This sector is India's most tax-buoyant and the key to manufactured exports. The growth rate in the booming service sector was 8.4 percent per year in the six years preceding 2003/4 and subsequently rose to the 9–10 percent range. This was impressive, but could not have been the source of the growth spurt. To add grist to the mill, India began implementing a wide range of reforms and opening up its economy to the rest of the world following a balance-of-payments crisis in 1991. The reforms had major negative fiscal consequences; but eventually forced manufacturing firms to restructure.

The explanation in this chapter of the 2003 growth takeoff harks back to the reforms of 1991 and their lagged effects. Public finances deteriorated after 1997 not because of fiscal profligacy but because of the cumulating (macro-fiscal) cost of the 1991 reforms. The lagged (microeconomic) benefit appeared in the shape of better firms and banks, which underpinned the post-2003 growth resurgence. This explanation emerged from analysis carried out for two World Bank reports on India, one in 2003 and the other in 2006.[2] Its essence is the macro-micro *interdependence* between fiscal and debt outcomes and firm-level restructuring decisions, instead of the one-way *causality* from fiscal profligacy to lower growth posited by most of the then prevalent analyses. Box 6.1 sets out the analytical links between the India story and chapters 2 and 3.

Table 6.1 contains a timeline that divides 1985–2007 into five subperiods. The first subperiod serves as a benchmark. While growth picked up in the late 1980s, fiscal deficits rose and government debt became unsustainable.[3]

**Box 6.1**  India—Analytical Interlude

The conundrum motivating this chapter is how India escaped a macroeconomic crisis in spite of deteriorating fiscal fundamentals and then, in apparent defiance of economic logic, shifted abruptly to rapid growth in the early 2000s. The "solution" appeals to key ideas in Chapters 2 and 3 as well as Annex 2.

First, with primary deficits increasing and real interest rates beginning to exceed growth rates during the early 2000s, government debt was, by definition, on an unsustainable path (as is evident from equation (A9')). But this was unlikely to morph into insolvency because India had built up a big cushion of foreign exchange reserves after its 1991 balance of payments crisis: high liquidity gives the government time to remedy the situation. In contrast, Russia in 1998 (as we shall explore in Chapter 7) had both unsustainable debt dynamics *and* low reserves with the market, signaling exceptionally high levels of default and devaluation risk.

Second, India's experience brings out the distinction between *unsustainability* and *insolvency* referred to in Box 3.1. Debt dynamics had become unsustainable in large part because of *reform costs*: import and financial repression taxes were cut substantially, with the latter contributing to rising real interest rates. Therefore, once *reform benefits* appeared in the shape of faster growth and higher future taxes, the present value of future primary surpluses would increase, ensuring solvency.

But, third, a myopic international capital market may not attach sufficient importance to primary surpluses in the distant future and may force a crisis as a self-fulfilling prophecy. India was sheltered from this possibility because of its high reserves and the decision to go slow on capital account liberalization. Besides, state-owned banks held a large fraction of government debt and this would prevent a disorderly selloff.

Fourth, the eventual growth takeoff captures two features of *the macro–micro linkages* so essential to a healthy government intertemporal budget constraint (GIBC): (i) allowing for long lags while these linkages play out, with macro-fiscal reform costs being borne first and microeconomic benefits coming much later (high foreign exchange reserves and gradual capital account liberalization lower vulnerability in the interim); and (ii) path dependence, meaning one has to be careful about attributing good (or bad) economic outcomes during a particular period to policy actions undertaken during that period itself. This was the case during the late 1990s when economic outcomes began deteriorating.

Fifth, India's Tenth Plan document covering 2002–7 had a growth target close to 8 percent compared to the 5.4 percent average growth rate actually achieved during the Ninth Plan (India, Planning Commission 2002, p. 30, table 2.7). This was a substantial step up, begging two interlinked questions: (i) Could the big required increase in the savings rate, estimated by the Tenth Plan document at 6 percentage points of GDP, be achieved without first raising the growth rate itself? (ii) How to counter diminishing marginal returns to capital? Box 2.2 showed that not only might the savings rate have to be raised substantially to achieve a higher growth target, it would have to be raised continually so long as the growth target was in excess of the steady-state growth rate. This meant paying attention to policies that would induce self-sustaining growth. Trade liberalization and easing domestic entry barriers raised product market competition and stimulated higher productivity in India—as in Poland's early transition—helping speed up growth and facilitating the rise in the savings rate, as captured in Figure 2.1 for India and China.

This led to a balance-of-payments crisis in 1991, which became a turning point for the Indian economy. The first steps were taken to convert it from a virtually closed to an open economy—but with slowness on opening up the capital account, which would later prove a saving grace. The reforms included liberalizing external trade, foreign direct investment, and domestic investment; initial steps on tax reform, the easing of financial repression, and liberalization of the domestic capital market. And, determined to avoid the embarrassment of another balance of payments crisis, the government decided to build up foreign exchange reserves, adopt a more flexible exchange rate, and shift toward the issuance of long-term rupee debt.

Economic outcomes were highly encouraging during the Eighth Plan period—the first five years after the start of reform—as shown in the third row of the table.[4] But things turned upside down during the Ninth Plan period, with a return to unsustainability in the government's debt dynamics. And then, against all odds, growth took off in 2003/4. It would have been difficult to pinpoint a cause in terms of *proximate* policy reform; but cumulatively there had been substantial reform since the 1991 balance of payments crisis.

The events depicted in the table provoke three questions:

1. With the government debt-to-GDP ratio above 80 percent and unsustainability creeping back into its debt dynamics, how did India avoid a crisis after 1997 when emerging markets such as Russia and Argentina fell victim to major crises with much more "modest" numbers?

2. Was the government to blame for fiscal profligacy and slowing growth during the Ninth Plan period?

3. Why did growth take off in 2003 when just about everyone was predicting a crisis?

**Table 6.1** Economic Timeline for India 1985–2007

| Subperiod | Defining Event(s) | Outcomes |
|---|---|---|
| 1985/6–1989/90 (benchmark period) | Fiscal deficit jumped to 9–10% of GDP in second half; growth accelerated to the 6% range. | Debt-to-GDP ratio rose by 25 percentage points and dynamics became unsustainable in the late 1980s.[a] |
| *1990/1–1991/2* (turning point) | Balance of payments crisis, triggered by oil price hike linked to the Iraqi invasion of Kuwait and falloff in transfers from nonresident Indians. | Rupee devalued July 1991. Growth slowed and debt-to-GDP ratio rose another 7 percentage points. |
| 1992/3–1996/7 (Eighth Plan period) | Crisis spurred macroeconomic and structural reform: the latter aimed at opening up the economy. | Growth recovered, fiscal deficits were cut, and debt-to-GDP ratio fell from 81 to 68 percent. |
| 1997/8–2001/2 (Ninth Plan period) | Reform momentum slowed, accompanied by accusations of fiscal profligacy and concerns about a crisis. | Growth slowed, fiscal deficits rose, and the debt-to-GDP ratio returned to 81 percent. Unsustainability crept into debt dynamics with significant primary deficits, and real interest rates catching up with growth rates. |
| 2002/3–2006/7 (Tenth Plan period. *Growth takeoff after 2003*) | Twelfth Finance Commission gave a fillip to state-level fiscal reform. Fiscal Responsibility and Budget Management Act became effective mid-2004, aimed at lowering indebtedness and increasing government saving. Tax reform and revenue mobilization picked up. | Growth took off starting in 2003, and debt-to-GDP ratio started falling after peaking at 87 percent in 2003/04. *The growth acceleration had no proximate policy cause.* |

[a] Throughout this chapter, "debt" will refer to the consolidated debt of the central government and the state governments.

## How Did India Avoid a Macroeconomic Meltdown After 1997?

The answer begins in 1991. There is no good explanation for why the balance of payments crisis that year did not translate into a full-blown macroeconomic crisis. Government debt was on an unsustainable course (according to Buiter and Patel 1992), reserves were low, and the exchange rate fixed—classic ingredients for a full-blown macroeconomic crisis. In emerging markets as diverse as Argentina, Russia, and Turkey, this combination proved lethal and led to triple debt-cum-banking-cum-exchange rate crises, with defaults in Argentina and Russia. Since a debt crisis did not occur in India in 1991, we can infer that even though the government's debt was on an unsustainable trajectory—calling for reform and a shift in policies—it was deemed solvent. Primary surpluses could always be raised in the future. Besides, India's inflation track record was decent and it has never defaulted on its sovereign debt. Its citizens have had high confidence in public institutions, especially the banks. India is debt-tolerant in the parlance of Carmen Reinhart, Kenneth Rogoff, and Miguel Savastano (2003). These are valid reasons why a major crisis was averted in 1991; but they involve ex post facto rationalization.

Ironically, it is easier to explain why India did not have a debt crisis after 1997 in spite of the rash of papers predicting dire consequences for the fiscal accounts.[5] Unsustainability reminiscent of the late 1980s had crept into the government's debt dynamics. Not only were primary deficits large, but, with financial repression substantially reduced, the knock-on effect of higher real interest rates began to feed through. T. N. Srinivasan (2002, p. 68) wrote, "When the economy seems to be at last on the verge of achieving sustained and rapid growth, jeopardizing it is unconscionable."[6] But a crisis was avoided during the Ninth Plan period even as other emerging market countries with seemingly better fiscal fundamentals succumbed to crises—and for good reason.

The big difference between the Ninth Plan period and pre-1991 was the government's decision to shift to rupee-denominated debt and build up foreign exchange reserves following the 1991 crisis. The big differences between India and emerging market countries which had endured a crisis during 1997–2001 were that India had high reserves relative to short-term external debt, and a flexible exchange rate; the government was debt-tolerant with long maturity debt denominated mainly in local currency; and balance sheet currency mismatches in firms and banks were largely absent. The last was clearly facilitated by the slow approach to capital account liberalization. In its 2003 development policy review, the World Bank stressed that even though India was not on the verge of a crisis, the public finances were not conducive to maximizing growth prospects and had jeopardized the attainment of the Tenth Plan growth targets, as India's Planning Commission itself had concluded. Part of this was because of the standard problems associated with high fiscal deficits, including crowding out and macroeconomic uncertainty. Besides, developmental and capital expenditure had been cut and government savings had fallen. But international liquidity was at safe levels. Foreign exchange reserves had grown from a paltry $4 billion at the end of 1989/90 to $75 billion by end of 2002/3. The ratio of broad money to reserves had fallen from 37 to just 4.7, and the ratio of short-term external debt to reserves from 3.65 to just 0.18 over the same period. With this level of liquidity and India's good credit history, a speculative attack was unlikely, notwithstanding the fiscal deterioration.[7]

## Was the Government to Blame for the "Bad" Outcomes of the Ninth Plan Period?

There were two parts to the blame game that began during the Ninth Plan period: slowing reform and fiscal profligacy. While the much-lauded Eighth Plan period was reform-intensive, the reforms were *gradual* with two implications. First, the reforms may not have garnered the credibility and mass needed to alter the behavior of firms and banks fast enough. Second, the reforms began to bite only during the Ninth Plan period on two fronts: the easing of financial repression, which meant rising interest payments on government debt; and trade liberalization. Only after 1996 did tariffs fall enough to put pressure on firms to become more efficient, as we shall see later in this chapter. The Ninth Plan period bore the brunt of the cost of the reforms which had begun in 1991.

To shed light on the accusation of fiscal profligacy, I shall make use of equation (iv) in Box 3.2, rewriting it to bring out the effects of the reforms. This equation is about how the debt-to-GDP ratio, $d$, changes over time. The primary deficit can be expressed as capital expenditure ($k$) plus noninterest current expenditure ($n$) minus the sum of indirect taxes like customs and excise duties ($\tau$) and other revenues ($t$), all expressed as ratios of GDP. Financial repression essentially means the government borrows at rates lower than it would have paid in a free market. This can be captured by writing the nominal interest rate paid by the government as $i = i^m - \phi$, where $i^m$ is the liberalized market nominal interest rate and $\phi > 0$ is the implicit financial repression tax wedge. This gives us:

$$\dot{d} = \left[ k + n - (\tau + t) \right] + \left[ \left( i^m - \phi \right) - g^N \right] d, \qquad (6.1)$$

where the first term on the right-hand side (RHS) in square brackets is the rewritten primary deficit. The second term captures the implicit revenue from financial repression, which is simply $\phi d$, while $g^N$ is the nominal rate of growth of GDP. Table 6.2 organizes fiscal data in line with equation (6.1). The first column gives the various components of the fiscal deficit. The next two columns give actual outcomes during the benchmark period and what happened in the Eighth Plan period relative to the benchmark.

Let's start with revenues in row 3. These fell, from an annual average level of 19.4 percent of GDP during the benchmark period, by 1.5 percentage points during the Eighth Plan period, that is, to an annual average level of 17.9 percent of GDP. Since the annual growth rate of real GDP went up by 0.2 percent (last row), we can infer that all the revenue reduction was because of changes in tax policy. Indeed, the tax reform led to a significant reduction in customs and excise duties ($\tau$) as a result of lowering tax rates in order to make the economy more efficient and competitive.

Now let's look at interest payments in row 5. These went up by an average of 1.3 percent of GDP *even though* the fiscal deficit fell substantially from

Table 6.2 Fiscal Adjustment 1985/6–2006/7 (Annual averages for each subperiod)

| % of GDP | Benchmark 1985/6–1989/90 | 8th Plan | 9th Plan | 10th Plan |
|---|---|---|---|---|
| | | *Relative to Benchmark* | | |
| 1. Capital expenditure | 6.6 | −2.9 | −3.3 | −3.1 |
| 2. Noninterest current exp. | 18.3 | −1.9 | −0.6 | −1.1 |
| 3. Revenues | 19.4 | −1.5 | −2.5 | −0.4 |
| 4. *Primary deficit (1+2−3)* | 5.4 | −3.3 | −1.5 | −3.8 |
| 5. Interest payments | 3.8 | +1.3 | +1.9 | +2.3 |
| 6. *Fiscal deficit (4+5)* | 9.2 | −2.0 | +0.4 | −1.5 |
| **Real GDP growth %/yr** | **6.4** | **+0.2** | **−1.0** | **+1.5** |

*Source*: Pang, Pinto, and Wes (2007); World Bank.

9.2 percent of GDP during the benchmark period to 7.2 percent of GDP during the Eighth Plan period. This should have cut borrowing requirements and lowered, not raised, interest rates, as well as interest payments on government debt. Indeed, we shall see later in this chapter that the debt-to-GDP ratio fell by 2.5 percentage points per year during the Eight Plan period. Therefore, we can attribute all the 1.3 percentage points of GDP increase in interest payments to the gradual elimination of financial repression. Adding puts the total reform-related revenue loss from indirect taxes and implicit financial repression taxes at about 3 percentage points of GDP.[8] The government reacted to this hole on the revenue side of its accounts by cutting capital expenditure by an almost identical 2.9 percentage points of GDP to compensate, as row 1 in the table attests.

This brings us to the much-maligned Ninth Plan period. Notice from the table that revenues *fell* by 1 percentage point relative to the Eighth Plan period and that interest payments *rose* by 0.6 percentage points of GDP. Since the reforms were gradual, we can conclude that the reform-induced revenue losses were at least the 3 percentage points of GDP computed for the Eighth Plan period, and probably closer to 4 percentage points. The growth rate fell by over 1 percent and the fiscal deficit rose by over 2 percent of GDP relative to the Eighth Plan period, leading to the accusations of slowing reform and fiscal profligacy.

The charge of profligacy arose from the salary award recommendation of the Fifth Pay Commission for government employees, which began to be implemented in 1997; but the impact of this was to raise government spending at best by 1.3 percent of GDP, as shown by the rise in noninterest current expenditure relative to the Eighth Plan period—about a third of the reform-induced revenue losses.[9] Besides, part of the problem is the way government sector wages are set in India—with no real increase for several years, followed by an abrupt adjustment. The year 1997 just happened to coincide with such an adjustment, leading to an upward jump in the government wage bill, the effect of which would then attenuate until the next big wage award. Moreover, primary spending was cut by some 4 percent of GDP during the Ninth Plan period compared to the benchmark period (3.3 percent capital, 0.6 percent noninterest current expenditure), hardly indicative of profligacy.

If we now return to equation (6.1), it is easy to see what happened to fiscal developments during the Ninth Plan period: Table 6.2 shows that the

---

**Box 6.2** What Exactly Does "Unsustainable Debt Dynamics" Mean?

Let me reproduce equation (A9') from Annex 2: $\dot{d} = pd + (r - g)d$, where $d$ is the government debt-to-GDP ratio, $pd$ is the ratio of the primary fiscal deficit to GDP, $r$ is the real interest rate, and g is the real growth rate. It follows that if $pd$ > 0, that is, a primary deficit exists, and $r$ > g, that is, real interest rates are above growth rates, then $\dot{d} > 0$ for any positive starting level of $d$. In the absence of policy change, the debt-to-GDP ratio will be on an unobstructed upward trajectory.

Does this mean debt dynamics are unsustainable? Mechanically, yes, because $d$ can rise without limit. But we need to temper this with more information. For example, if the debt-to-GDP ratio $d$ is 20 percent to begin with and the government is investing heavily in infrastructure, then even if the debt-to-GDP ratio is rising by 3 percentage points of GDP per year, that may not be immediate cause for concern.

Now take India. At the start of the Ninth Plan period, $d$ was around 70 percent and the primary fiscal deficit, $pd$, about 4 percent of GDP. Since we know all the other variables in equation (A9'), we can calculate the implied real interest rate, $r$. It turns out (Pinto and Zahir 2004, p. 1041, figure 2) that the implied real interest rate was well below the growth rate during the Eighth Plan period, helping to more than offset the impact of primary deficits on $d$; but with financial repression easing, real interest rates rapidly caught up with growth rates during the Ninth Plan period.[a] This meant that the debt-to-GDP ratio would grow at least by 4 percentage points a year starting from an initial level of 70 percent, and this was definitely unsustainable without a substantial pickup in growth rates or a deliberate fiscal policy correction.

---

[a] A similar analysis is contained in Rangarajan and Srivastava (2005).

---

primary deficit went down from 5.4 percent of GDP in the benchmark period to 2.1 percent during the Eighth Plan period and then rose to 3.9 percent during the Ninth Plan period. This, together with rising interest rates as the liberalization of the government debt market progressed and the marked slowdown in growth, is what injected unsustainability into the government's dynamics. Box 6.2 probes this further.

More evidence is presented in Table 6.3, which contains a debt decomposition similar to that undertaken for Kenya in Chapter 5. In the table, changes in the debt-to-GDP ratio are assigned to primary fiscal balances, growth and interest rates, exchange rates, and other factors. Results are shown for the five subperiods identified in the timeline table, with the impact of each determinant annualized.[10]

**Table 6.3** Factors Accounting for Rising Indebtedness 1985/6–2006/7 (Annual average, % points of GDP)

|  | Benchmark | Crisis[a] | 8th Plan | 9th Plan | 10th Plan |
|---|---|---|---|---|---|
| Change in debt | 3.5 | 3.6 | −2.5 | 2.5 | 0.0 |
| *Contribution from* |  |  |  |  |  |
| 1. Primary deficit | 5.4 | 3.8 | 2.1 | 4.0 | 1.6 |
| 2. Real GDP growth | −3.7 | −2.4 | −4.7 | −3.6 | −6.2 |
| 3. Real interest rate | −0.3 | −2.0 | 0.3 | 2.8 | 2.9 |
| 4. Real exchange rate | 0.2 | 1.9 | 0.1 | 0.3 | −0.3 |
| 5. Other factors | 1.8 | 2.4 | −0.4 | −0.9 | 2.0 |

[a] "Crisis" refers to the balance of payments crisis and its aftermath, 1990/1–1991/2.

*Source*: Pang, Pinto, and Wes (2007); World Bank.

In contrast to other emerging markets, especially the ones suffering a serious crisis, the real exchange rate impact (except for the crisis period) was small while costs of financial sector recapitalization were insignificant and therefore do not appear in the table.[11] Two points are of interest: the contribution of the real interest rate to indebtedness kept growing over the Eighth, Ninth, and Tenth Plan periods as financial repression eased (row 3). By the Tenth Plan period, the real interest rate was increasing government debt by 3 percentage points of GDP a year, at a time when global interest rates were at historic lows and the primary deficit substantially reduced relative to the Ninth Plan period. This is proof that the easing of financial repression was driving the higher interest payments. The second point is the tangible impact of the growth acceleration after 2003. Faster growth alone was reducing the debt-to-GDP ratio by over 6 percentage points of GDP per year during the Tenth Plan period. The primary deficit had dropped below the level of the Eighth Plan period—a result driven by higher growth and increasing revenue mobilization.

Therefore, a more benign—and better-supported—interpretation of what happened during the Ninth Plan period would say: fiscal deficits rose and the government's debt dynamics deteriorated after 1997 because the reform-induced revenue losses intensified and real interest rates rose as financial repression eased. And the compensating cut in capital expenditure, which was maintained throughout the period shown in the table, contributed to slowing growth via its negative effect on private investment.[12] But there were two other reasons that private investment slowed: higher real interest rates as monetary policy was tightened in response to the East Asian crisis after 1997; and the pressure on firms to restructure, which came from growing import competition. This brings us to the microfoundations for growth and the 2003 growth takeoff.

## Why Did Growth Take Off in 2003?

Growth took off only in 2003 because it took until then for the firm-level restructuring, which began in earnest in 1997, to bear fruit. That is what I picked up in conversations in November 2005 in Mumbai, India, with the CEO of a major private bank, the head of a prominent credit rating agency, and the chief economist of an industrial powerhouse. All pointed to import competition traceable to the reduction in tariffs as a major driving force. This story begs two questions. First, why didn't firms begin restructuring in 1991 itself with the onset of reform? Second, what accounts for the big pickup in private investment toward the tail end of the Eighth Plan period, that is, before restructuring purportedly began in 1997, shown for the years 1995/6 and 1996/7 in Figure 6.1?[13] The answers to these two questions are connected.

The reason firms did not begin restructuring immediately is related to the gradual nature of the reforms. Import competition was inhibited by a slow fall in the effective import tariff rate (customs duties divided by total imports), which fell from 50 percent in 1990/91 to 30 percent in 1996/7. However, it had become clear by then there would be no backtracking on import liberalization, and by 2004/5 the effective tariff rate had dropped to just 8 percent. Another important reason delaying restructuring was that incumbent firms appeared to have pressed their advantage in the years soon after 1991. Contemporary accounts attribute the private investment boom of the Eighth Plan period not to business fundamentals, but to the industrial and financial organization then prevalent in India. The landscape was dominated by a few large industrial houses that exploited their special relationships with the state-owned development finance institutions, or DFIs. The DFIs provided long-term investment funds, while working capital came from state-owned commercial banks.

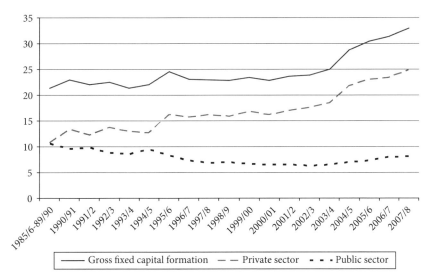

**Figure 6.1** India: Investment-to-GDP (%) 1985/6–2007/8
*Source*: Ministry of Finance, *Economic Survey*.

Nachiket Mor, R. Chandrasekhar, and Diviya Wahi (2006) described the scramble following the 1991 liberalization as follows:

> In part led by the consortium financing system but largely because neither industrialists nor bankers had any experience in operating in liberalised environments, almost every project that was submitted for financing was accepted. As a consequence, the system created capacity (which is quite possibly what showed up as growth numbers) in industry after industry—steel, man-made fibre, paper, cement, textiles, hotels, and automobiles received a major share of the large loans given principally by the DFIs and partly by the CBs [commercial banks]....excess capacities...[emerged]...in the manufacturing sector, particularly textiles, chemicals, food and beverages, and metals industries.[14]

In a similar vein, Rakesh Mohan (2004) observed: "The exuberance of investment activity in the mid-1990s also led to the creation of over capacity in industry, including some uncompetitive capacity that led to erosion of profits which, in turn, perhaps explains the poor performance of the stock market during this latter period."

Profitability as measured by the return on assets (ROA) for a sample of firms listed on the Bombay Stock Exchange was high initially, in the 12 percent range, as shown in Figure 6.2, but then steadily eroded as a result of

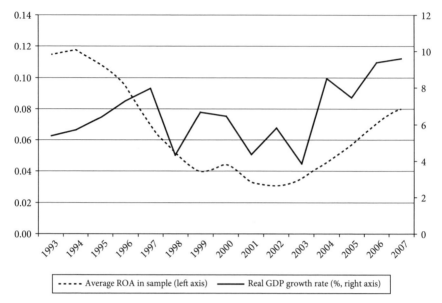

**Figure 6.2** India: Corporate Profit and GDP Growth Rate 1993–2007
*Source:* Mody, Nath, and Walton (2011, p. 14, figure 5).

growing import competition reinforced by homegrown competition. The deregulation of domestic industry and the progressive removal of entry barriers led to a rapid increase in the number of private companies from 249,181 in 1992 to 449, 730 in 1997.[15]

After a substantial increase during the last two years of the Eighth Plan period, private investment began losing its upward momentum during the Ninth Plan period. Naushad Forbes (2002) attributed the slowdown over the period 1996–9 to

> poor investment decisions of the boom years as a major cause ... Used to operating in a shortage economy where profits were limited by how much one could make, firms invested heavily in sectors like steel, fertilizers, cement, petrochemicals, and aluminum ... Capacity increased much faster than the market ... It is only in the last four years as industrial growth has fallen and industry has come under the dual pressure of competition from imports and falling margins that firms have been forced to look at which activities they really wish to retain.

The common thread in narratives of developments during the 1990s is that import competition eliminated easy profits, forcing incumbent companies into serious restructuring around 1997.[16] It took a total of six years for the restructuring to show up in the 2003 growth takeoff. The micro story thus mirrors the macro one: private investment during the Eighth Plan period was helped by domestic deregulation and established business relationships, which gave incumbent firms a chance to go on an investment binge that boosted profitability because of the slow pace of trade liberalization. In contrast, private investment during the Ninth Plan period was hurt by falling profits as import competition intensified, and by sustained cuts in public infrastructure investment because of the "crowding-in" effect of such spending. Thus, the private investment boom during the Eighth Plan period was not sustainable while the consequent difficulties firms experienced during the Ninth Plan period acted as a spur for serious restructuring.

## Solving the Puzzle

We return to the puzzle of how a growth takeoff occurred in 2003 on the heels of a sustained deterioration in the government's debt dynamics and what was widely expected to be a fiscal crisis. The explanation offered here rests on reinterpreting the deteriorating fiscal and debt outcomes during the six years preceding the 2003 growth takeoff. These were the result, not of fiscal profligacy, but of reform-related revenue losses from trade, excise, and financial repression taxes, which intensified after 1997 because of the gradual nature of the reforms. The growth takeoff which followed was the lagged benefit of the reforms and flowed from the restructuring under-taken by firms. The driving force was the pressure on the profit margins of incumbent Indian firms from import competition and liberalized domestic entry.

The long lags involved—six years after the reforms began in 1991 for firms to start serious restructuring and another six before the growth take-off—raises the question of transition costs. In Figure 6.3, the lower graph shows the actual debt-to-GDP trajectory over 1991/2 to 2004/5. The debt-to-GDP ratio fell and then began rising again in 1997/8 before beginning to fall again in 2003/4, when the growth spurt began, in line with the discussion earlier in this chapter. The upper graph shows what would have happened to the debt-to-GDP ratio had government capital expenditure (capex) been

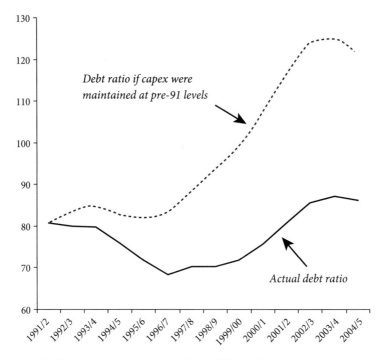

**Figure 6.3** India: Government Debt-to-GDP (%) 1991/2–2004/5
*Source:* Calculations based on World Bank data.

kept at its pre-1991 levels, with all other variables held constant.[17] The gap between the two graphs thus captures the cumulative cost of reforms as capital expenditure was cut to offset reform-related reductions in revenues. By 2003/4, the year growth resumed, this cost amounted to a staggering 38 percentage points of GDP.

Given the magnitude of these costs, it is something of a miracle that India did not suffer a devastating macroeconomic crisis. This underlines the salutary role of capital controls and gradual domestic financial liberalization. Had India liberalized its capital account and domestic financial system immediately after the 1991 crisis, the results could have been disastrous, judging by the experience of emerging markets with open capital accounts and unsustainable debt dynamics.

An important question is whether the firm-level restructuring which began in 1997 has yielded permanent benefits. Hiroko Oura (2007) surveys studies estimating India's long-run potential growth using a growth accounting framework similar to that set out in Annex 1. Potential growth over the medium term is put at around 8 percent. An interesting finding is that TFP growth accelerated from 2003. The IMF's Fall 2006 World Economic Outlook estimated TFP growth for 2002–05 at 3.2 percent compared to 1.5 percent for 1982–2001, while Tushar Poddar and Eva Yi (2007) estimate TFP growth for 2003–05 at 3.5 percent, more than twice that for 1980–9 or 1990–99. Oura notes that there is no identifiable proximate cause in terms of closely preceding reforms—but this is not greatly surprising given the long lags involved before firm-level restructuring began and before the benefits appeared.

## Lessons from India

The first lesson from India's experience is that it is hard to capture the complicated links between the public finances and growth. The failure to anticipate India's growth spurt was due in part to interpreting the deteriorating macro-fiscal outcomes after 1997 as bad policy rather than the accumulating fiscal costs of reform. The empirical growth literature includes macroeconomic variables like fiscal deficits and inflation on the right-hand side of the growth regression, which, in India's case, would have led to the inference of weak growth because of deteriorating fiscal fundamentals. This approach is unable to capture the intertemporal aspects of the government's budget constraint or allow for positive microeconomic effects that might appear after a longer lag than one would typically encounter in regression frameworks.

Second, long lags and considerable upfront reform costs may be involved before growth takes off and it becomes evident that government debt is on a sustainable course. Market myopia could derail the adjustment process if creditors confuse temporary unsustainability with insolvency and decide to pull out (as might have been the case with India over 1997–2002 had the capital account been fully open). Equally importantly, long lags may incorrectly suggest that reforms are not working.

Third, the chances of a full-blown crisis were minimized because India took a cautious line on capital account liberalization and domestic financial liberalization. A powerful argument against premature capital account liberalization is that it could lead to bad investments and vulnerability to a crisis, especially when the domestic financial system is weak, a result immortalized by Carlos Diaz-Alejandro's 1985 paper (covered later in Box 8.1). India's experience shows that, in addition to avoiding such vulnerability, slow capital account liberalization can help in two respects: it cushions the adjustment of firms and banks to a more open economy by lowering the risk of a disruptive crisis; and it permits a more gradual replacement of trade and financial repression taxes with more efficient taxes, which is an important consideration if trade and financial repression are a significant source of revenue to begin with, as was the case in India.

Fourth, rules of thumb on 'safe' levels of debt and cross-country comparisons of macro-fiscal fundamentals are of limited value. India avoided a crisis after 1997 despite unflattering comparisons on fiscal and debt indicators with countries that ended up suffering major crises. Its strategy of self-insuring after 1991 (building up reserves, shifting toward local currency debt) foreshadowed the post-2000 policies of countries like Brazil and Turkey: a topic that will be discussed in Chapter 9. In all three countries—India included—public investment cuts fueled concern about the impact on long-run growth via the so-called 'fiscal space' argument, which I shall address in Chapter 8.

## Postscript

India's rapid growth was maintained until the Great Recession of 2008–9, as were the positive trends in savings, investment, and the profitability of the nonfinancial sector. It also rebounded quickly from the effects of the global financial crisis. But growth slowed to 5 percent in 2012/13, the lowest in a decade, and is expected to remain at this level during 2013/14. Formidable development challenges remain, from strengthening governance and institutions (at the national and subnational levels) to increasing government saving, improving infrastructure, and reforming labor markets—not to mention capitalizing on India's favorable demographics. Urgent priorities include implementing an efficient Land Acquisition Bill (for compensating private owners of land needed for public use, such as roads, and perceived as critical for the next stage of industrialization); ratifying and implementing the Goods and Services Tax, which requires a constitutional amendment and is needed for additional revenue mobilization; and energy sector pricing and regulation reform to enable more investment in the power sector. Indeed, the shortage of electricity is viewed as the most serious constraint on economic growth.

Remember the discussion on solvency versus sustainability in Boxes 3.1 and 6.1? The appearance of unsustainability in the early 2000s in India was temporary, related to the fiscal costs of the reforms motivated by the 1991 balance-of-payments crisis, with the subsequent growth takeoff and expected higher future taxes ensuring solvency—the main point of this chapter. As it turns out, the IMF has lowered India's potential growth rate from the 8–9 percent range to the 6.5 percent range in its February 2013 report (IMF 2013), with the implementation of the Goods and Services Tax (GST) seen as the key step in returning revenues to levels that prevailed before the global financial crisis, and ensuring more favorable debt dynamics. But microeconomic reforms to restore India's potential growth to the 8–9 percent range are equally important. These need to focus on true domestic contestability supported by improved regulation and governance along the lines set out by Philippe Aghion and Ashoka Mody and their respective coauthors. In other words, the policy task has returned to the soundness of the government intertemporal budget constraint while nurturing favorable macro–micro linkages via the micropolicy trio. The task is much harder this time around because India is now more open in terms of trade and financial linkages than it ever has been. Ensuring growth with financial stability in this environment is going to be a major challenge, but can draw on the foundation constructed after the 1991 crisis, described in his 2011 book by Rakesh Mohan.

## Notes

1. The two reasons singled out by the World Bank (2003a) for a crisis being unlikely were that India had built up a huge cushion of foreign exchange reserves; and that the capital account was being only very slowly liberalized, while the banking system was largely state owned.
2. The reports were both *development policy reviews*, comprehensive assessments of the policies of the Indian government in the realms of growth and poverty reduction. I worked on the macro fiscal with Gaobo Pang, Marina Wes, and Farah Zahir.
3. See the insightful paper 1992 paper by Willem Buiter and Urjit Patel.
4. For the unsuspecting reader, the word "plan" for the period under observation does not have the connotations of central government control over the economy that existed in the 1960s and 1970s.
5. Acharya (2001, 2002a, 2002b), Ahluwalia (2002a), Srinivasan (2002).

6. Professor Srinivasan was not alone in expressing misgivings about growth. See also Ahluwalia (2002b), India, Planning Commission (2002, ch. 2), World Bank (2003a), and Pinto and Zahir (2004).

7. Numbers from Table 1, Pinto and Zahir (2004).

8. Estimates from Giovannini and de Melo (1993) and Kletzer and Kohli (2001) suggest that the lost taxes from *financial repression alone* might have been of the order of 3 percent of GDP.

9. The pay award was labeled the "single largest adverse shock to India's strained public finances in the last decade" and an act of "fiscal profligacy" without parallel (Godbole 1997, Acharya 2001).

10. Thus, during the benchmark period, the debt-to-GDP ratio rose by 3.5 percentage points per year, with the primary deficit contributing 5.4 percentage points per year; whereas over the Eighth Plan period, the debt-to-GDP ratio fell by 2.5 percentage points per year, etc.

11. Real exchange rate collapses and the fiscal costs of bank bailouts were the main factors raising the debt-to-GDP ratio in emerging markets suffering a crisis. Growth collapses played a small role. Budina and Fiess (2004).

12. Reserve Bank of India (2002) shows that public investment in infrastructure is complementary to private investment.

13. The starting point for Figure 6.1 is the average investment rate over the benchmark period.

14. Material in square brackets added.

15. Topalova (2004, p. 28, table 1).

16. The role of competition is emphasized in econometric investigations by Aghion, et al. (2005), Mody, Nath, and Walton (2011), and Topalova and Khandelwal (2011).

17. Growth might have gone up had government investment not been cut; but interest rates would also have been higher, lowering growth. It would be reasonable to assume that a government scrambling to open up the economy, put the public finances on a manageable trajectory, and achieve faster growth would have assessed the tradeoffs.

# CHAPTER 7

# Russia Rewrites the Book

*Russia, he said, has achieved macroeconomic stabilization....The IMF is virtually certain, he declared, that real growth is underestimated and will soon show up in official figures...What are the prospects for Russia? In general, Fischer argued, the real GDP tends to turn up within two years of a serious stabilization.*

—Summary of address by Stanley Fischer in *Final Report: U.S.-Russian Investment Symposium*, Harvard University, January 1997

The position Stanley Fischer staked out that January 1997 was eminently reasonable. Russia had already endured a 40 percent decline in output over 1990–95. With inflation being licked, it was only logical to expect that output would bottom out and start growing again.

Alas, the reality on the ground refused to oblige. Just three months before Fischer's Harvard speech, in October 1996, I had visited Russia to prepare a country risk assessment for the International Finance Corporation (IFC), the World Bank Group's private sector wing. Boris Yeltsin had just been reelected president in a tense, second-round runoff against his Communist Party challenger, Gennady Zyuganov. A year had elapsed since the implementation of an exchange rate-based stabilization program that was seeking to bring inflation down from over 200 percent in 1994 to single-digit levels by 1997. The government was finding it difficult to meet its fiscal deficit targets and establish credibility, as evidenced by exceptionally high real interest rates on ruble T-bills. Banks were more interested in the lucrative ruble T-bill market than in lending to the real sector. And a system of arrears and widespread barter was getting established. In the midst of this impossible combination, optimism had emerged that Russia was on the verge of a resumption of sustained growth—all because inflation was coming down.

One conclusion emerged unambiguously from that visit. The microfoundations for a resumption of growth were nonexistent, the visible decline in inflation notwithstanding. Imagine the US government borrowing at interest rates of more than 50 percent per year or more, General Motors selling 60 percent of its cars and trucks on a barter basis, Kraft foods doing the same and paying its workers in mayonnaise! That's what happened across the board in Russia during 1996 and 1997, with astronomically high real interest rates, a rapidly appreciating real exchange rate, and widespread payment arrears and barter becoming a normal way of doing business.

In addition to numerous banks and securities companies, domestic and foreign—which had sprouted to take advantage of exorbitant interest rates on ruble T-bills and make money trading the IOUs and quasi-monies that had developed as result of arrears and extremely tight monetary policy—the enterprises I visited included a giant truck maker, a float glass company, a company making engines for railway locomotives and light motors for high-speed coastal boats, a company specializing in optical instruments, and a company which made margarine, mayonnaise, and other oil-based products, as well as processed meat products and animal and bird feed. These enterprises were scattered all over Russia yet recited an identical litany of complaints—about payment arrears, starting with the government; payment in kind rather than cash, utilizing complicated barter chains and promissory notes; the collapse of distribution networks; crippling interest rates; and the real appreciation of the ruble. Their stories jived with what I picked up from the banks and the securities companies. My October 1996 report concluded: "Inflation has been brought down sharply in Russia. *However, growth is unlikely toresume and attain sustainable levels of 4–5 percent any time soon.* My guess is that 1999 or 2000 is the earliest, based on a gut-feel comparison with Poland..."[1]

It would have been hard to comprehend what the microeconomic situation in Russia was like at that time without actually having traveled around the country and talked to people making decisions about whom to lend to or whether or not to invest. The barter deals were not simple two-party transactions but involved long chains linking several companies. A new form of industrial organization developed around noncash settlements, complete with its own specialized intermediaries and IOUs, with managers reportedly spending as much as 30 percent of their time organizing these transactions. I shall return to this idiosyncratic phenomenon of noncash settlements and barter later in the chapter and show how it ended up fueling instability in the government's debt dynamics by shrinking cash tax payments and killing growth prospects. Box 7.1 sets out the analytical links to Chapters 2 and 3, and makes a connection to chapter 8 as well. Later, Box 7.2 discusses the then prevailing textbook wisdom on stabilization and how the Russian crisis of 1998, or Russia 1998, challenged it.

---

**Box 7.1** Russia—Analytical Interlude

The reader might throw a mild fit if I were to say that Russia's experience over the 1995–9 period is a profound illustration of the importance of the government intertemporal budget constraint and the micropolicy trio in attaining genuine stabilization and creating a platform for growth. What relevance can an ex-communist country in transition and dominated by natural resource wealth have for other emerging markets?

The answer is twofold. First, these very features of Russia (not to mention its status as a nuclear power) led economists to treat it as a special case, leading to a serious misdiagnosis, when in fact the behavior of the government, firms, and banks was rational given the incentives they faced. Second, one learns more about behavior from exceptions than from the rule, because the parameters influencing behavior are at extreme levels.

Russia 1998 above all illustrates the peril of trying to diagnose a country's problems from afar, based on the conventional wisdom. Most recognized there was a serious fiscal problem. Most recognized that the spread of barter and arrears was correlated with tax evasion. But very few recognized that barter, arrears, tax evasion, the sky-high real interest rates and the eventually explosive trajectory of government debt as growth prospects vanished were interconnected.

And that is the real story of Russia 1998: that, ultimately, stabilization is not just a macroeconomic problem but rests both on the GIBC and the micropolicy trio—a combination that, together with managing volatility, also creates the best foundation for economic growth.

Russia 1998 occurred in the midst of the EM crises of 1997–2001 and thus serves as a bridge to the macroeconomic policy debates and lessons presented in Part Three of this study. This crisis was the result of unsustainable government debt dynamics combined with low foreign exchange reserves in the presence of a fixed exchange rate, and is an example of the so-called "first generation crisis model" set out in Table 8.2 of Chapter 8.

## Refining the Textbook

Economists take a dim view of high inflation for good reason. It is a sign of macroeconomic uncertainty, and therefore a deterrent to investment and growth: private investors in fixed capital are notoriously averse to uncertainty. In addition, there is a long-standing result that the variance of relative prices goes up (and therefore their information content as a guide to where to invest goes down) with inflation surprises.[2] And inflation is known to hurt the poor more than the rich because the latter are better able to hedge themselves against its consequences: inflation is a regressive tax.

Traditionally, there has been a strong link between fiscal deficits and inflation in developing countries. Deficits tended to be money-financed owing to limited capital market access. Besides, fiscal deficits tended to result more from poor governance and wastage than from investing in public goods for the future. These features are particularly true of the 1960s to the 1980s, the period from which many of the empirical results in the macroeconomic growth literature were extracted. Box 7.2 presents the resulting framework, which, as I witnessed firsthand, dominated macroeconomic policy prescription by the IMF and World Bank until the emerging market crises of 1997–2001.

The framework in Box 7.2 represented the state of the art on policy when Russia embarked on its stabilization program in the mid-1990s, attempting to lower inflation from over 200 percent in 1994 to single-digit levels by 1997. The initial level of inflation evoked Stanley Fischer's admonition, contained in the paper summed up in Box 7.2, that "inflation is merely a symptom of a government out of control" (Fischer 1993, p. 507). Russia pegged its ruble to the US dollar as a nominal exchange rate anchor for bringing inflation down rapidly. It also progressively liberalized external access to its ruble T-bill market to augment funding sources, but was finding it difficult to adhere to its fiscal deficit targets. As a result, real interest rates remained stubbornly high with arrears and barter becoming pervasive. At the same time, the ruble was appreciating significantly in real terms, a typical consequence of exchange rate-based stabilization programs, as we shall see later in this chapter.

Few economists would dispute the proposition that bringing inflation down from triple-digit levels is a *necessary condition* for sustained growth as Russia was attempting to do. But a problem could arise when it is treated

**Box 7.2** Stabilization and Growth: The Thinking before the Crises of 1997–2001

The inspiration for policy advice on macroeconomic stabilization and growth prior to the emerging market crises of 1997–2001 came from models like:

Growth = f(inflation, fiscal surplus, black market premium),

where "f" stands for function. "Growth" in the above "model" could be measured by real GDP growth; or the growth in capital, labor, and human capital inputs; or by the Solow residual left over from the kind of "growth accounting exercise" described in Annex 1. The objective of the empirical growth literature has been to explain growth as thus measured by the variables on the right-hand side of the above equation.

Fischer's 1993 paper in the *Journal of Monetary Economics* is a prime example. Employing cross-sectional and panel regressions in a cross-country study covering 1961 to 1988, he concluded that a "stable macroeconomic environment, meaning a reasonably low rate of inflation and a small budget deficit, is conducive to sustained growth" (Fischer 1993); and that the weight of evidence pointed to a causal flow from high inflation to low growth, rather than vice versa. The channels through which inflation reduces growth include reduced investment as well as a lowered rate of productivity (TFP) growth measured by the Solow residual, while larger budget surpluses are associated with more rapid growth through greater capital accumulation and greater productivity growth. But Fischer observes toward the end of his paper that "a high deficit by itself is not a certain indicator of later trouble....it would take supplementary studies of the...debt dynamics..." to draw an appropriate conclusion.

The "model" shown at the beginning of this box has serious shortcomings. First, it is hard to know which variables are driving which, something that is known as *endogeneity*. For example, faster growth could mean more taxes, hence lower fiscal deficits; it could also mean higher real money demand and hence lower inflation. Second, the right-hand-side variables are interrelated and this could impede clear policy prescription. For example, in countries where the government on net buys foreign exchange from the private sector, the black market premium on foreign exchange is an implicit tax on exports. Eliminating it by floating the currency would normally be considered a positive step; but this could actually raise inflation, which is the tax on money, unless other tax instruments are readily available or there is a substantial reduction in the fiscal deficit.[a]

Using fiscal deficits and inflation as proxies for macro stability is unsatisfactory in three crucial respects: first, it does not fully capture the government intertemporal budget constraint and related concerns like solvency and debt sustainability (recall Box 3.1). Second, it does not allow for cumulative lagged effects. And third, it ignores the microfoundations for growth and how these are influenced by the macro-fiscal situation. These issues were prominent not just in Russia but also in India and even Kenya (recall Chapters 5 and 6).

Its shortcomings notwithstanding, the above framework for empirical growth survived the 1997–2001 emerging market crises intact, as shown in William Easterly's 2005 paper for the *Handbook of Economic Growth*.

---

[a] Kharas and Pinto (1989) and Pinto (1991).

as a *sufficient condition*. Fischer's confidence in his 1997 Harvard speech about growth responding to stabilization flowed from results reported in his 1996 paper with Ratna Sahay and Carlos Vegh. Page 47 of this paper explains: "inflation falls substantially...as fiscal deficits are brought under control....after two years growth is positive....reducing high inflation is a precondition for the revival of growth." The paper went on to claim that for transition countries, "stabilization appears close to being both a necessary and sufficient condition for growth" (p. 59).

However, as underlined by Russia's meltdown in August 1998, which occurred in spectacular fashion six months after annual inflation was lowered to single-digit levels, achieving low inflation does not mean either that the government is in control or that a platform for growth is being established. This crisis helped rewrite the book on macroeconomic stabilization in two ways. First, it shifted the focus from current inflation and fiscal deficits to the government intertemporal budget constraint and fiscal solvency in particular. If inflation is coming down but concerns about credibility and the creditworthiness of the government persist, then private investors who buy Treasury bills and bonds are likely to push real interest rates to levels inimical to growth and hence fiscal solvency. Second, the crisis also brought home the pivotal importance of the microfoundations of growth. If these are weakened by the high real interest rates and an appreciating real exchange rate that accompany the pursuit of low inflation, this would have negative effects on fiscal solvency by lowering growth and tax payments, and would eventually derail the stabilization. In other words, a serious stabilization must pay close attention to the macro–micro linkages discussed in Chapter 3, an important theme pursued below in this chapter.

Treating the conquest of inflation as a sufficient condition for growth implicitly assumes that everything else will fall into place—that firms and banks will start humming again, policy credibility will be restored, public debt will be placed on a sustainable trajectory, and growth will take off and persist. As it turned out, Russia did not address its fiscal problems even while continuing to squeeze inflation out. Low inflation can be achieved in the presence of a large fiscal deficit, but not for long if the government is issuing debt at an interest rate which exceeds the growth rate and there is a ceiling on the stock of bonds the market is willing to hold—a result recognizable as Sargent and Wallace's (1981) unpleasant monetarist arithmetic. Besides, the high interest rates could ruin growth prospects, especially when accompanied with an appreciating real exchange rate. This is exactly what transpired in Russia, as explained later in this chapter.

On the positive side, the huge, unexpected economic rebound that occurred on the heels of Russia's 1998 crisis brought home the importance of hard budgets for the government and private sector, import competition, and competitive real exchange rates, that is, the micropolicy trio, in underpinning both fiscal solvency and growth. This is economic lesson *numero uno* from the experience of the transition countries of Central and Eastern Europe.[3]

## Was the East Asian Crisis to Blame?

Optimism was widespread in early 1996 that Russian growth would restart that year. Typical was this quote from Economist Intelligence Unit (1st quarter 1996): "As the EIU has long been predicting, 1996 is expected to be the year in which Russia finally achieves real GDP growth....This opinion is shared by most other forecasters..."[4] As it turns out, real GDP ended up falling by 3.4 percent in 1996; but outcomes over the first ten months of 1997 appeared to confirm Fischer's January 1997 prediction. The liberalization of the ruble T-bill (better known by its Russian acronym, GKO) market to ease foreign investor participation put interest rates on a downward path and swelled foreign exchange reserves to a record $25 billion (a significant level pre-Lehman for a 400-odd billion-dollar economy). It looked like Russia might at last see the beginnings of positive growth; in fact, official statistics put growth at 0.9 percent for the year. By February 1998, Russia had attained the Holy Grail of single-digit inflation; but it endured a comprehensive public debt, exchange rate, and banking crisis only six months later.

An obvious candidate for explaining this reversal was the East Asian crisis, which spilt over in October 1997, subjecting the ruble to a speculative attack. The central bank CBR lost a significant amount of reserves defending the ruble's peg to the dollar, as maintaining the peg was central to Russia's inflation reduction strategy. The situation then quietened down until the end of January 1998, when the foreign exchange market encountered another round of turbulence. The third and final round of turbulence began in mid-May, coinciding with the intensification of Indonesia's political and economic crisis triggered by the departure of President Suharto. This culminated in the

Russian meltdown of August 17, 1998, with eventual real GDP growth of minus 4.9 percent for the year.

Should one then conclude that the spillover from the East Asian crisis scuttled the Fischer–Sahay–Vegh (FSV) hypothesis that inflation reduction was sufficient for growth? No, for two reasons. First, Russia had a fundamental fiscal problem in the shape of a chronic shortfall in tax collections, which forced additional debt issuance to compensate: the government was trying to lower inflation, which ruled out printing money. Second, as I had discovered during my October 1996 visit, the microfoundations for growth were nonexistent. The net effect was that inflation was being squeezed out, even as government debt was mounting, and enterprise restructuring was stalling, with real interest rates rising to impossible levels. As a result, growth prospects evaporated and debt dynamics became unsustainable, culminating in the August 1998 meltdown.

By the time the East Asian crisis spilled over in October 1997, the system of noncash settlements and barter had become firmly entrenched. Portfolio investors were talking of a disconnect between the *macroeconomic* accomplishments of falling inflation and interest rates and the notable *microeconomic* absence of enterprise restructuring in an atmosphere of rising barter and falling tax revenues—which begged the question of whether the inflation reduction was sustainable.[5] This question was answered unequivocally on August 17, 1998, when Russia devalued the ruble and defaulted on its debt.

## Russia's Fundamental Fiscal Problem

Russia's fundamental fiscal problem was not that it had a primary fiscal deficit with a real interest rate exceeding the real growth rate—so did India toward the late 1990s. The real problem was that there was little hope that this situation could be remedied without a drastic change in polices; it was not going to self-correct. But correcting the situation required that the problem be acknowledged in the first place. However, the deterioration in the government's debt dynamics was masked by the real appreciation of the ruble. Let's take a closer look, starting with the numbers in Table 7.1.

The second and third columns of the table show a fairly significant primary fiscal deficit coupled with large interest payments over 1995–7, while the growth rate was either highly negative (1995 and 1996) or positive but

**Table 7.1** Public Finances and Economic Growth in Russia 1995–8

| Year | Primary Deficit (percent of GDP) | Interest Payments | | Government Debt | | Real GDP Growth (percent per year) |
|------|------|------|------|------|------|------|
| | | Percent of GDP | Percent of revenues | Billions of dollars | Percent of GDP | |
| 1995 | 2.2 | 3.6 | 28 | 170 | 50 | −4.0 |
| 1996 | 2.5 | 5.9 | 47 | 201 | 48 | −3.4 |
| 1997 | 2.4 | 4.6 | 38 | 218 | 50 | 0.9 |
| 1998 | 1.3 | 4.6 | 43 | 242 | 75 | −4.9 |

*Source:* Kharas, Pinto, and Ulatov (2001).

small (1997). The real interest rate on ruble T-bills averaged 50 percent per year—this is not a typo—over these two years. Based on equation (5.2), the government debt-to-GDP ratio should have been on an explosive path. Yet the table shows that the ratio barely budged, even though debt grew by close to $50 billion between 1995 and 1997—a sizable number for what was then an approximately $400 billion economy. This paradox can be solved by bringing in the currency composition of the government's debt and the real exchange rate: if a sufficiently large fraction of the government's debt is in foreign currency ("dollars"), and the ruble appreciates sizably in real terms against the dollar, this would result in a capital gain to the government and lower the debt-to-GDP ratio.

If we plug equation (5.3), which gives the real interest rate on government debt as the weighted average real rates on ruble and dollar debt, into equation (5.2) and rearrange terms, we get a new equation (see Box 5.2):

$$\dot{d} = pd + (\tilde{r} - g)d - \left[(1-w)\rho d\right], \qquad (7.1)$$

where the last term on the right-hand side in square brackets captures the effect of the real appreciation of the ruble on debt dynamics (recall that $(1-w)$ is the share of dollar-denominated debt in total government debt and $\rho$ is the appreciation of the dollar-per-ruble real exchange rate). Over the 1995–7 period, with the ruble appreciating rapidly in real terms, the product of $(1-w)$ and $\rho$ times the debt-to-GDP ratio $d$ was high enough to offset the upward push of the primary deficit, the real interest rate stripped of real appreciation,

$\tilde{r}$, and negative or low growth on the government's indebtedness. For example, in 1996, the share of foreign currency debt in Russian government debt was 69 percent, meaning $(1-w)$ was 0.69; the real exchange rate had appreciated by 22 percent, meaning $\rho$ was 0.22; and the debt-to-GDP at the beginning of the year was 50 percent. Thus, the effect of the real appreciation alone was to reduce the debt-to-GDP ratio by 8 percentage points!

The ruble appreciated a cumulative 60 percent between July 1995, when the stabilization began, and July 1997. Roughly speaking, this means imports were about 40 percent cheaper than domestically produced goods by then, and the only way to offset this would have been for Russian firms to become superefficient; but this was clearly not happening. In fact, these firms were also coping with astronomically high real interest rates and the proliferation of barter and arrears, a point to which I shall return. Where did the real appreciation come from? The answer: it was an artifact of the stabilization program itself. This is a common occurrence when governments seek to lower inflation from very high levels by fixing the exchange rate, as Russia did in mid-1995.[6] For example, if the inflation rate is 200 percent to begin with and the exchange rate is fixed, implying that its rate of depreciation drops instantly to zero, inflation is not going to fall to zero instantaneously.[7] In Russia's case, it took two-and-a half years for inflation to reach single-digit levels. In the interim, imported goods became much cheaper, making life hard for the enterprise managers. The real exchange rate contined to appreciate until July 1997, after which it stabilized.

When the exchange rate came under attack following the spillover of the Asian crisis in October 1997, one option would have been to devalue the ruble; but since the exchange rate peg was the lynchpin of the stabilization program, the central bank chose to defend it. Besides, there seemed to be a deep-seated belief that squeezing inflation out would lead to growth, as noted earlier in this chapter. Only when it became evident that the situation was impossible did Russia abandon the ruble's peg to the dollar. It did this on August 17, 1998, simultaneously announcing a forced restructuring of much of its ruble debt. The ruble's subsequent collapse had a sizable effect on the debt-to-GDP ratio, as shown in the sixth column of Table 7.1; but not before a valiant IMF-led rescue effort to save Russia's stabilization program, which I discuss next.

## Market Anxiety and the July 1998 Rescue Package

Even though Russia's government debt-to-GDP ratio, at around 50 percent during 1995–7, was well within the Maastricht criterion of 60 percent, the market seemed anxious.[8] And notwithstanding the attainment of single-digit inflation in February 1998, its assessment of default and devaluation risk became gloomier as the year progressed. With the real exchange rate stabilizing, the underlying unsustainability in the government's debt dynamics became obvious by mid-May: by then, the marginal real interest rate was projected at over 25 percent, with real growth forecasts having been reduced to the 0–1 percent range for the year.[9]

Table 7.2 shows the devaluation and default risk premiums demanded by GKO investors, extracted from an expression based on equation (5.1). The default risk premium (additional compensation or "spread" being demanded by the market relative to a similar maturity "risk-free" United States Treasury bond, both denominated in dollars) was estimated at 5 percent, and the devaluation risk premium at 23 percent, on May 15, 1998, when

**Table 7.2** Trends in Default and Devaluation Risk Premiums prior to the August 17, 1998 Crisis

|  | 1-year GKO Yield (% per year) | Default Risk Premium (% per year) | Devaluation Risk Premium (% per year) |
|---|---|---|---|
| May 15—Indonesian political and economic crisis intensifies | 40 | 4.8 | 23 |
| **July 13—IMF-led rescue is announced** | 102 | 8.5 | 82 |
| July 14 | 58 | 8.1 | 39 |
| July 20—IMF Board approves rescue package, $4.8 billion released | 52 | 7.8 | 32 |
| July 24—GKO–Eurobond swap completed | 66 | 10.0 | 45 |
| August 14—last working day (Friday) before default and devaluation announced Aug. 17, 1998, a Monday | 145 | 23.8 | 110 |

*Source:* Based on Table 8 in Kharas, Pinto, and Ulatov (2001).

---

**Box 7.3**  Russia's July 1998 Rescue Package

Toward the end of June, Russia began discussions began with the International Financial Institutions (IFIs) on an emergency package, which was announced on July 13, 1998. It had three components:

- Fiscal and structural reforms designed to quickly achieve primary fiscal surpluses, eliminate nonpayments (described in the subsection on macro–micro linkages), and spur growth.
- A $22.6 billion financing package including a liquidity injection of $5.5 billion from the IMF upon approval of the package by the IMF Board on July 20— eventually reduced to $4.8 billion—in order to save the ruble's peg to the dollar and what were perceived as hard-won stabilization gains.
- A debt swap out of GKOs into long-maturity dollar Eurobonds (the "GKO– Eurobond swap"), to substantially lower interest payments on government debt while simultaneously lengthening maturities, thereby lowering rollover risk.

---

*Source*: Box 1, page 10, Kharas, Pinto, and Ulatov (2001).

---

the intensification of the Indonesian crisis pushed one-year GKO yields to 40 percent.[10] The GKO yield, default, and devaluation risk premiums all subsequently maintained an upward trend until July 13. That was the day the IMF-led rescue package was announced; Box 7.3 describes it. Something remarkable happened the very next day: the yield on the GKO fell sharply, with almost all the decline explained by a reduction in the devaluation risk premium; the default risk premium fell only marginally from 8.5 percent to 8.1 percent, as shown in the table. This is an important point to which I shall return.

Then things headed south quickly. On July 24, a swap from "expensive" ruble GKOs to "cheap" dollar-denominated Eurobonds was completed. The swap had been conceived as an ingenious means of reversing the government's unsustainable debt dynamics: since the exchange rate is fixed, why not borrow via long-term Eurobonds at around 12 percent instead of short-term GKOs costing well over 50 percent? In one stroke, interest payments would be brought down sharply and rollover risk substantially eliminated, giving the government breathing room to implement fiscal reform. But exactly the opposite happened when the swap was completed: the one-year GKO yield went up and the default risk premium jumped sharply from 8.2 percent the previous day to 10 percent. Thereafter, the situation spiraled out of control. On Friday August 14, GKO yields reached 145 percent and the default risk premium 24 percent. This led to the government's decision to devalue and default on August 17, 1998.

I shall explain how this sequence of events unfolded. Remember the dramatic decline in the devaluation risk premium the day after the IMF-led rescue package was announced, with the default risk premium barely budging? The only way to square this with the elements of the rescue package is to conclude that the market had developed genuine misgivings about fiscal solvency. The expectation of a large official loan with the first disbursement to come about a week after the announced package meant the central bank's reserves would go up, temporarily increasing liquidity. This would reduce the pressure to devalue, explaining the reduction in the devaluation risk premium; but the source of the liquidity injection was a big dollop of implicitly senior debt from the international financial institutions to a government bedeviled by solvency problems, that is, insufficient primary fiscal surpluses in present value terms to service all its debt. This meant that all other claims—including ruble T-bills as well as dollar-denominated debt issued by the Russian government—were made less attractive, as the official creditors were first in the queue.

In these circumstances, attempting to prop up an insolvent country's fixed exchange rate through an increase in the central bank's reserves financed by a loan from senior creditors becomes the perfect time for junior debt holders to exit. This is exactly what the holders of GKOs did, leading to a run on reserves and the meltdown of August 17, 1998. In effect, official loans were financing capital flight and an exit from the ruble *at the overvalued pre-crisis exchange rate*. The debt swap worsened the situation. It ended up dumping more Russian government dollar-denominated paper (the Eurobonds issued in exchange for the ruble T-bills, the GKOs) onto the market, lowering the price of such claims. As it turns out, Russian commercial banks were sitting on significant sums of dollar-dominated Russian government paper which they had bought on margin; when the prices of these assets fell, they faced margin calls which they met by selling their GKOs and asking the central bank to convert the ruble proceeds into dollars. This only hastened the pace of reserve loss by the central bank, accelerating the crisis.

## Macro–Micro Linkages

A close examination of the macro–micro links over the period 1995–8 would have revealed close connections among the following features of the Russian economy: elusive growth notwithstanding rapidly declining inflation; the growing entrenchment of barter and arrears; and the steadily worsening debt dynamics, ending in the August 17, 1998 crisis.

This is what happened: the government wanted to eliminate high inflation by pegging the ruble to the dollar and controlling credit aggregates, but was conflicted about the social consequences of possible mass bankruptcy in the manufacturing sector. So it maintained budgetary subsidies of the order of 8 percent of GDP while turning a blind eye to arrears on tax payments and on contributions to the social extra-budgetary funds. It also put pressure on the energy monopolies, Gazprom (gas) and RAO UES (electricity), not to disconnect enterprises delinquent on their energy bills. How did the energy monopolies (some of the most profitable companies in Russia) react? They became delinquent on their tax payments, leading to a chronic shortfall in fiscal revenues.

Trying to achieve single-digit inflation in this milieu meant issuing more debt than planned at extraordinarily high interest rates. With taxes flagging, inadequate expenditure control, and sky-high real interest rates, the government itself resorted to arrears on its payments to suppliers and to various forms of IOUs even as it sought to root out inflation.[11] Its example was quickly followed by enterprises, giving them the perfect excuse to deliberately run up tax arrears that could be settled at a substantial discount through offset schemes orchestrated by the government itself, which incorporated tax forgiveness through the use of inflated notional prices when taxes were paid in kind.

One study estimated the implicit subsidies embedded in tax offsets, energy payment arrears, and energy settlements in kind (at off-market prices) at between 7.5 and 12 percent of GDP, leading to total subsidies to manufacturing companies of the order of 15–20 percent of GDP.[12] Profitable, cash-rich enterprises joined the bandwagon. They also ran up tax arrears which could then be settled at a discount in kind; bought monetary surrogates from struggling enterprises—which had received these from the government in exchange for their unsaleable goods—at a discount, redeeming them at full face value to pay their taxes; and shifted profits to intermediaries set up and owned by them through the arbitrary and opaque transfer pricing that came to epitomize noncash settlements. This was an ideal environment in which to strip assets for personal enrichment.

Cliff Gaddy and Barry Ickes (1998) coined the term "Russia's Virtual Economy" to describe these strange goings-on; but the Russian economy of the time was a very real one in which intelligent people were responding rationally to the cripplingly high real interest rates, the fast appreciating real exchange rate, and the large sums of money to be made by gaming the system. Failure to appreciate this would lead to huge mistakes in diagnosis. The most egregious was the notion that squeezing out inflation in these circumstances would stimulate growth.

A close second was the idea that barter and arrears were driven by tax evasion, which was the prime hypothesis during my October 1996 visit. The government just needed the political will to crack down on tax cheats and all would be well. That very October, an emergency tax commission known by its Russian acronym VChK ("vecheka") was set up under the Prime Minister to do precisely this; but it went nowhere and was allowed to lapse. This was a tacit admission that nonpayments were part of a political bargain to keep unviable manufacturing firms afloat: the biggest tax delinquents—oil, gas, electricity, railways—were a prime source of the implicit subsidies in nonpayments. Going after them was simply not credible without hardening budgets for the manufacturing companies—something the government was not willing to do. Eventually the system unraveled because it placed government debt on an explosive path.

Even though interest rates fell during the first ten months of 1997, the new system of nonpayments—not paying taxes and energy bills and dealing with offsets—had by then become a bad habit. Real interest rates on ruble debt began rising again after the East Asian crisis spilled over in late 1997, and then continued to rise with devaluation and default risk, as shown in Table 7.2, leading eventually to the August 1998 meltdown.

## What about Oil Prices?

Russia is a major oil and gas exporter, and oil price movements were significant over the 1995–8 period. What impact did these price movements have on the crisis? Suppose oil prices go up by 25 percent as they did in 1996. Then exports and foreign exchange reserves would go up, leading to an appreciation of the exchange rate. Not so simple. The current account surplus in 1996 was around $11 billion, and the sum of government external borrowing and portfolio inflows was $13 billion. This means that the central bank's reserves should have gone up by $24 billion, but they fell by $2 billion. In other words, capital flight was around $26 billion. This scale of capital flight should have put downward pressure on the real exchange rate; but it appreciated by 22 percent in 1996. The reason, as discussed earlier in this chapter, was that the exchange rate was fixed as part of the stabilization program but inflation came down much more slowly.

One would also expect a 25 percent rise in the oil price to raise fiscal revenues and hence lower the need for debt issuance; but this did not happen for two reasons. First, the taxes on oil at that time were specific, that is, linked exclusively to the volume of oil exports, and did not vary with the oil price; and, second, there was an indirect impact through nonpayments. To the extent that oil companies had become tax delinquents (in "retaliation" for being forced to subsidize manufacturing companies), more debt would need to be issued by the government. In other words, the effect of oil price movements was eclipsed by capital flight, the effects of the stabilization program, the nature of oil taxation, and nonpayments.[13]

## Lessons from Russia

First, the Russian crisis of 1998 helped rewrite the book on the links between macroeconomic stabilization and growth. It showed that squeezing out inflation was not enough to get growth going; one needed to adopt a broader approach which pays attention to the collateral impact of lowering inflation on the government's debt dynamics and growth prospects of firms, as transmitted by real interest rates and the real exchange rate. While the high real interest rates in Russia over the period 1995–7 were tangible, fueling noncash settlements not just by firms but also by the government, the real appreciation of the ruble tended to be ignored because Russia never had a current account problem; but it had a profound effect on firms' ability to export and be competitive. The real appreciation of the ruble coexisted with asset stripping instead of enterprise restructuring, and masked the deterioration in the government's debt dynamics. It therefore failed the Dornbusch–Werner criterion of being on an equilibrium path, discussed in Box 3.4.

Second, the Russian crisis of 1998 underlined the importance of understanding the macro–micro linkages. Taking the time to talk to enterprise managers would have shown that they were not restructuring, and that the high real interest rates and the real appreciation of the ruble which accompanied the macroeconomic stabilization were hurting even though the balance of payments appeared to be under control. This, in turn, fed back into the fiscal accounts via lower taxes, which necessitated even higher debt issue, raising interest rates further, and adding to the credit woes of firms, feeding barter and arrears. Asset stripping intensified in the resulting opaque world. To borrow from the Dornbusch–Werner insight in Box 3.4, neither the government nor firms nor workers appeared to be winning; the only winners were the barter intermediaries, opportunistic managers who siphoned out profits, and the big Moscow banks and foreign investors who had a lock on the equities and government securities market. The August 1998 devaluation and default would reverse these winner and loser roles!

The third lesson is about the importance of hard budget constraints. The large subsidies embedded in noncash settlements sabotaged growth prospects by skewing managerial incentives away from restructuring to asset stripping; and made the government's debt trajectory untenable by raising interest rates and contributing to an ever-growing tax shortfall. In contrast, Poland was quick to slash enterprise subsidies and then proceeded to shut off soft loans from the state-owned banks, as noted in Chapter 4. There was an unambiguous signal from the government that there would be no bailout. Thus, Poland's focus was overwhelmingly on the fiscal outcomes, and single-digit inflation was finally attained in 1998, six years after the resumption of growth. Ironically, Russian firms were either paying their workers late or in kind so the subsidies did not help them, pointing to an important lesson: that the government should have focused on helping vulnerable individuals instead of bailing out unviable firms, which, in Russia's case, eventually only helped corrupt managers enrich themselves and led to a debt crisis.

The fourth lesson is on the inadvisability of official loans being used to prop up a fixed exchange rate when the market is signaling strong and justified concerns about a country's solvency. The prime issue here is the negative interaction between the seniority of the official loan and fiscal insolvency.

This is how it was articulated in the analysis of Russia in 1998 in Kharas, Pinto, and Ulatov (2001, p. 43)

> A debt-based [official] liquidity injection that aims to boost confidence could worsen public debt dynamics while offering heavily exposed [private] investors a convenient selling opportunity.... the financing portion of the package could actually trigger a crisis if the market is sufficiently skeptical about the implementation of fiscal and structural reforms. This argument is even stronger if the [official] liquidity injection involves debt that is perceived to be senior to existing claims of private creditors.

Interestingly, Christophe Chamley and I argue that a similar negative interaction underlay the chaotic developments in Greece during its official bailout starting in April 2010, showing that this lesson is a hard one to grasp.[14]

The fifth lesson, typified by the GKO–Eurobond swap, is that financial engineering will not work if the market has fundamental misgivings about a country's fiscal situation. Annex 3 contains more details on the mechanics of the swap, and compares it with the Argentine debt swap, which took place some three years later and also failed to work. I shall confine myself to three points about the economics of the swap. First, on the underlying *intuition*. With short-term ruble Treasury bills (GKOs) at 50 percent and long-term dollar Eurobonds at 12–15 percent, the swap had irresistible appeal as a vehicle for cutting interest costs while reducing rollover risk.

Second, on the *analytics* of the swap, which showed that the intuition was wrong on three counts: (i) the GKO–Eurodollar interest differential, while substantial, was not an arbitrage opportunity waiting to be exploited but rather a signal of the market's assessment that holding GKOs was fraught with devaluation and default risk; (ii) by analogy with the Modigliani–Miller theorem in corporate finance, a market-based swap could never lower the present value of a government's indebtedness as no creditor would voluntarily let this happen; and (iii) solvency concerns meant that the government might need to devalue as a way of lowering the real burden of ruble debt (by definition, dollar-denominated debt cannot be "taxed" through a devaluation). Swapping out of ruble into dollar debt would reduce the outstanding stock of ruble debt (the "tax base") and thereby call for a larger devaluation (the "tax rate") to balance the government's budget. Anticipating this, ruble debt holders would exit, with the speculative attack on the central bank's reserves forcing a crisis.[15] The moral: not only will financial engineering not compensate for weak fiscal fundamentals, it could actually backfire.

Third, on the *unintended portfolio consequences* of the swap. As I noted earlier in this chapter, the swap increased the supply of Russian government dollar-denominated debt, lowering its price and triggering marginal calls on big Moscow banks, which had borrowed against their holdings of such debt. This forced them to liquidate their ruble T-bills and convert the proceeds into dollars to meet the margin calls, depleting the central bank's limited reserves and hastening the crisis.

Ironically, notwithstanding the gloomy predictions, post-meltdown economic performance turned out to be surprisingly strong. Initial forecasts were of a *decline* in real GDP of 7–10 percent for 1999, but Russia ended up with *positive growth* of over 5 percent in 1999. In fact, industrial production rebounded just a few weeks after the meltdown, by October that very year. The immediate factor was the large real depreciation accompanying the collapse of the ruble, which shut down imports and switched domestic demand toward Russian-made goods. An equally important factor was the hardening of the government's own budget constraint as the default shut it out of the domestic and international capital markets. The government began insisting on cash tax payments by the energy monopolies; as a chain reaction, budgets hardened throughout the economy, forcing managers to begin running their companies instead of negotiating barter deals and tax offsets.

Overall, the Russian crisis of 1998 was an eye-opener in that it shifted attention from a focus on low inflation and fiscal deficits to the health of the government intertemporal budget constraint and macro–micro linkages in the pursuit of sustainable growth. Even though there was a tendency to regard Russia as a special case because of oil, its being in the midst of a complicated transition from central planning to a market system, and the idiosyncratic proliferation of barter and noncash settlements, closer examination revealed orthodox behavior on the part of the government, the energy monopolies, and enterprise managers, all of whom were responding rationally to the economic incentives and constraints they faced. Indeed, there are remarkable similarities in the determination to defend fixed exchange rates, the emergence of unsustainable government debt dynamics, and the futile last-minute attempt to fend off a crisis through ill-advised and costly sovereign debt swaps, between Russia in 1998 and Argentina a couple of years later. The response to the Argentine crisis in 2000–2001 might well have been designed differently had a timely and careful analysis of the Russian crisis of 1998 been undertaken; at the very least, repeating the same mistakes would have been avoided, a point made in Box 7.4.[16]

---

**Box 7.4**  Russia 1998 and Argentina 2001

The Independent Evaluation Office of the IMF identified ten lessons from its postmortem of Argentina 2001.[a] Four macroeconomic and crisis management lessons were identified and are reproduced verbatim below:

"**Lesson 2.** The level of sustainable debt for emerging market economies may be lower than had been thought, depending on a country's economic characteristics. The conduct of fiscal policy should therefore be sensitive not only to year-to-year fiscal imbalances, but also to the overall stock of public debt.

**Lesson 7.** The catalytic approach[b] to the resolution of a capital account crisis works only under quite stringent conditions. When there are well-founded concerns over debt and exchange rate sustainability, it is unreasonable to expect a voluntary reversal of capital flows.

**Lesson 8.** Financial engineering in the form of voluntary, market-based debt restructuring is costly and unlikely to improve debt sustainability if it is undertaken under crisis conditions and without a credible, comprehensive economic strategy. Only a form of debt restructuring that leads to a reduction of the net present value (NPV) of debt payments or, if the debt is believed to be sustainable, a large financing package by the official sector has a chance to reverse unfavorable debt dynamics.

**Lesson 9.** Delaying the action required to resolve a crisis can significantly raise its eventual cost, as delayed action can inevitably lead to further output loss, additional capital flight, and erosion of asset quality in the banking system. To minimize the costs of any crisis, the IMF must take a proactive approach to crisis resolution, including providing financial support to a policy shift, which is bound to be costly regardless of when it is made."

These were exactly the same lessons as those that arose from Russia 1998! First, being within the Maastricht ceiling of 60 percent of GDP was not cause for comfort; the market signals on default and devaluation risks also mattered. Second, the catalytic approach tends to fail when reserves are augmented with senior official loans in the presence of a fiscal solvency problem because this could hasten a speculative attack by private (junior) bondholders—as outlined in the fourth lesson from the 1998 Russian crisis on designing an international rescue package. Third, the alluring market-based GKO–Eurobond swap backfired—it was too good to be true. And, fourth, procrastination in addressing the fundamental fiscal problem, which was facilitated by continuing private capital inflows in the expectation of a bailout, only led to a much bigger debt burden when the crisis inevitably occurred.[c]

---

[a] Independent Evaluation Office (IEO) of the IMF (2004), Executive Summary.

[b] The "catalytic approach" refers to the idea that the IMF's seal of approval will bolster confidence and persuade private creditors to roll their loans over instead of exiting and possibly precipitating a crisis. It is more likely to work when the country is facing a liquidity or confidence problem rather than a fundamental debt sustainability or insolvency problem.

[c] See Pinto and Ulatov (2012).

## Epilogue

If there were ever such a thing as an *Emerging Markets Crises Hall of Fame*, Russia 1998 would surely occupy pride of place. Contagion from it led to a spike in emerging market sovereign bond spreads in the fall of 1998 as global credit risks were repriced. The hedge fund managed by Long-Term Capital Management (LTCM) had placed large, highly leveraged bets on the expectation of falling spreads.[17] Given the size of its on-balance sheet ($125 billion) and off-balance sheet ($1.25 trillion in various derivatives) transactions, LTCM posed a systemic risk and had become too big to fail. The New York Federal Reserve was forced to organize a bailout whereby 14 banks invested $3.6 billion for a 90 percent stake in LTCM. At the same time, the Federal Reserve Board eased monetary policy aggressively by cutting interest rates thrice in quick succession, to preempt a possible recession.[18]

Economic contagion was not the only fallout. A political blame game began, with the crisis threatening to become an issue in the 2000 US presidential elections. Michael Dobbs and Paul Blustein wrote: "The finger-pointing over 'Who lost Russia?' threatens to spill over into next year's US presidential election campaign. Foreign policy advisers to George W Bush are attempting to link Vice President Gore to the failure of economic reform in Russia . . ."[19] This was only one of a multitude of press articles to carry the title, "Who Lost Russia?," as a Google search reveals.

As it turns out, Russia was not lost, just badly diagnosed. The 1998 crisis provided the spur for reforms which at last hardened budgets throughout the economy and reversed the real overvaluation of the ruble. Even the increase in dollar-denominated debt of $16 billion that had been incurred in a futile defense of the ruble over the last ten weeks before the meltdown was fortuitously recovered: this was identical to the loss in net present value terms that Russia's London Club creditors were forced to take in August 2000 on their holdings of Russia's Soviet-era debt (debt incurred prior to January 1, 1992), with the IMF throwing its weight behind Russia. Above all, hard budgets and fiscal prudence were maintained by the government when oil prices subsequently rose starting in the year 2000, instead of reverting to the old system.

We are left with two enduring lessons. First, serious stabilization must rest on a bedrock of fiscal solvency, which both depends upon and promotes strong microfoundations for growth. Second, when eminent economists get it wrong, the fault is less likely to be with economics than with their not having enough time to really understand the intricate workings of an economy, or trying to understand it from a safe distance. This is a field in which the country economist has a natural advantage.[20]

## Notes

1. Pinto (1996). Italics added.
2. Parks (1978). Bruno and Easterly (1998) found a negative association between inflation crises and growth; but causality and harmful effects of low-to-moderate inflation on growth were hard to establish.
3. As an oil exporter and a country blessed with every element in the periodic table, Russia faces a raft of other challenges related to lessening its dependence on natural resources, not coincidentally combined with a complicated political transition. My focus is on the lessons from its failed stabilization.
4. *EIU Country Report: Russia*, 1st quarter 1996. Page 8 forecast real GDP growth of 3 percent for 1996 and 4 percent for 1997. Actual outcomes were -3.4 percent for 1996 and +0.9 percent for 1997.
5. My notes from Dow Jones/Sachs Second Annual Russia investment conference, March 1997.
6. Russia did not literally fix the exchange rate. It had a target nominal depreciation rate and managed the ruble within a narrow, prespecified band around a central ruble per dollar rate.
7. See Dornbusch and Werner (1994, p. 273).
8. The Maastricht criteria defined under the umbrella of the February 1992 Maastricht Treaty are economic conditions European Union countries must meet in order to adopt the euro. They stipulate, among other things, that gross government debt should not exceed 60 percent of GDP.
9. See Kharas, Pinto, and Ulatov (2001, p. 16).

10. For details on how these calculations (which are quite simple) were done, see Kharas, Pinto, and Ulatov (2001).
11. Over the 1995 to mid-1998 disinflation, noncash settlements accounted for as much as 50 percent of spending by regional governments, while money surrogates and offsets averaged over 20 percent for federal government noninterest spending (Pinto, Drebentsov, and Morozov 2000a, b).
12. Pinto, Drebentsov, and Morozov (2000b).
13. See Table 45.3 in Pinto and Ulatov (2012), and the related discussion.
14. See Chamley and Pinto (2011).
15. You will find a formal argument in Aizenman, Kletzer, and Pinto (2005), and the references therein.
16. See Pinto, Gurvich, and Ulatov (2005), Aizenman, Kletzer, and Pinto (2005), Mussa (2002), and Pinto and Ulatov (2012).
17. For contagion effects from Russia, see Dungey, et al. (2006). For an assessment of the impact of Russia 1998 on LTCM, see Jorion (2000).
18. Details in Dungey, et al. (2006).
19. "Policymakers Debate: 'Who Lost Russia?'" *The Washington Post*, September 12, 1999, p. A1.
20. Most of the points in my 2001 Brookings paper with Homi Kharas and Sergei Ulatov were first raised in the weeks prior to the design of the failed July 1998 rescue package.

# PART THREE

# Policy Debates and Lessons

Emerging markets were plunged into successive crises between 1997 and 2001. The Russian crisis of 1998 was a major part of the story, even threatening to bring down the US financial system, as noted in Chapter 7. Competing explanations were proffered for the crises, with *debt intolerance* arguing it was the fault of the countries themselves, and *original sin* blaming the inability of these countries to issue long-term external debt in their own currencies. A fierce debate erupted on *fiscal space*. Chapter 8 takes stock, with Brazil's experience after 1999 illustrating two key ideas: first, that fiscal fundamentals dominate financial engineering, in the sense that better debt structures in terms of maturities and currencies cannot be achieved unless fiscal credibility is first established. Otherwise, the market will exact an exorbitant price. Second, reestablishing fiscal credibility will unavoidably take a toll on growth in the short run as governments are forced to cut even public infrastructure investment in order to raise primary fiscal surpluses. Crisis prevention is definitely better than cure, and much less costly.

Chapter 9 documents the remarkable response of emerging markets to their crises. They took steps few economists would have anticipated, leave alone for the length of time that they did. They crossed a threshold with a permanently positive change in government behavior and a heightened awareness of the importance of the government intertemporal budget constraint. They adopted what I call a package approach to self-insurance that is closely connected to self-financed growth, or to the idea that fast-growing countries tend to rely more on their own savings than foreign savings. This reconnects us to the ideas explored in Chapters 2 and 3.

Chapter 10 sums up and draws lessons for low-income countries from emerging markets while recognizing the special constraints these countries face.

# CHAPTER 8

# Emerging Market Crises of the Last Decade: A Watershed

*Crises have been a constant of market capitalism.*

—Easterly, Islam, and Stiglitz (2000)

The Russian crisis of 1998, which formed the subject of Chapter 7, was preceded by the East Asian crisis of 1997–8 and followed by crises in Brazil, Argentina, and Turkey. In this chapter, I focus on the common elements of these crises as well as their impact on the theoretical literature, and the policy debates they inspired. The East Asian crisis will be referred to only fleetingly. Not only am I less well acquainted with it, it differs from the others in two respects: first, there was no fundamental fiscal problem in the sense that the government's debt dynamics were under control—although substantial fiscal costs were incurred in bailing out the private banks once the exchange rate collapsed; and East Asian countries, by and large, enjoyed quick, "v-shaped" recoveries relative to the longer and more complicated adjustments in Brazil and Turkey.[1] Therefore, I shall focus on the latter countries, mostly because they offer clear illustrations of the main points I want to make.

Together with Russia 1998, these crises rewrote the book on macroeconomic stabilization while raising profound questions about the nature of the international debt and capital markets, as well as the ability of emerging markets to manage sovereign debt and the public finances to spur growth. The exchange-rate crisis literature was augmented with new models. Two distinct controversies arose, around *original sin* and *fiscal space*, which I shall illustrate with Brazil's experience. But it ended in a triumph centered on what I loosely call "self-insurance," discussed in Chapter 9. After the crises of 1997–2001, emerging markets went far beyond simply building up a cushion of foreign exchange reserves in their quest for self-insurance, as we shall see. This response was pivotal in enabling countries like Brazil and Turkey to weather the global financial crisis, not simply without collapsing, but displaying considerable resilience.

## The Crisis Literature Augmented

The exchange-rate crisis literature is about the collapse of a fixed exchange rate brought about either by weak macroeconomic fundamentals, shifting market confidence, or both. Three generations of crisis models have evolved, which I describe in Annex 4. Up until the Exchange Rate Mechanism (ERM) crises of 1992–3, the literature was dominated by a speculative attack model conjured up in a 1979 paper by Paul Krugman.[2] In Krugman's so-called *first generation* model, a speculative attack on reserves is spurred by inconsistent fundamentals: a fiscal deficit financed by credit is not consistent with the zero inflation implied by a fixed exchange rate, leading to a depletion of foreign exchange reserves and an eventual abrupt collapse of the exchange rate. But in a 1994 paper, Maurice Obstfeld argued that Krugman's model could not fully explain the ERM crisis of 1992–3 and the experience of Sweden in particular.

## Second Generation Models

Obstfeld's central idea is that the government has options to address actual or perceived unsustainability in macroeconomic policies. It balances the *pain* of holding on to a fixed peg (in the form of high interest rates leading to pressures on private sector balance sheets or the exacerbation of high unemployment, for example) with the *gain* of letting it go (the pain will be avoided without a big effect on the government's credibility either because other important countries have acted similarly or because the move will be seen as "sensible"). The ambiguity about how the government will respond gives rise to "multiple equilibria." Market expectations are molded by perceptions of which policy option the government will choose, affecting positions taken by investors, which could, in turn, force the hand of the government. This circular logic could lead to a crisis as a *self-fulfilling prophecy* triggered by shifting market sentiment, irrespective of fiscal fundamentals. Such models are often referred to as *second generation* models.

Obstfeld makes two key points:

1. Governments can borrow reserves "subject only to the government's consolidated intertemporal budget constraint." I quote Obstfeld 1994, p. 200: "Ultimately, accounts of crises based on limited foreign reserves must also be based on overall fiscal weakness: were the public fiscal position robust, it would be credible and feasible to borrow sufficient reserves to repurchase a large portion of the high-powered money supply and thereby fend off any attack."

2. One should beware of the essentially false dichotomy between "fundamentals" and "purely" self-fulfilling expectations. The two feed off each other.

The pivotal importance of the government intertemporal budget constraint (GIBC) stressed in Obstfeld's point 1 is aptly illustrated by Russia 1998 and Argentina 2001, where fixed exchange rates coexisted uneasily with unsustainable debt dynamics.[3] In Russia's case, borrowing reserves in the form of implicitly senior loans from the international financial institutions hastened the end of its exchange rate peg *because* of its fiscal solvency problems. Obstfeld's point 2 tells us we should be looking both at fundamentals as well as market signals on devaluation and default risks for emerging markets. No point in saying, "Fiscal fundamentals are okay, after all the gross government debt-to-GDP ratio is less than the Maastricht criterion of 60 percent," as was the case in Russia prior to the August 1998 meltdown. The market signals were highly negative and, on closer inspection, so were Russia's fiscal and growth fundamentals.[4]

## East Asia and the Third Generation

The *third generation* crisis model was motivated by the East Asian experience of 1997–8. This highlighted balance sheet mismatches in currencies and maturities (typified by short-term dollar debt financing long-term local currency assets), international illiquidity (insufficient foreign exchange reserves), and moral hazard (the private sector makes bad investment decisions but is confident the government will bail it out). As a result, even if the government is not *currently* running large fiscal deficits, *prospective* deficits may be high on account of contingent liabilities related to the fiscal costs of bailing out banks and private firms.

An important catalyst for the East Asian crisis was financial liberalization combined with actions taken by central banks to sterilize capital inflows, which raised interest rates at home. With implicit exchange rate guarantees, private firms and banks naturally preferred to borrow in foreign currency, leading eventually to large currency and maturity mismatches on private sector balance sheets.[5] Insufficient international illiquidity, manifested in a high ratio of broad money to foreign exchange reserves, made East Asian countries vulnerable to capital flow reversals that would force a devaluation. If interest rates were raised to make domestic currency assets more attractive, this would have put a strain on banks' balance sheets by increasing nonperforming loans; if the exchange rate were allowed to collapse, the real burden of dollar-denominated debt would rise on corporate balance sheets, forcing them into bankruptcy, and hurting the banks as well. This made it impossible to defend the fixed exchange rate against speculative attacks, forcing its abandonment as well as costly public bailouts, as wholesale bankruptcy of the corporate and financial sectors would have been politically unacceptable.[6]

Table 8.1 contains the sizable gross fiscal bank bailout costs for several East Asian countries for the first five years, starting from the crisis year of 1997, as a percentage of average nominal GDP over this period. As an example, Indonesia's public debt went up from an average of 35 percent of GDP during the three years between 1995 and 1997 to 94 percent of GDP by the end of 1998, the year its political and financial crisis came to a head. But consider this: the rupiah/US dollar exchange rate went from 2436 on July 11, 1997 to a high of 16,800 on June 17, 2008, a depreciation of close to 600 percent. The rupiah subsequently rebounded, but with even half this kind of depreciation the currency mismatches on the balance sheets of firms and banks would have increased the real burden of dollar-denominated debt, spurring bad loans and forcing a big bailout. Indeed, a widely documented finding is that a significant part of the increase in emerging market indebtedness during the

**Table 8.1** Bank Bailout Cost during the East Asian Crisis

| Country | Gross Fiscal Cost 1997–2001 (percent of average nominal GDP) |
|---------|-------------------------------------------------------------|
| Indonesia | 56.8 |
| Korea | 31.2 |
| Malaysia | 16.4 |
| Philippines | 13.2 |
| Thailand | 43.8 |
| Vietnam | 10.0 |

*Source:* Laeven and Valencia (2008).

crises of the last decade was explicable by real exchange rate collapses in conjunction with dollar-denominated debt and the fiscal costs of bank bailouts.[7]

## Common Elements

Table 8.2 summarizes the essential features of the three generations of crisis models, which I use as a backdrop for extracting the elements common to the emerging market crises of 1997–2001. A central feature was the existence of a fixed exchange rate: Argentina had a constitutionally mandated hard peg; Russia and Brazil, soft pegs designed to lower inflation; and East Asia, implicit exchange rate guarantees—in other words, the private sector acted as though the existing exchange rate with the US dollar would be fixed in perpetuity, a belief the central bank did nothing to shake.

There were other important commonalities: unsustainable debt dynamics (Russia and Argentina); balance sheet mismatches (Argentina, East Asia); and low international liquidity (all). A final prominent common factor was open capital accounts and international financial integration. The tempting question is whether this last factor amplified financial fragility, eventually resulting in a sizable increase in public debt even in countries where large fiscal deficits were not a chronic problem. The answer is yes. Balance sheet mismatches could not develop unless the private sector both perceived that foreign borrowing was cheaper and had easy access to it.

The vulnerability stemming from private sector balance sheets, so essential to the third generation model with its corollary of private sector bailouts, was not entirely novel: Carlos Diaz-Alejandro's classic 1985 paper

**Table 8.2** Crisis Models—Essential Features and Consequences

| Type | Essential Features | Consequences |
|---|---|---|
| First Generation (Latin America 1970s and 1980s) | Fiscal fundamentals key. Fixed exchange rate, open capital account, limited foreign exchange reserves. Credit-financed fiscal deficit. | Speculative attack on reserves followed by float after which fiscal deficit is financed by the inflation tax. Crisis timing predictable. |
| Second Generation (ERM crisis 1992–3) | Confidence, market psychology key. Fixed exchange rate, open capital account, and low international liquidity (i.e., low levels of foreign exchange reserves relative to liquid claims on them). Conflict between external (e.g., maintain fixed parity) and internal (e.g., reduce unemployment) policy goals. | Multiple equilibria related to multiple government policy options; government's hand can be forced by positions taken by investors, leading to crisis as a self-fulfilling prophecy. Crisis timing arbitrary. |
| Third Generation (East Asian crisis 1997–8) | Confidence, market psychology, balance sheet mismatches for firms and banks, key, possibly moral hazard as well. Fixed exchange rate, open capital account, low international liquidity. | Sudden stop in capital inflows linked to contagion, spillovers, fundamentals, or all three, leads to real exchange rate collapse with disastrous consequences including widespread bankruptcy (on account of currency mismatches) and recession. Government may be forced to bail out private sector leading to big increases in public debt. |

*Source:* My interpretation of Krugman (1999), Jeanne (1999), Frankel and Wei (2005).

anticipated many of the features of the East Asian crisis, as shown in Box 8.1. A premature financial liberalization could lead to a boom in private external borrowing, currency mismatches on private balance sheets, and a severe misallocation of resources. This eventually results in a plethora of bad loans and a financial collapse. When banks are bailed out, public debt goes up and moral hazard gets ingrained: banks will be tempted to take risky bets again in the future, confident that public resources will be used to prevent

---

**Box 8.1** Diaz-Alejandro (1985)—Déjà Vu All Over Again

Carlos Diaz-Alejandro's brilliant 1985 paper does not have a shred of algebra in it, yet is rightly deemed a classic, anticipating the 1997–8 East Asian crisis and the third generation crisis model in all their essential aspects. His paper was motivated by the experience of the Southern Cone countries, starting in the mid-1970s, as they sought to lower inflation while opening up their capital accounts. By 1983, these countries were embroiled in a ruinous public debt problem as a result of bailing out the private sector. Their experience is typified by what happened to Chile:

- 1979: Chile fixes peso–dollar exchange rate to lower inflation and gradually opens up capital account.
- 1981: Capital account liberalized, but interest and inflation rates slow to converge to US levels so private capital comes flooding in. Current account deficit of 14 percent of GNP (gross national product, now replaced terminologically with GNI or gross national income) appears, while domestic savings collapse. Banking supervision slow to develop, owing to idea that financial markets and private borrowers will self-regulate: "only in 1981 were significant regulatory powers given to the Superintendency of Banks" (p. 8). By November, two important private banks and several *financieras* are on the verge of collapse.
- Late 1981, 1982: Central bank bails out private sector by expanding credit.
- June 1982: Peso is devalued, goes from 39 per dollar to 74–80 pesos per dollar by January 1983. Real GNP falls by 14 percent in 1982.
- 1983: Chilean government takes over private external debt in spite of strong ex ante assertions to the contrary. "Apparently, the Chilean government caved in under pressure from the bank advisory committee..." (p. 12). Public debt, which was modest, balloons as a result of "an explosive amount of contingent liabilities to both foreign and domestic agents, who held deposits in, or made loans to the rickety domestic financial sector."

---

them from going bust. As a result of the subprime mortgage crisis in the USA, we now know that even sophisticated financial systems with experienced, state-of-the-art supervision are prone to moral hazard and crashes. The takeaway for emerging markets is that fragility is an unavoidable aspect of financial systems, calling for constant vigilance and updating of regulation to keep pace with innovation: the Southern Cone crisis that inspired Diaz-Alejandro's 1985 paper occurred in a far simpler world without derivatives and sovereign bond markets.

The aftermath of the 1997–2001 emerging market crises proved controversial, with competing hypotheses in the form of "original sin" and its polar opposite, "debt intolerance," springing up to explain why emerging markets were vulnerable to debt crises.[8] *Original sin* argued that emerging markets' vulnerability to crises stemmed from their inability to borrow long term in their own currency. *Debt intolerance* argued that emerging market debt crises were self-inflicted: countries with high inflation and bad credit histories were prone to macroeconomic collapses and default even when they had relatively low levels of debt. Another controversy that arose was on "fiscal space." This was the idea that emerging markets were shooting themselves in the foot by raising primary fiscal surpluses at the expense of public investments in infrastructure in order to lower public debt, but paradoxically endangering fiscal solvency because of the harmful consequences for future growth and taxes. Indeed, a substantial increase in primary surpluses occurred across emerging markets in response to the crises of 1997–2001.[9]

## Original Sin

The *original sin* hypothesis argues that emerging markets cannot do much on their own to counter vulnerability stemming from bad debt structures because it is neither their fault nor within their control. Barry Eichengreen, Ricardo Hausmann, and Ugo Panizza argue, in their 2002 paper, that the fundamental problem is the inability of emerging markets to issue long-term external debt in their own currencies; they typically do so in hard currencies like the US dollar. Furthermore—and this is where the notion of an inherited sin comes in—the authors posit that this costly inability has nothing to do with the domestic policies or institutions in emerging markets, but flows instead from the absence of a market for such debt instruments, whose birth is inhibited by network externalities.[10] The resulting currency mismatch increases the potential impact of an external shock on a country and its output volatility because the mismatch amplifies the effect of any real exchange rate collapse (which could be brought about by a sudden stop, for example, as was the case in Indonesia in 1997–8).

This idea is pursued in a comprehensive examination of public debt in Latin America published in 2007—see Box 8.2. If the payoff to financial engineering is high both for borrowing governments and investors, why have appropriate debt instruments not developed spontaneously? An impediment already mentioned is the prevalence of "network externalities" in launching and marketing new types of instruments—it is too costly for one country to

> **Box 8.2** Living with Debt
>
> The central message of IDB (2007) is that *debt structure* is more important than *debt levels* in determining vulnerability to a crisis. The report argues that currency composition and maturity go hand in hand in determining the probability of a debt default and hence borrowing costs. This message is reiterated in Chapter 11 of IDB (2007) on approaches to fiscal sustainability, which stresses that standard approaches ignore debt structure even though this may be more important than debt levels in determining debt sustainability.
>
> Based on the preceding diagnosis, the report advocates contingent debt contracts with equity-type features, inflation-indexed debt instruments, and a shift toward domestic currency-denominated debt to limit the risks of sovereign finance and enable the use of sovereign debt as an instrument for growth. The idea is to let debt service vary with a country's ability to pay over the business cycle and avoid exposure to exchange rate changes. Governments will obviously benefit but so will investors because of the fall in default risk.

go it alone. Chapter 14 of the 2007 IDB (Inter-American Development Bank) study suggests that the International Financial Institutions (IMF, World Bank, Regional Development Banks) can play a role in helping with the coordination, setup costs, and marketing. This idea echoes the recommendation in Eichengreen, Hausmann, and Panizza (2002) that the International Financial Institutions (IFIs) and rich countries kick-start the market by issuing debt denominated in an index of emerging market currencies and then arrange swaps with emerging markets to reduce or eliminate the currency mismatch.

*Original sin* generated strong reactions. Carmen Reinhart, Kenneth Rogoff, and Miguel Savastano wrote in their 2003 paper on debt intolerance: "the notion that the 'original sin' of serial defaulters can be extinguished through some stroke of financial engineering, allowing these countries to borrow in the same amounts, relative to GNP, as more advanced economies, much less at the same interest rates, is sheer folly." *In essence, a country's track record on default and its fiscal fundamentals are more important than its debt structure.*

Morris Goldstein and Philip Turner (2004) were more charitable, agreeing that currency mismatches pose a threat but disagreeing that emerging markets are to be absolved of all blame. Their solution is twofold: improve policies, for example, by adopting flexible exchange rates to raise awareness of exchange rate risk; and strengthen institutions to monitor and control currency mismatches. IFIs should both measure and report currency mismatches and, if deemed excessive, make their reduction over the medium term a condition for loans from the IMF. There is no quick fix and a decade may elapse before tangible improvements are secured.

My own assessment, honed during the course of the internal debates at the World Bank, consists of two points, which I shall illustrate later in this chapter using Brazil's experience: first, policy credibility and fiscal fundamentals dominate the debt structure identified by IDB (2007). Second, contrary to the impression perhaps unwittingly conveyed in IDB (2007), debt structure for emerging markets—or indeed *any* country—is not a one-sided policy decision by the government. The market has its say.[11] No emerging market deliberately chooses short-term, dollar-denominated debt. This is an outcome forced upon it by the demand for, and supply of, various debt instruments a government may wish to issue, with the options constrained by fiscal fundamentals and credibility. Consider the following statement in a 2004 paper by Federico Sturzenegger and Holger Wolf: "prices in Argentina increased 312,000 million times between 1970 and 2002, which might forgive not just foreign but Argentine investors as well for not accepting long-term bonds denominated in pesos."

Credibility rears its head in another form: how to enforce compliance with the underlying contracts when special debt instruments are designed. Governments can manipulate inflation or output statistics in cases where debt is indexed to inflation or GDP: even the best-designed instruments can be defaulted on. This possibility is illustrated by allegations that the official Argentine statistics agency, the Instituto Nacional de Estadística y Censos (INDEC), underreported the inflation rate to save on interest payments on inflation-indexed debt. To quote Carmen Reinhart and Kenneth Rogoff from a June 24, 2008 *Wall Street Journal* article: "Already, a good share of Argentina's debt is in default. What else do you call it when a government that owes over $30 billion in inflation-indexed debt manipulates its consumer-price statistics?"

## "Fiscal Space," or: Growth Foolishly Foregone

If *original sin* blames the international capital markets (absence of suitable debt instruments) and *debt intolerance* blames the countries themselves (debt problems are self-inflicted by bad credit and inflation histories, which tend to linger), *fiscal space* blames the IMF and World Bank. The fiscal space controversy arose in the context of Latin American countries—most of which would have been classified as debt intolerant by Reinhart, Rogoff, and Savastano. The idea is built around the notion that any government which refrains from making an investment in a project with a high economic and social rate of return is acting foolishly. And it is the IFIs who are behind this because they dictated the macroeconomic adjustment programs which were a staple of Latin America in the 1980s and 1990s. The costly nature of these programs was articulated thus by Cesar Calderon, William Easterly, and Luis Servén (2004, p. 133): "fiscal adjustment through public infrastructure compression can be largely self-defeating in the long-run, because of its adverse effect on growth and hence on the debt-servicing capacity of the public sector."

The authors blame the IFIs for focusing on short-run stabilization and fiscal deficits and ignoring long-run solvency. Instead of raising primary surpluses at the expense of infrastructure in order to lower indebtedness, fiscal space argues that it would make sense to borrow even more and invest in infrastructure. Why? Because long-run solvency would be strengthened as a result of the positive effect on future growth and taxes even though the immediate effect would be to raise the debt-to-GDP ratio further. The key condition, derived in work by Servén (2007, pp. 12–13), is that the marginal financial return to the government, namely, user charges plus the tax collected on the marginal product of the extra spending on infrastructure, exceed the user cost of capital given by the marginal cost of borrowing plus the rate of capital depreciation. This is a variation on the result in project economics that any investment where the rate of return exceeds the marginal cost of financing is worth undertaking. In other words, so long as infrastructure projects which raise future taxes and growth sufficiently to offset borrowing costs are available, governments have fiscal space. Ergo, cutting public investments to raise primary surpluses makes no sense.

However, the seemingly watertight argument of Calderon, Easterly, and Servén breaks down in practice. First, for their argument to work, we would need perfect capital markets in the sense that the government can easily (i.e., without a big jump in interest rates) borrow against future earnings from taxes and user charges, *even if these materialize in the distant future*, as is typically the case with investments in most components of infrastructure, mobile telephony being an exception. But we have learned painfully that capital markets are myopic and imperfect. The market may react badly to even a temporary rise in the debt-to-GDP ratio, pushing up interest rates. This could completely derail the economics of the project because the effective capital cost would include the impact of the rise in interest rates on the entire stock of inherited debt, which is more likely to be the case the shorter the maturity of the debt: a prominent feature in debt-intolerant countries.

Second, the argument requires a certain stability in external conditions; but as the global financial crisis has demonstrated, shocks exogenous to emerging markets—this one originated in the United States—have adverse fiscal consequences and some fiscal space needs to be reserved for shock absorption.

Third, one has to look at the entire balance sheet of the government, not just at the marginal project. Implicit in the Calderon–Easterly–Servén argument is the idea that the management of the public finances as a whole is exemplary: that revenue mobilization is adequate, user fees set correctly, and only good public investment projects selected. This is seldom the case. State-owned electricity companies often make losses because electricity prices are set too low, and governments often invest in white elephant projects. In this sense, public debt sustainability problems in debt-intolerant countries have similar effects as the corporate debt overhang, in that even profitable public investment infrastructure projects may have to be foregone until indebtedness is lowered and creditworthiness reestablished.[12]

## Brazil's Experience

Brazil's annual inflation rate exceeded 40 percent some 60 percent of the time over the period 1958–2001, and it was in a state of external debt default or restructuring 25 percent of the time between 1824 and 1999, inducing Reinhart, Rogoff, and Savastano (2003) to classify it as "debt intolerant."[13] After six unsuccessful stabilization programs over the previous decade, Brazil launched the *Real Plan* in July 1994, which succeeded in achieving single-digit inflation. In tandem, the government began shifting toward domestic currency debt. Then, as a result of the spillovers from the 1997–1998 East Asian and 1998 Russian crises, Brazil abandoned its peg to the dollar in early 1999, with the *real* depreciating from 1.19 reais per dollar in November 1998 to 1.91 reais per dollar in February 1999. It switched to a flexible exchange rate, complementing this with efforts to build up foreign exchange reserves and significantly higher primary fiscal surpluses. The crisis year 1999 would prove a positive turning point, but only after a long lag.

I shall appeal to Brazil's experience over 1994 to 2008 to make two points: first, that there is really no way of speeding up the attainment of a better debt structure and higher creditworthiness based on financial engineering alone along the lines of IDB (2007); and, second, that countries with debt-intolerance problems may have to forego even profitable public investment opportunities until they have first convinced the markets of their creditworthiness. The existence of fiscal space for such investments is illusory when countries are debt intolerant. To set the stage, recall the conclusion in Chapter 3 that the creditworthiness of the government was a more plausible candidate for being the binding constraint in Brazil over the period 1998–2004 than the level of national saving put forward by Hausmann, Dani Rodrik, and Andres Velasco (2005).

## Financial Engineering Is No Shortcut

Brazil launched a sustained shift toward domestic currency debt in the mid-1990s to combat original sin; but the market did not stand passively by, as we shall see. Suppose, for argument's sake, that the government had been successful in its quest to issue debt at fixed nominal interest rates in its own currency, the *real*. Now consider an exogenous shock—such as a reversal of capital inflows—that led to a large real depreciation of the *real* and forced the central bank to raise interest rates. The real burden of the existing stock of government debt would then decline as a result of the accompanying higher inflation, with debt fixed in nominal terms. Had the debt been in dollars, its real burden would have increased, hitting the government with a multiple whammy: an upward jump in its debt-to-GDP ratio, slowing growth and fiscal revenues on account of the exogenous shock, and rising interest rates. This example captures the advantage of being able to issue debt at fixed nominal interest rates in the government's own currency: it has desirable shock-absorption properties as opposed to the amplification that would result with dollar debt.

The results associated with Brazil's shift toward domestic currency debt, starting in the mid-1990s, underline two hard facts: first, debt structure is not a one-sided policy choice but heavily influenced by a government's reputation and solvency *as perceived by the market*. The government may decide a shift to local currency debt is in its best interests; but the market could exact a heavy price for going along with this. Second, there is little chance of a shortcut to reduced vulnerability and lower indebtedness based on financial engineering *alone* for countries with debt-tolerance problems. Indeed, Brazil continued to encounter headwinds in lowering government indebtedness even though the shift to local currency debt was part of a package that included a switch to flexible exchange rates and higher primary surpluses, starting in 1999.

The first point about the market exacting a heavy price is captured by the fluctuating share of nominal, unindexed local currency debt in total local currency Brazilian government debt. The higher this share, the greater the shock absorption benefits of shifting toward local currency debt described earlier in this chapter. A higher share of unindexed debt also indicates that investors are more confident about the future course of inflation and the public finances. The share of unindexed debt fell from a peak of 60 percent in 1996, when credibility, following the successful stabilization of 1994, was high, to less than 10 percent in 2002, as a result of political uncertainty and fears of a default in connection with the presidential election that summer. It then rose to around 30 percent in 2006 as confidence was slowly restored.

In fact, the bulk of local currency debt between 1997 and 2008 was indexed either to the SELIC (overnight interest rate of the Brazilian central bank) or the exchange rate, blurring the distinction between dollar-denominated and local currency debt. This conveyed the desire of investors to be protected against the possibility of an inflation surprise or devaluation—which could stem from either public finance problems or vulnerability to a sudden stop or both. In their assessment of macroeconomic events in Brazil between 1999 and 2003, Francesco Giavazzi, Ilan Goldfajn, and Santiago Herrera respond to the puzzle of why high real interest rates persisted in spite of the rise in primary surpluses and hardening of subnational government budgets after 1999 thus: "real rates are temporarily high and will come down over time, provided fiscal policy keeps being consistent."[14] In other words, it takes persistence to convince the market about the soundness of the government intertemporal constraint or it will sabotage a shift toward local currency debt, either by demanding a high level of indexation or an exorbitantly high real interest rate in the absence of indexation.

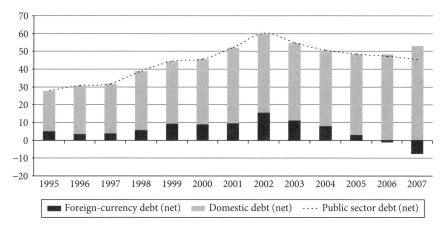

**Figure 8.1** Brazil: Net Public Sector Debt-to-GDP (%) 1995–2007
*Source:* Central Bank of Brazil.

The second point about the absence of a shortcut based on financial engineering comes out in Figure 8.1, which depicts the net debt of the public sector as a ratio of GDP as well as its currency composition.

After 1995, new public borrowing was largely in the domestic market and in local currency; the increase in the ratio of dollar-denominated debt to GDP between 1998 and 2002 was mainly because of the depreciation of the *real*. In addition to shifting toward local currency debt (albeit with a large proportion of it indexed), Brazil moved from a primary *deficit* averaging 0.3 percent of GDP over 1996–8 to a *surplus* of 3.3 percent over 2000–03. This commendable fiscal effort was bolstered by the federal government's negotiating stringent deals with state governments, with a view to avoiding future bailouts of the latter, epitomized by the Minas Gerais affair in early 1999. The then Governor of this state, which boasted the second largest number of voters in the country, declared a moratorium on debt service payments to the federal government which violated an agreement struck between the previous administration of that state and the federal government. The then President responded by organizing a coalition of other governors to denounce the moratorium as irresponsible. At the same time, the national Treasury adhered strictly to the earlier contract signed between the federal government and the state, whereby it applied revenue shares that would normally be transferred to Minas Gerais directly to its debt service. This nipped the problem in the bud and signaled the uncompromising determination of the federal government to impose fiscal discipline.[15]

The hardening of budget constraints for subnational levels of government and the sustained, large increase in primary surpluses should have lowered borrowing requirements (recall Kenya's experience in Chapter 5). But net indebtedness over 2005–7—a period sufficiently removed from the political turbulence of the year 2002, which I discuss below—was far higher than during the three years which preceded the 1999 crisis, as shown in Figure 8.1. This is partly because real interest rates remained stubbornly high and partly because growth did not take off. In fact, the higher primary surplus was achieved mainly by raising taxes. Such a move could deter private investment and long-run growth by lowering private returns to capital. This could keep real interest rates high, if it lowers future taxes and primary surpluses, and inhibit the movement to a good equilibrium characterized by higher private investment and growth. This idea was expressed succinctly in the OECD's 2006 report on Brazil:

> Nevertheless, fiscal adjustment has been achieved at the expense of cutting back on public investment and by increasing the tax burden. The revenue-to-GDP ratio rose by about 5 percentage points during 2000–05 to nearly 37.5% in 2005—a level that is one of the highest among countries with comparable income levels. *A durable reduction in public indebtedness on the back of a retrenchment of current expenditure, rather than tax hikes, would serve to facilitate a swifter fall in real interest rates and to permit the channelling of domestic saving to finance growth-enhancing investment.* It would also lay the groundwork for removing distortions in the tax system, including by broadening tax bases. (OECD 2006, p. 12)

This quote bemoaning the cuts in public investment and the increase in taxes is a perfect segue into the second controversy, over fiscal space.

## Fiscal Space—Illusory for Debt-Intolerant Countries

Brazil raised its primary surplus by an average of 3.6 percentage points of GDP during the four years 2000 to 2003 which followed its 1999 crisis, as compared to 1996–8. It then ramped it up further in 2004 and 2005 in a remarkable display of political stamina. One would have expected such a large, sustained fiscal effort to convince the markets that the government had no intention of defaulting; but Brazil's interest payments actually *rose* from an average of 7 percent of GDP during the three years before the crisis, to over 8 percent of GDP in the three which followed. The market is not simply unforgiving, to borrow Guillermo Calvo's expression; it can be merciless. As Figure 8.2 shows, in spite of the big ramp-up in the primary surplus after 1999, bond spreads were pushed to default levels in 2002. This last incident merits a comment.

Fears of debt repudiation were rife in 2002 because the candidate of the Brazilian Workers' Party, Luiz Inácio Lula da Silva, was expected to win the presidential election. Bond spreads rose to over 2000 basis points by the end of July 2002 as polls "indicated that Lula would win the presidential election .... can [investors] be certain that a Brazil run by a president with a past record of sympathizing with default will not take the easy way out?" This quote is from an insightful commentary by John Williamson (2002), who argued that Brazil was the victim of a confidence or multiple equilibria situation, reminiscent of the second generation crisis model shown in Table 8.2. Fundamentals were sound: primary fiscal surpluses had been raised substantially, budget constraints hardened for the state governments, and a flexible exchange rate adopted in 1999. Williamson was, in part, responding to a wager by Morris Goldstein (2003) that there was a 70 percent chance that Brazil would be forced to restructure its debt by the end of 2003.

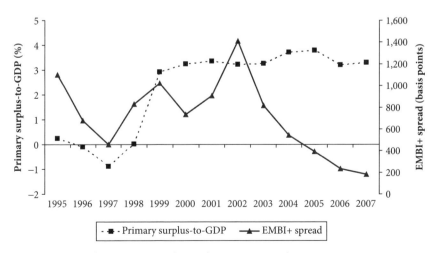

**Figure 8.2** Brazil: Primary Surplus and EMBI+ Spread 1995–2007
*Source:* Central Bank of Brazil and Bloomberg.

Compared to a starting position of unsustainable debt dynamics and a fixed exchange rate prior to 1999, Brazil had floated its currency and raised primary fiscal surpluses significantly by July 2002. Based on market reaction, it had evidently not yet succeeded in shedding its debt-intolerant image; but the fact that it had taken serious corrective steps was not in doubt. Lula ended up winning the election. The default fears proved groundless and bond spreads then subsequently fell, but only slowly. In the interim, a $30 billion loan was secured from the IMF; recall point 1 earlier in this chapter, from Obstfeld's 1994 classic on multiple equilibria: that if fiscal fundamentals are strong, market confidence can be shored up by borrowing reserves. Nevertheless, the market remained jittery, captured by the declining share of unindexed local currency debt, and it would have been foolhardy to have attempted a debt-financed increase in public expenditure on infrastructure in these circumstances. The overwhelming priority was to restore creditworthiness via higher primary fiscal surpluses. The dominant nature of this priority was captured elegantly by Olivier Blanchard's chapter in the 2005 Giavazzi–Goldfajn–Herrera volume. He cautioned that raising interest rates to keep inflation within its target range could backfire by raising perceptions of default risk and worsening inflation expectations if this fueled expectations of higher currency depreciation.[16]

But the concern lingers that long-run growth may have suffered. Brazil's primary surplus was increased on the back of tax increases; infrastructure spending had already been cut to the bone—by 1998, the year before the crisis, it was less than 1 percent of GDP, with total public investment less than 4 percent of GDP.[17] Both responses, raising taxes and cutting infrastructure investment, would reduce aggregate demand as well as returns to private investment, lowering growth. On the positive side, Brazil hardened budgets for its state governments and the private sector. The bet was that following this course would eventually convince markets that Brazil was no longer debt intolerant, lowering interest rates and spurring growth.

The intriguing question is to what extent the fiscal adjustment path chosen by Brazil was forced upon it by its credit and inflation history. Why could it not have cut marginal tax rates and increased public expenditure on infrastructure projects with high rates of return instead of doing the opposite? The simple answer is that the debt markets would not have let it to do so and that Brazil's "debt-intolerant" history was an important factor. Any attempt to borrow without a restoration of fiscal credibility would have probably resulted in a spike in interest rates, reflecting not high rates of return to capital (as argued by Hausmann, Rodrik, and Velasco—see Chapter 3) but high default risk. A second consideration is the politics of fiscal adjustment. As the 2006 OECD report noted, Brazil had developed an inflexible spending pattern focused on pensions and wages at the expense of public investment. Thus, market myopia combined with political realities ruled out a higher-quality fiscal adjustment.

India's fiscal adjustment after its 1991 balance-of-payments crisis provides an interesting contrast. India cut tax rates and gradually eased financial repression with a significant loss in revenues and a visible deterioration in its government debt dynamics around the turn of the millennium; but this proved remarkably pro-growth—albeit with a long lag, as noted in Chapter 6. The debt markets were willing to give India the benefit of the doubt that future primary surpluses would be sufficiently high as a result of faster growth and higher revenue mobilization. But, in common with Brazil, India also cut government capital expenditure, which contributed to a growing infrastructure gap that has become the biggest constraint on private investment today.

There is another important difference: India's capital account has been and is being liberalized slowly. The high fiscal costs of India's reforms (which in Chapter 6 were estimated at 38 percentage points of GDP between 1991 and 2004) begs the question of whether emerging markets with open capital accounts can incur such reform costs without succumbing to a macroeconomic crisis. Indeed, an open capital account does appear to be strongly associated with debt intolerance; it is clearly not sufficient for becoming debt intolerant, as evidenced by the experience of East Asian countries. Because of its slow approach to capital account liberalization, India was able to avoid a crisis when its debt dynamics worsened after 1997; and the toxic combination of real exchange rate collapses and currency mismatches was preempted, unlike in the Latin American and East Asian emerging markets.

## Crossing a Threshold

Four main points emerge from this chapter. First, a combination of fixed exchange rates, open capital accounts, and market concerns about fiscal fundamentals is pretty much fatal. Second, addressing fiscal fundamentals in a way that assuages market concerns about default risk becomes, perforce, the top priority *even* if this has negative consequences for growth in the short run—as when primary surpluses are raised by reducing public spending on infrastructure. The markets don't care. A corollary is that no amount of financial engineering will restore confidence or sustainability if the fiscal fundamentals are not addressed. Third, as competing hypotheses for the travails of emerging markets over the 1990s and early 2000s, debt intolerance appears more persuasive than original sin. Fourth, long lags are likely to be involved in overcoming debt intolerance; prevention is better than cure.

As will become evident in Chapter 9, emerging markets crossed a threshold during the first decade of the new millennium in spite of the dismal start to it. For the first time in several decades, they took matters into their own hands. They learned from their mistakes and implemented reform focusing on the soundness of the government intertemporal budget constraint and responding to the vulnerabilities unearthed by the three generations of crisis models by building up foreign exchange reserves, shifting to flexible exchange rates, and strengthening financial sector regulation and supervision. The results from this self-insurance package were surprisingly positive, as we shall see in Chapter 9, indicating the lessons are of enduring value.

## Notes

1. This does not mean East Asia escaped unscathed. Cerra and Saxena (2005) present evidence of permanent output losses in all the countries.
2. See also the extensions in Flood and Garber (1984).
3. Luis Servén and Guillermo Perry (2005) document the 2000–1 Argentine crisis.
4. Referring to Obstfeld's 1994 paper, Paul Krugman admitted in a 1999 volume in honor of Robert Flood (Krugman 1999) that "I was wrong; Maury Obstfeld was right." But the two points just discussed suggest both were right.
5. On East Asia 1997–8, see Claessens (2005, pp. 236–7, figure 6.2). See also Chang and Velasco (2000).
6. Various aspects of the third generation model were inspired or developed by Dooley (2000), Krugman (1999), Chang and Velasco (2000), and Burnside, Eichenbaum, and Rebelo (2001). See also Claessens (2005), Frankel and Wei (2005), and the seminal paper of Diaz-Alejandro (1985).
7. IMF (2003), Gill and Pinto (2005), IDB (2007).

8. Original sin: Eichengreen, Hausmann, and Panizza (2002). Debt intolerance: Reinhart, Rogoff, and Savastano (2003).
9. As shown in Table 4.3 in Gill and Pinto (2005).
10. "Network externality" in this case means that the first country to issue long-term debt externally in its own currency is going to face huge costs because of the novelty; this cost declines as more countries join the bandwagon. But there is no mechanism for sharing the subsequent benefit with the first mover, leading to a stalemate and calling for intervention.
11. However, the external debt structure for low-income countries may be largely determined by policy since official creditors predominate.
12. The concept of the debt overhang owes its origin to Stewart Myers in the corporate finance literature (Myers 1977). The idea is that if a firm's income is not sufficient to service its existing debt, it will find it difficult to attract new financing even for investment projects with a positive net present value. This is because much or possibly all the net present value could be appropriated by the existing debt holders. Thus, the firm will end up foregoing profitable new investment opportunities and its growth will suffer.
13. Table 1 in Reinhart, Rogoff, and Savastano (2003). Their study focuses on a country's total (public plus private) external debt, not its public debt.
14. Giavazzi, Goldfajn, and Herrera (2005, p. xx).
15. I am grateful to Alvaro Manoel for unearthing this story for me. See also Giavazzi, Goldfajn, and Herrera (2005, pp. xv–xviii and fn 5).
16. Blanchard noted that a higher proportion of dollar debt in total government debt would increase the chances of this outcome. But note that much of *real* debt was indexed, as pointed out earlier in this chapter, and therefore similar to dollar debt.
17. Figure 2.14 c., Easterly and Servén (2003, p. 40).

# CHAPTER 9

# Self-Insurance and Self-Financed Growth

In the 1980s, most emerging markets exhibited low financial integration, rampant capital controls combined with fixed exchange rates and active monetary policy, and low levels of international reserves.... This configuration changed dramatically as emerging markets learnt...from the crises of....1997–2001.

—Aizenman and Pinto (2011)

On April 30, 2008, less than 18 months after the OECD's sobering diagnosis quoted in Chapter 8, Standard & Poor's raised Brazil's sovereign credit rating to investment grade. Even more astounding, this rating was reaffirmed in April 2009 when assessments of the global economy were at their bleakest following disastrous first-quarter output results and stock market collapses in the richest countries, marking the nadir of the global financial crisis. And in early December 2009, Fitch raised Turkey's credit rating by two notches from BB- to BB+, just below investment grade. According to a Reuter's news report from Istanbul, the reason was Turkey's "resilience to the crisis and the easing of earlier restraints such as inflation. Fitch added Turkey had shown that its credit fundamentals and debt tolerance are stronger than previously thought."[1] Not bad for a country which, like Brazil, had been classified as debt intolerant by Reinhart, Rogoff, and Savastano (2003). Ironically, this upgrading in default risk occurred in 2009, the year in which the Turkish government ran its first primary fiscal deficit since 2000!

## Turkey: Dismay to Delight

Turkey's 2000–01 experience is worth dwelling upon for two reasons: first, together with Brazil, its experience provides a cogent illustration of how self-insurance worked. Second, its 2000 program, which ended in failure, marked the last serious attempt by an emerging market to stabilize by using the nominal exchange rate as an anchor.[2]

The previous year, 1999, had been a difficult one, with an output contraction of 6 percent, real interest rates above 30 percent, and the taking over of eight vulnerable banks. Securitizing the "duty losses" of the banks—the counterpart of interest rate subsidies commercial banks were required to offer on various directed credits mandated by the government—had added substantially to Turkey's public debt. Inflation in 1999 had come in at 65 percent. The government decided to do something drastic, as outlined in its Letter of Intent to the IMF, dated December 9, 1999.[3] The Letter of Intent starts by decrying Turkey's 25-year history of high inflation, its large fiscal deficits, and its volatile and relatively low growth. It recognizes the costs in terms of credibility, exorbitant real interest rates, and the harmful effects on the private sector. The Letter of Intent is eye-catching in that it diligently incorporates the lessons from the earlier crises in Russia and Argentina, articulating what any practitioner at that time would have regarded as a state-of-the-art stabilization program.

The centerpiece was the adoption of a crawling peg aimed at lowering inflation to 25 percent in 2000, with a preannounced monthly rate of depreciation against the dollar and a three-year horizon for achieving single-digit inflation. But, learning from Argentina, the Letter of Intent recognized in paragraph 30 the "need to avoid to be locked into a monetary and exchange rate framework that—while appropriate for disinflation—may lead to unnecessary rigidities in the long run, a problem that has affected many emerging markets in recent years. Hence, there is a need for a transparent and pre-announced exit strategy from this exchange rate regime."[4] And, learning from Russia, it laid out a comprehensive fiscal program to place public debt on a sustainable trajectory bolstered with structural reforms covering several areas, including pension liabilities, tax policy and administration, the banking sector, agricultural subsidies, and privatization (with the proceeds intended to pay down public debt).

Good things happened in 2000: growth rebounded to plus 6 percent and the public sector's net debt-to-GNP ratio fell slightly.[5] But end-year inflation came in at 39 percent compared to its 25 percent target, leading to a real appreciation of the lira. Two other problems developed: first, the current account deficit widened to 5 percent of GNP, substantially above the target of 1.8 percent, because of the 16 percent real appreciation of the lira and rising oil prices; recall Dornbusch and Werner's (1994) admonition about the virtual inevitability of a real appreciation when the nominal exchange rate is used as an anchor for price stabilization, encountered with a vengeance in Russia over the 1995–8 period. Second, the commercial banks developed substantial exchange rate exposures as a result of borrowing abroad and investing in lira assets, owing to much higher interest rates at home.

## Why the 2000 Program Failed

The real appreciation, which occurred as the result of using the exchange rate as an anchor for lowering inflation, was reminiscent of the stabilization program which preceded Russia's 1998 crisis, while the currency mismatch on the banks' balance sheets fueled by the domestic–foreign interest differential had shades of Indonesia 1997–8. Even though nominal lira interest rates more than halved compared to the triple-digit levels of 1999, they remained in the 40 percent range. This, plus the preannounced path of the Turkish lira exchange rate, set up a classic one-way bet which made it profitable to borrow in dollars and invest in Turkish T-bills. Box 9.1 sets out the arithmetic.

The resulting foreign exchange and interest rate exposures on the banks' balance sheet proved fatal. The currency mismatch made banks vulnerable to any depreciation of the lira triggered by a speculative attack, while raising interest rates in a defense of the exchange rate would have inflicted capital losses on banks holding lira government debt at fixed interest rates. If banks needed to close out their open foreign exchange positions in a hurry, they would be forced to sell lira government securities and use the proceeds to buy dollars from the central bank. This would set up a vicious circle of a fall in the market value of their holdings of lira government debt, possible margin calls on dollar borrowing collateralized with such debt, hence further sales to obtain the necessary dollar liquidity, and so on—the now-familiar deleveraging cycle augmented with the depletion of the central bank's reserves.

---

**Box 9.1**  Arithmetic of the One-Way Bet

By definition, a real appreciation of the lira against the dollar means that

$$\hat{e} < \pi - \pi^*, \tag{i}$$

where $e$ is the nominal exchange rate in lira per dollar, $\pi$ is Turkish inflation, and $\pi^*$ is US inflation. The rate of depreciation of the lira, $\hat{e}$, was given by the pre-announced path under the macroeconomic program and, by construction, was much less than the prevailing Turkish inflation, since the whole point was to lower inflation. As a result, the lira would tend appreciate in real terms against the dollar until such time as Turkish inflation equaled US inflation plus the preannounced depreciation of the lira (which would also be lowered over time in pursuit of single-digit inflation). But this alone does not make it worthwhile to borrow in dollars and invest in Turkish lira T-bills: it depends eventually on interest rates. The condition for making this worthwhile is:

$$i > i^* + \hat{e}, \tag{ii}$$

where $i$ is the rate of interest on Turkish T-bills and $i^*$ is the interest rate at which Turkish banks can borrow dollars. The right-hand side of (ii) is the effective lira cost of borrowing dollars because it takes into account the depreciation of the lira against the dollar. If the inequality holds, you can make money by borrowing dollars and investing in lira T-bills.

How does this profitability condition connect to the real appreciation of the lira under the stabilization program? Multiply both sides of (i) by -1, add $(i - i^*)$ to both sides and rearrange to get:

$$i - (i^* + \hat{e}) > (i - \pi) - (i^* - \pi^*) = r - r^*, \tag{iii}$$

where $r$ and $r^*$ are the real interest rates in lira and dollars respectively.

It follows from (iii) that if the real interest in Turkey is higher than that in the USA—which is what you would expect—condition (ii) must also hold. In other words, if the real exchange is appreciating AND real interest rates at home are higher than in the USA, the one-way bet mentioned at the beginning of this chapter would be profitable, fueling open foreign exchange positions or currency mismatches in commercial banks and setting them up for a fall, with attendant bailout costs, should the exchange rate eventually collapse.

---

Besides, foreign banks would become reluctant to roll over credit lines and syndicated loans.

This is exactly what happened in November 2000, and the lira was eventually floated in late February 2001 after some $10 billion was used up in defending the crawling peg—a fortune in those days. The crisis in Turkey thus conformed to a classic emerging market pattern: an attempt to remedy

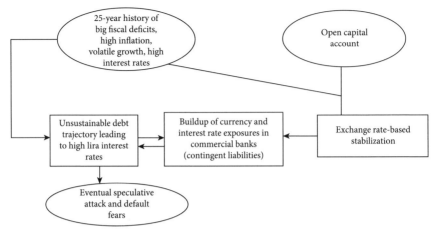

**Figure 9.1** Why Turkey's Exchange Rate-Based Stabilization Failed

a history of high inflation and some instability in government debt dynamics is made via an exchange rate-based stabilization program in the presence of an open capital account, leading eventually to a full-blown exchange rate-cum-banking-cum-public debt crisis, as in Russia in 1998. *What it demonstrates is the great difficulty in using the exchange rate as a nominal anchor to bring inflation down successfully when the country has a bad macroeconomic history and the capital account is open.* Figure 9.1 illustrates the vicious cycle. Turkey 2000 really had little chance, notwithstanding a conscientious attempt to avoid Argentina's and Russia's mistakes.

Real interest rates stayed at exceptionally high levels in spite of the February 2001 float. And by August 2001, the spread on the 2007 Eurobond had more than doubled to 1100 basis points from the level prevailing before the November 2000 speculative attack. The expectation was that, by the end of 2001, net public debt would rise by 20 percentage points of GNP compared to the end of 2000 because of the high real interest rates and the anticipated costs of cleaning up the banks, generating default fears.

## An Astonishing Turnaround

In spite of the failure of the 2000 program and the dismal outcomes of 2001, Turkey avoided a default and eventually stabilized, but with a floating rather than a fixed exchange rate! How did it accomplish this? The crucial step was to shift policy attention from the exchange rate to a comprehensive approach to the government intertemporal budget constraint. But did not the December 1999 Letter of Intent aim to do exactly this? Could just the exchange rate regime have made such a difference?[6] The answer is twofold: first, a flexible exchange rate would make banks mindful of exchange risk compared to a preannounced crawl or a fixed peg, and weaken incentives for mismatched currency positions. Second, even though the December 1999 Letter of Intent made all the right noises, it takes time to establish fiscal credibility. Credibility ultimately comes from putting the government intertemporal budget constraint on a sound footing by getting the government's debt dynamics under control and taking steps to minimize contingent liabilities in the financial sector. This is achieved neither instantaneously nor permanently; recall the terrible time Brazil had in restoring creditworthiness in spite of a large increase in its primary surplus after 1999. The *Real Plan* stabilized prices in 1994, but it took another 14 years for Brazilian government debt to be declared investment grade.

Restoring fiscal credibility demands that default fears be lowered by ramping up primary fiscal surpluses; this will then bring interest rates down by lowering the risk premium demanded by lenders. Faster growth would help, but is unlikely to materialize in a crisis atmosphere. Like Brazil after its January 1999 float, Turkey substantially ramped up the primary fiscal surplus of the public sector from some 3 percent of GDP in 2000 to the 5–6 percent of GDP range. In his 2003 retrospective, Kemal Dervis, who took over as Minister of Treasury—a post he held from March 2001, the month after the exchange rate collapse, to August 2002—attributes Turkey's eventual success to four factors (Dervis 2005):

1. Using the back-to-the-wall effect of the crisis to "frontload structural reforms" by quickly pushing through 19 important structural reform laws or regulations.

2. Adopting a dirty float mindful that a big collapse of the exchange rate would have a ruinous effect on banks and corporations because of their liabilities denominated in dollars. Central bank reserves boosted by a big loan from the IMF would be used to prop up the exchange rate combined with "talking up" the exchange rate to prevent a free fall.

3. Rejecting a forced debt restructuring because 60 percent of public debt was held internally and choosing to ramp up the primary fiscal surplus substantially instead. Even though this would reduce aggregate demand, it was expected to be outweighed by the positive effect on "expectations about debt dynamics and debt sustainability, which has an expansionary effect" (Dervis 2005, p. 94). In other words, the credibility effect of a high primary surplus would lower interest rates, very similar to the Brazilian strategy discussed in Chapter 8.

4. Reaching an agreement with trade unions on wage increases.

But keep in mind that Dervis was in office for just a little over a year; this is too short a period to overcome a 25-year history of macroeconomic volatility. The IMF (2001, p. 11) noted somewhat rhetorically in its June 2001 postmortem after the exchange rate collapsed: "What has kept interest rates high? The most obvious reason is the public finances, the high level of indebtedness as a result of the crisis, and therefore the risk of monetization (or failure to rollover debt)." What made the difference eventually was the dogged adherence to the higher primary surplus that Dervis insisted upon. At last something was working, and this something was to do with the government intertemporal budget constraint, not inflation reduction based on fixing the exchange rate; inflation expectations and default risk would fall once the private sector was convinced that public debt was on a sustainable trajectory, lowering interest rates by setting in train the virtuous dynamics noted in point 3.

So, while Turkey's resilience and credit-rating upgrade during the global financial crisis is impressive, it was no accident. Like Brazil, Turkey had learnt from the last round of emerging market crises and took the preventive measures indicated, enabling it to cross a threshold. These measures, which I club under the title "self-insurance," are responses to the vulnerabilities implicit in the successive generations of crisis models shown in Table 8.2.

## Self-Insurance: Skepticism to Success

Few economists would have put serious money on the bet that emerging markets would do well during the global financial crisis just because they self-insured in response to their own crises.[7] To understand why the success of self-insurance comes as a surprise, you have to go back to 2003, when Ricardo Caballero summarized the state-of-the-art methods for insuring emerging markets. Caballero's starting point was that countries can self-insure against fluctuations over the business cycle; but doing so against the ruinous effects of sudden stops was not feasible because of the extreme volatility and large size of capital flows. The necessary insurance markets and instruments did not exist: available instruments might hedge the annual fiscal revenues of a commodity-exporting country against oil or copper price risk, but not against a sudden stop.

Caballero therefore proposed new instruments in his 2003 paper, centered on contingent bonds, including structures involving collateralized debt obligations (CDOs), whereby several tranches of bonds would be issued under the CDO with the proceeds used to purchase the contingent bonds issued by emerging markets—essentially, an asset-backed structure. The contingency would be defined by a variable not under the country's control such as the international price of copper or oil, or high-yield spreads. This would avoid moral hazard and the need for country-specific knowledge; Caballero (2003) notes in this context that "issuing external debt in local currency, while extremely appealing on insurance grounds, is unlikely to provide the solution in the magnitude required, precisely because it fails this requirement," yet another blow to the *original sin* hypothesis. The purpose of tranching would be to define senior tranches that would focus on the contingency itself, isolating it from country default risk, making these instruments appealing to pension funds and insurance companies; while specialist emerging market funds would take the default risk associated with the more junior tranches. The international financial institutions (World Bank and IMF, for example) could play a catalytic role in helping these markets to develop by addressing the network externalities which arise in connection with pioneering new financial instruments—an approach similar in spirit to that espoused in IDB (2007) and discussed in Chapter 8.

Now that we have the luxury to review these ideas with the wisdom of hindsight, how do they stack up? The revelations unearthed by the global financial crisis about financial markets and derivatives are hardly a vote of confidence in financial engineering and instruments like CDOs. The whole infrastructure has come under attack, from instruments, to regulation, to credit-rating agencies, to incentives and compensation structures biased toward manipulation and excessive risk-taking; virtually nothing has gone unscathed. And, on the positive side, self-insurance, which Caballero argued was too costly and unequal to the task, has served emerging markets well during a natural experiment far more exacting than anyone might have imagined at the beginning of this decade, namely, the global financial crisis. To quote Caballero (2003, p. 4):

> these economies are self-insuring through costly accumulation of large international reserves and stabilization funds. Most individuals would be "underinsured" if they had to leave a million dollars aside for a potential automobile collision and the liabilities that would follow, rather than buying insurance against such event; countries are no different. Underinsurance is what greatly amplifies these countries' recessions.

### Why Did Self-Insurance Work?

Self-insurance worked in spite of all the misgivings voiced earlier in the decade because emerging markets went considerably beyond just accumulating foreign exchange reserves, hedging via existing instruments, or aiming for a higher share of domestic currency debt for the government. The key has been the central role accorded to the government intertemporal budget constraint in the broad sense, which means including the anticipation of contingent liabilities associated with private sector balance sheets. A sudden stop will almost inevitably require a large real depreciation (as the country would probably be running a surplus on the capital account and most likely a deficit on the current account prior to its occurrence). If there are large currency mismatches on private balance sheets—that is, liabilities in dollars and assets in local currency—then the real depreciation might cause a spike in bad bank loans and a credit crunch, leading to a costly recession and a deterioration in the government intertemporal budget constraint as the government steps in to bail out the private sector.

But a recession is not preordained: if currency mismatches are limited and the public finances are sustainable, the combination of the expenditure-switching effects of a real depreciation and the boost to aggregate demand from a fiscal stimulus could help support domestic output and minimize the effects of even a large adverse external shock. How do we know? Because of what happened to countries like Brazil and Turkey during the global financial crisis. Even Nigeria, plagued by three decades of weak governance and bad economic management, managed to stave off a big collapse in output in 2009 because of the fiscal savings and foreign exchange reserves it had built up following the about-turn in fiscal policies in 2004 described in Chapter 3.

Is self-insurance too costly? Let us take India. It built up reserves to approximately 25 percent of GDP by 2007. If we extravagantly assume a spread of even 300 basis points in dollar borrowing costs for the Indian government relative to the US government (in reality, it is likely to be much smaller given India's investment grade sovereign credit rating), the fiscal cost of carrying these reserves would be less than 1 percent of GDP; not bad if it can tide you through the biggest economic crisis since World War II!

To sum up:

- Self-insurance as implemented by emerging markets after 1997–2001 went far beyond simply increasing reserves or using hedging instruments.

- The focus shifted to the soundness of the government intertemporal budget constraint based on addressing fundamental fiscal problems and hardening budgets for both the government and the private sector. As Brazil's experience after 1999 (sketched out in Chapter 8) showed, this is a necessary condition for reaping the benefits from a better mix of local and foreign currency in public debt.

- And, as illustrated by the East Asian crisis of 1997–8, it would be a mistake to overlook contingent liabilities in the private sector—manifested typically in high loan-to-deposit ratios on the liability side of commercial banks' balance sheets, currency mismatches, and asset bubbles (especially in real estate).[8]

## Convergence to Self-Insurance

Here is something truly interesting: emerging markets which suffered crises during 1997–2001 all resorted to "self-insurance" in spite of widely differing initial conditions and history: East Asia, with no history of government debt sustainability problems (with the exception of Philippines at that time) but with contingent liabilities from its banks' exposures; and Russia, Brazil,

Argentina, and Turkey, which had government debt sustainability problems, with Argentina and Turkey also exhibiting vulnerable private banks. The hallmark of this convergence to "self-insurance" was the evident realization by emerging markets that they would have to fend for themselves in restoring soundness to the government intertemporal budget constraint. Outside attempts to help in the form of statutory approaches to debt resolution (such as the unsuccessful attempt to establish a Sovereign Debt Restructuring Mechanism discussed in Annex 5) or through the promotion of new debt instruments with equity-type features, such as the GDP-indexed bonds mentioned in Chapter 8, did not take off.

In their pursuit of crisis-proofing, emerging markets sought to remedy the twin sources of vulnerability from unsustainable government debt dynamics and low foreign exchange reserves relative to the claims on them. Table 9.1 sets out the policy goals and instruments which formed part of their

**Table 9.1** Self-Insurance: A Package Deal

| Goal | Instrument(s) | Comments |
|---|---|---|
| 1. Restore sustainable debt dynamics and lower risk premia (*First generation*) | • Raise primary surpluses for prolonged period.<br>• Strengthen fiscal institutions. | Might have to cut even good public investments owing to debt intolerance and myopic markets |
| 2. Lower contingent liabilities associated with private sector (*Third generation*) | • Shift to flexible exchange rates (avoid exchange rate guarantees).<br>• Monitor private external borrowing and currency mismatches.<br>• Strengthen financial institutions. | Flexible exchange rates will reduce incentive for currency mismatches. But direct, macro-prudential controls may also be needed by central bank on volume of private external debt and loan-to-deposit ratios of commercial banks. |
| 3. Insure against shifting market sentiment and possible sudden stops (*Second generation*) | • Build up foreign exchange reserves.<br>• Restrict currency mismatches on government and private balance sheets. | "Ideal" level of reserves will depend upon short-term external debt, flexibility of exchange rates, and extent of currency mismatches. |

.

self-insurance package, which, not surprisingly, are evocative of the three generations of crisis models.

## Backstopping Liquidity

If you look at the IMF reports on Turkey issued just before the September 15, 2008 Lehman Bros bankruptcy plunged the world into the global financial crisis, and then again more recently, two features appear curious. First, high current account deficits were projected over the medium term in the reports issued before Lehman. I would have expected these to have been revised downwards substantially after the global crisis intensified and the credit crunch took effect. But the IMF's September 2010 Turkey country report continued to project current account deficits of the order of 5 percent of GDP into the medium term. Second, Turkey's reserves went up from some $25 billion in 1999 to over $70 billion by the end of 2007; but reserves have consistently been less than short-term external debt plus maturing long-term debt, contrary to the so-called "Guidotti–Greenspan rule" advanced in 1999. Such insufficiency of reserves has been strongly linked by empirical studies to macroeconomic crises and sudden stops.[9] Nevertheless, Turkey was not expected to comply with the Guidotti–Greenspan rule: in the September 2010 IMF country report, Turkey's gross foreign exchange reserves were projected at just 80 percent of short-term external debt for 2014.

Then how does one explain Turkey's elevation to a BB+ credit rating from BB- in 2009, in spite of the expectation of large current account deficits and its persistent "violation" of the Guidotti–Greenspan rule?[10] The answer is twofold: first, the shift to flexible exchange rates does not simply dull the incentives for currency mismatches, thereby lowering contingent liabilities; it also means, by definition, that countries need a smaller amount of reserves. Second, there appears to be a hierarchy in market assessments of risk and vulnerability, with the government intertemporal budget constraint (fiscal solvency in its extensive form, including contingent liabilities from the private sector) given more prominence than international liquidity.

The notion that Guidotti–Greenspan may have lost some of its sheen, with fiscal solvency taking center stage in an era of *flexible exchange rates*, makes considerable sense. The successive generations of crisis models were developed for *fixed exchange rate* regimes and their collapse; in these models, shifting market sentiment and international liquidity may be as important as fiscal solvency. But in the new dispensation of flexible exchange rates, international liquidity appears to be taking a backseat to the government intertemporal budget constraint. In his 1988 classic on the debt overhang, Paul Krugman noted: "There is no such thing as a pure liquidity problem; it must arise because of doubts about solvency"; this comment is evocative of Obstfeld's first point in Chapter 8. With the widespread switch to flexible exchange rates and the focus on both the government and private sector's balance sheets in the new age of self-insurance, Krugman's claim acquires new meaning.

Let me spell out a caveat lest we fall into the trap of dismissing the importance of international liquidity. The global economy is going to experience considerable volatility over the next few years. As it is, government debt in the advanced G20 countries is expected to reach 115 percent of GDP by 2015, some 40 percentage points above pre-global crisis levels.[11] If another round of panic sets in, with Germany and the USA in particular acting as a safe haven, emerging markets will be adversely affected through no fault of their own. There is always going to be a question around how much self-insurance is enough, and, here, the IMF's Flexible Credit Line (FCL), discussed in Annex 6, would be a valuable backstop.[12] Indeed, the ability of solvent emerging markets with good fundamentals to engage in swaps with the central banks of the rich countries or tap into the IMF's FCL might explain why market investors appear more relaxed about international liquidity.

## Self-Insurance and Growth Policy

That the comprehensive approach to self-insurance outlined earlier in this chapter has strong links to the elements in the growth policy package spelled out at the end of Chapter 3 should not be surprising. A sound government intertemporal budget constraint requires good growth prospects and adequate future taxes, which call for the micropolicy trio of hard budgets, import competition, and competitive real exchange rates. The macro–micro linkages inherent in this description are fundamental to both self-insurance and growth. Taking steps to limit contingent liabilities from the banking system while keeping the government's own debt dynamics under control needs strong financial and fiscal institutions. The latter are essential for managing domestic and external sources of volatility, as Chapter 3 underlines. The rest of this chapter sets out the links between self-insurance and growth policy, beginning with the notion of "self-financed growth."

## Self-Financed Growth

"Self-financed growth" refers to the empirical finding that fast-growing developing countries have tended to rely substantially on their own savings in order to build up their domestic physical capital stock and spur growth. Joshua Aizenman, Artur Radziwill, and I examined the self-financing hypothesis, that is, that national savings remain the dominant financing source for the domestic physical capital stock in spite of financial globalization.[13]

We constructed "self-financing ratios" for various countries using a ten-year horizon, as follows. Suppose the estimate of the capital stock in some initial year, t, is 100. We add the cumulative national savings over a 10-year period to this initial capital stock, let's say it is 30. Now suppose the cumulative investment over the same period is 35. Then the self-financing ratio for year (t+10) is 130 divided by 135, that is, 96 percent.[14] These calculations were made for 47 developing countries and 22 OECD countries for the period 1981–2001, meaning that self-financing ratios were constructed for every year starting in 1991 and ending in 2001. This enabled us to see how the self-financing ratio varied over the 1990s in response to growing financial integration.

The main findings were: first, the average self-financing ratio for developing countries did not change much over the 1990s, global financial liberalization notwithstanding. Second, there did not seem to be a growth bonus associated with greater external financing of the domestic capital stock. To the contrary, countries with higher self-financing ratios grew significantly faster! Third, more volatile self-financing ratios were associated with lower growth; but this result disappeared when a proxy for the quality of institutions was included in the cross-country regressions. These regressed per capita growth on the self-financing ratio, its square, its volatility, and the quality of institution measure. But the strong, asymmetric effect of self-financing on growth persisted: a rise in the self-financing ratio from 1.0 to 1.1 raised average per capita growth from 2.8 percent to 4.4 percent while a drop from 1.0 to 0.9 lowered per capita growth from 2.8 percent to 2.2 percent.[15]

These findings sit uneasily with the hype surrounding financial globalization, which was at its peak in the mid-1990s. Andrew Crockett, the then General Manager of the Bank for International Settlements, observed in early 1998 in a speech at the 33rd SEACEN Governors' Conference that private debt and portfolio inflows into emerging markets had increased from less than $40 billion per year between 1983 and 1990 to $200 billion between 1993 and 1997 as a consequence of financial liberalization: "These capital inflows have provided additional resources to supplement domestic savings and support high levels of investment." But, with the wisdom of hindsight, open capital accounts and premature financial liberalization were important factors in the 1997–2001 emerging market crises. The effects in "debt-intolerant" countries like Turkey and Brazil took almost a decade to unravel. In contrast, East Asian emerging markets, which ran large current account surpluses and relied on national savings, grew faster than those in Latin America, where the reliance on foreign savings and capital inflows was higher. The former also rebounded much more quickly from the 1997–2001 crises.

Self-financed growth is not a new idea. Martin Feldstein and Charles Horioka wrote a famous paper in 1980 asking how internationally mobile capital really was. In regressing investment rates on national savings rates for 21 OECD countries using data from 1960 to 1974, they consistently found coefficients close to 1.0 and stable over time. These results were evocative of a closed economy, suggesting capital was not as mobile across borders as might have been assumed; if it were, one would expect a close to zero correlation between national saving and national investment. This finding became enshrined as the "Feldstein–Horioka puzzle." But there is an important difference. A country consistently running a large, but constant, current account deficit as a ratio of GDP would register a coefficient of 1.0 when the investment rate is regressed on the saving rate in the Feldstein–Horioka framework; however, its self-financing ratio would be less than 1 in the Aizenman–Pinto–Radziwill framework.

In related work, Eswar Prasad, Raghuram Rajan, and Arvind Subramanian examined the links between capital flows and growth in the financially globalized 1990s (Prasad, Rajan, and Subramanian 2007). Their starting point is twofold: the perverse flow of capital from poor to rich countries; and the allocation puzzle of Pierre-Olivier Gourinchas and Olivier Jeanne (2007), namely, that within the group of developing countries, net capital inflows tend to find their way to the slower-growing countries. Prasad, Rajan, and Subramanian find a positive correlation between average current account balances and average growth rates for developing countries after controlling for the standard growth determinants during the 1970–2004 period. Moreover, they find that this correlation is driven more by savings than investment: when savings-to-GDP is included in the growth regression, the coefficient on the current account balance becomes statistically insignificant and actually turns negative, but remains virtually unchanged when the investment rate is included, suggesting the dominant role of savings.

The explanation Prasad, Rajan, and Subramanian favor as to why savings are positively correlated with growth is that financial systems tend to be underdeveloped in developing countries. So, not all the savings are intermediated into investment, and part of it gets parked abroad via current account surpluses, leading to an accumulation of foreign exchange reserves. Alternatively, foreign exchange reserves could get built up either because countries want to avoid overvaluation or because they want a cushion against the volatility of capital flows.

Self-financed growth runs contrary to neoclassical economics, according to which capital should flow from rich to poor countries in order to equalize per capita incomes. In Chapter 2, we encountered one reason this may not happen: marginal returns may not be higher in poorer countries (even though they have lower capital-to-labor ratios) once technology, human capital and risk are brought into the picture, as shown in Robert Lucas's 1990 paper. But even in a situation where marginal returns are higher in poorer countries, the welfare benefits of financial integration may be limited, as reported by Pierre-Olivier Gourinchas and Olivier Jeanne in their 2006 paper and discussed in Chapter 2. Financial integration would help if it served to bridge the gap between the *levels* of total factor productivity (TFP) in poor and rich countries. For example, foreign direct investment could help narrow productivity gaps through technological spillovers; but it is far from obvious that letting foreign portfolio investors into the stock market or government Treasury bill market in developing countries can do this. This means that developing countries wanting to grow faster will need to focus both on raising national savings rates *and* creating conditions for faster TFP growth. Self-insurance in the sense laid out in this chapter helps with both.

## Does Self-Insurance Imply Self-Financed Growth?

Self-insurance is a defensive measure that minimizes the risk of bad outcomes from both external (shifting market sentiment, myopic investors interested in short-run returns) and internal (unsustainable government debt dynamics, balance sheet mismatches) sources of vulnerability. But it is also pro-growth. Fundamental to self-insurance by emerging markets has been their ability to raise primary fiscal surpluses. This by itself will not raise public saving unless current spending comes down. Indeed, emerging markets have tended to cut capital expenditure, which increases primary *surpluses* but not public *saving*.[16] However, sustained increases in the primary surplus will eventually help raise public saving by lowering the high interest payments on public debt as credibility is reestablished and devaluation and default risks reduced; the size of interest payments is a powerful obstacle to higher public saving. Hence, the fiscal component of self-insurance promotes higher public saving over time as credibility takes hold and interest payments come down—creating genuine fiscal space for growth-promoting infrastructure investments as opposed to borrowing even more for such projects when debt intolerance is an issue (as discussed in Chapter 8 in the Brazilian context).

By reestablishing credibility and (where relevant) restoring creditworthiness, self-insurance also reduces macroeconomic uncertainty for the private sector, which would further promote growth by lowering the cost of capital and lengthening business horizons, leading to an increase in private investment and faster growth. In this case, if consumption grows more slowly than output, savings rates will rise over time as we have seen in fast-growing countries like China and India. The combination of higher public and private saving should eventually feed into higher current account balances. Self-insurance in the broad sense thus acts to eventually promote both saving and faster TPF growth (via the micropolicy trio needed to spur growth in order to underpin sustainable government debt dynamics) in keeping with self-financed growth. By raising current account surpluses, it will also facilitate foreign exchange reserve accumulation.

In a 2005 review of the 1997–2001 crises and the then ongoing response of emerging markets, Indermit Gill and I noted: "the willingness of countries facing [public] debt sustainability problems to run persistently large primary fiscal surpluses, while adopting flexible exchange rates and strengthening fiscal institutions, stands out...paying attention to the GIBC [government intertemporal budget constraint] is vital....Assessing debt sustainability...requires looking at a range of complex factors, including contingent liabilities, the micro foundations for sustainable economic growth, and the vulnerability to exogenous shocks."[17] Our paper was an outcome of a study that had been asked for by the higher-ups in the World Bank in 2004. They were afraid that emerging markets were then on the verge of another serious debt crisis. The biggest positive surprise we found was the steps emerging markets were taking on their own, without waiting for the global community or IFIs to swing into action. And these steps centered on a package approach to self-insurance.

The point, ultimately, is a simple one: emerging markets wanting to self-insure cannot suddenly wake up one morning and decide they need to boost foreign exchange reserves. This decision would make sense only if bolstered by the determination to simultaneously minimize domestic sources of vulnerability from unsustainable government dynamics and private sector balance sheets, especially the banks. And while the paths may be long and differ from country to country, as illustrated by the varying experiences of India, Kenya, Poland, and Russia, it is hard to think of sustainable debt dynamics without the micropolicy trio of hard budgets, import competition, and competitive real exchange rates. This brings us full circle.

## A New Beginning for Emerging Markets

Emerging markets, even those traditionally regarded as crisis prone, have crossed a threshold with the remarkable resilience they displayed during the global financial crisis. Self-insuring, not simply by building up foreign exchange reserves, but by restoring soundness to the government intertemporal budget constraint, and strengthening fiscal and financial institutions while adopting flexible exchange rates, has been fundamental to this maturation. This package also means that emerging markets have taken enduring steps to manage the domestic sources of macroeconomic vulnerability that have plagued them for decades. Looking forward, we can therefore expect favorable macro–micro dynamics as lower risk premia reduce the cost of capital for the private sector, spurring investment and growth, and, in turn, bolstering fiscal sustainability.

## Notes

1. Alexandra Hudson, "Turkey-Upgrade." Reuters, December 3, 2009. Don't miss the allusion to "debt tolerance."
2. I was asked to look at Turkey's debt dynamics and creditworthiness in the summer of 2001, after my return from Russia, where I had served from 1998 to 2001. Some of this is based on that analysis.
3. Available at: <http://www.imf.org/external/np/loi/1999/120999.htm>.
4. With the wisdom of hindsight, Argentina held on to its fixed peg too long. Its 1991 Convertibility Plan mandated a one peso to one dollar peg, which successfully lowered inflation and led to strong economic performance, with Argentina becoming the darling of Wall Street. But as the years passed, currency mismatches in banks and an overvalued real exchange rate developed, which, together with loose fiscal policy, contributed to the crash and default of 2001–2002. See Servén and Perry (2005), and Mussa (2002).
5. Turkey was then using the concept of GNP rather than GDP as a measure of aggregate economic activity. GNP equals GDP plus net factor income from abroad (interest, dividends, etc.) and is now known as Gross National Income, GNI.
6. Recall the discussion of Fischer's 2001 paper on bipolarity in exchange rate systems in Chapter 1.
7. Just to remind the reader: I shall use "global financial crisis" to refer to the crisis and Great Recession of 2008–9.
8. I do not cover contingent liabilities emanating from the financial sector and asset bubbles in real estate; but this subject is of sufficient importance to merit a mention. The reader may want to look at Aizenman and Pinto (2011, 2013), which summarizes the emerging market experience with external financial integration over the past two decades and the evolving policy response in line with the content of Table 9.1.
9. See the survey by Green and Torgerson (2007).
10. Turkey was further elevated to investment grade by Fitch Ratings in early November 2012 (although S&P and Moody's refrained from doing so).
11. Debt numbers from Olivier Blanchard and Carlo Cottarelli, "The Great False Choice, Stimulus or Austerity." *The Financial Times*, August 11, 2010.
12. Gill and Pinto (2005) argued that there was no real alternative to self-insurance by emerging markets because there seemed to be little investor appetite for contingent debt instruments; and because of the limited resource base of the international financial institutions. The latter at least has changed, with substantial additional resources given to the IMF after the global financial crisis.
13. Aizenman, Pinto, and Radziwill (2007). The paper was Joshua Aizenman's idea, inspired by a conjecture of Michael Mussa's that financial globalization may have led to a maximum of 10 percent of the physical stocks of capital in developing countries being financed by foreign savings.
14. Suitable adjustments would be needed for depreciation. For details and caveats, see Aizenman, Pinto, and Radziwill (2007).

15. If the country is running current account surpluses on average, the self-financing ratio would exceed 1.

16. To see this, recall the accounting identities public saving = revenues minus current spending; and primary surplus = revenues minus noninterest current spending minus capital expenditure.

17. Gill and Pinto (2005, pp. 114–15).

# CHAPTER 10

# Lessons for Low-Income Countries

*We are the music makers. And we are the dreamers of dreams . . .*
*Till our dreams shall become their present,*
*And their work in the world be done.*

—Arthur O'Shaughnessy

It's funny, how many developing countries have vision statements. Kenya's Vision 2030, published before its disastrous presidential elections of December 2007, aims for a growth rate of 10 percent per year. Rwanda's Vision 2020, published in 2000, posited a growth target of 7 percent per year. Spurred by its inclusion in the N-11 ("Next-11"), a group identified by the investment bank, Goldman Sachs, as having the potential to become global players, Nigeria's Vision 2020 embraces the goal of being among the top 20 economies in the world by 2020. The vision includes a GDP of at least $900 billion and a per capita income of at least $4000 by 2020.

Actually, it's not funny. We started out in Chapter 1 by saying that countries are not going to grow unless the political elite want growth. Therefore, the vision statements are a step in the right direction; but reality quickly rears its head. Any low-income country seeking growth rates of 7 percent or more over the long haul—not coincidentally the growth rate needed to double real GDP in a decade—must ask itself four questions: First, are national savings rates commensurate with the envisioned growth rates, and are conditions ripe for faster TFP growth (which would enable a smaller increase in national savings rates)? Second, do hard budgets and competition exist?

Third, is government debt on a sustainable trajectory, and are real exchange rates competitive?[1] Fourth, is the country reasonably insured against shocks, domestic and external?

The four questions feed into an intertwined macro–micro policy agenda capped by the need for good governance. The latter finds its most immediate expression in how the public finances are managed *and* in the willingness to enforce hard budget constraints and competition, which gets to the core of the political economy challenge *all* countries, advanced and developing, face. I shall answer the four questions briefly, drawing upon the preceding country stories and policy debates from emerging markets; and then dive into a more detailed discussion of what else low-income countries need to do.

## Savings Rates and TFP Growth

Raising national savings rates is a formidable challenge. Most low-income countries have savings rates in the region of 15 to 20 percent of GDP, inadequate for the growth rates enshrined in their visions. This poses a policy dilemma. As the graphs on India and China in Chapter 2 show, savings rates go up with growth rates. Besides, the cross-country evidence suggests that countries aiming to grow at 7 percent per year are looking at savings rates in the neighborhood of 35 percent of GDP. What should policy then initially aim for, faster growth or higher savings? Raising savings rates for low-income countries is going to be difficult because of their relative poverty, which points to the importance of official aid for low-income countries, a topic I shall address later in this chapter. Therefore, the major initial gains are more likely to come from faster growth—driven *not* by higher savings rates but as a result of higher efficiency *in using existing assets* as a consequence of hard budgets and competition; in other words, by making the microfoundations for growth stronger by putting carrots and sticks in place for faster TFP growth, outcomes we have seen in countries as varied as India and Kenya.

This makes intuitive sense. Private sector firms are unlikely to have the resources or stomach to make large new investments when reforms first begin. They are more likely to start by using existing assets better, and then taking the plunge into big new investments only when they are convinced that the reforms are there to stay. The government should focus on raising

TFP growth rates through hard budgets and import competition, while implementing policies to keep the real exchange rate competitive. As growth picks up, private savings rate could rise, reinforcing faster growth through the accumulation channel.

The preceding is an apt description of the savings–growth dynamics witnessed in India after 1991. Depending upon the initial conditions and speed of reform, one could encounter long lags between the start of reform and the appearance of sustained high growth. In the meanwhile, substantial fiscal costs of reform could be incurred. The Indian experience after 1991 underlines the interdependence between macro-fiscal outcomes and microfoundations of growth, and the likelihood of long lags. Fiscal costs of reform, including cuts in import tariffs, amounted to some 38 percentage points of GDP between 1991 and 2003; but the resulting increase in import competition forced manufacturing firms to become more efficient as the years passed. Nevertheless, it took 12 years for sustained faster growth to appear.

Long lags were involved in Kenya as well. From the prism of neoclassical growth, being poor is an advantage because it enables income convergence based on higher returns to capital. This is where the 1990 paper of Robert Lucas casts its long shadow. Once we allow for risk, returns in low-income countries may not be that high. A particularly important source of such risk is unstable politics and, in many cases, social division. This is the central lesson from the chapter on Kenya. The goals of reducing government indebtedness and spurring growth required political stability and social cohesion to be nurtured together with economic reform. Doing this successfully could yield high dividends as the cost of capital falls, business horizons lengthen, and government debt dynamics improve with falling interest rates and accelerating growth. Unfortunately, judging by its December 2007 presidential election reversal, Kenya's experience also shows how difficult it is to establish political and social stability in a country where the opposite has been the norm for decades.

The initial agenda, therefore, should focus on lowering country risk through improved governance and better political leadership while raising productivity via hard budgets and competition. To the extent that public savings can be raised by cutting wasteful current spending and raising revenues through better tax policy, as Kenya so successfully did, this is a worthwhile addition to the initial agenda.

## Hard Budgets and Competition

Poland's early transition experience is the gold standard for hard budgets and competition. And the efficacy of the micropolicy trio of hard budgets, competition, and competitive real exchange rates is no more visible than in the contrasting experiences of Poland and Russia. Poland's experience underlined an important lesson: that macroeconomic stringency alone will not deliver the goods. Its microfoundations for growth needed explicit attention, and privatization was not going to be enough. Russia's unsuccessful macroeconomic stabilization between 1995 and 1998 reinforced the perils of ignoring macro–micro linkages and failing to harden firms' budgets. Soft budgets fed insidiously into asset stripping at the micro level and into unsustainable debt dynamics at the macro level. Trying to squeeze inflation out in this milieu hit firms with a double whammy: exceptionally high real interest rates and an appreciating real exchange rate, killing growth prospects and eventually placing government debt on an explosive path, culminating in the default of August 1998. The default shut the government out of the capital markets, hardening its budget constraint and, through a chain reaction, the budgets for enterprises. It also resulted in a large real depreciation. However, Russia's economy turned around much faster than anyone would have bet after the crisis, attesting to the powerful impact of hard budgets and competitive real exchange rates. Fiscal and debt policy changed permanently for the better after the 1998 crisis, with no return to soft budgets.

## Sustainable Government Debt Dynamics

Stressing the importance of sustainable government debt dynamics might appear redundant after the preceding build up. Nonetheless, three points are worth highlighting. First, the foundation stone for stabilization is a government intertemporal budget constraint that is consistent with reasonable real interest rates and competitive real exchange rates. This would not be possible without good growth prospects based on the above-mentioned micropolicy trio, bringing macro–micro linkages into sharp relief. Second, macro–micro linkages play out differently in different countries. In Kenya, a decline in political risk between 2003 and 2007 fed into lower interest rates and faster growth, helping with the quest to cut government indebtedness. In India, the deterioration in the government's debt dynamics toward the end of the 1990s and early 2000s was the counterpart of the fiscal costs of reform and yielded benefits in the shape of more efficient manufacturing firms and substantially faster growth after 2003. Going slow on capital account liberalization provided a much-needed cushion against a macroeconomic crisis in the interim. But the deterioration in Russia's debt dynamics in 1998 reflected soft budgets and weakening microfoundations for growth, culminating in a massive debt crisis. Third, a solid government intertemporal budget constraint anticipates and limits contingent liabilities from the private sector, leading to the next set of lessons.

## Crisis Prevention is Better than Cure

The policy debates spawned by the emerging market crises of 1997–2001 centered on least-cost approaches, in terms of foregone growth, to restoring the creditworthiness of countries that had got into sovereign debt problems, typified by the debate over fiscal space laid out in Chapter 8. A controversy developed about cutting public investments to raise primary fiscal surpluses (which many countries were doing to lower public indebtedness), as this would lower future growth and tax revenues, hurting the government's debt dynamics. Then why did emerging markets do this? They had little option: borrowing even for growth-promoting public investments at the margin would probably have been "vetoed" by the markets through higher interest rates on the country's entire debt unless creditworthiness was first restored. The experiences of Brazil, Russia, and Turkey illustrated a cold, hard fact in overcoming bad credit and inflation histories. Countries must first restore creditworthiness (or eliminate debt intolerance) and lower fears of a default even if this means a poor alignment between fiscal policy and growth in the interim. Becoming "debt tolerant" calls for a persistent, time-consuming effort to improve fiscal fundamentals. It is far less costly to prevent debt intolerance than to cure it! A corollary is that financial engineering solutions for restoring creditworthiness through "better" debt structures are secondary to fiscal fundamentals, amply demonstrated by the failed debt swaps of Russia and Argentina, and Brazil's experience between 1999 and 2008, recounted in Chapter 8.

Pooling the results on overcoming debt intolerance with the experience of the East Asian countries over the same period emphasizes the importance of a comprehensive approach to self-insurance. Building up foreign exchange reserves is not enough. Nor is it enough to strengthen the government's balance sheet. Countries must watch out for contingent fiscal liabilities from private external debt. Flexible exchange rates, competent financial sector supervision, and even direct controls (or so-called macro-prudential regulations) are required to minimize currency mismatches on private balance sheets and keep external borrowing at manageable levels.[2]

## What Should Low-Income Countries Do?

At a minimum, low-income countries should take the lessons from emerging market experience on sovereign debt and growth seriously. But what else should they do to speed up growth? A recent book by Steven Radelet (2010) provides clues from Africa. He gives an upbeat account of 17 "emerging countries," opening with a glowing summary of Ghana's achievements over the past 15 years.[3] Kenya falls into a second-rung category of "threshold countries," those on the verge of making it. Radelet's main point is that this time things are different because a critical mass of reforms *and* countries has emerged with persistently good results since 1995. This stands in refreshing contrast to the 1960s, when widespread independence from colonial powers fueled euphoria about economic prospects that fizzled out in short order.

Radelet lists five reasons why he believes the good economic results could endure: (i) rise of more accountable and democratic governments; (ii) better economic policies; (iii) an end to the debt crisis; (iv) new technologies, in particular, cell phones and ICT (information and communications technology); and (v) emergence of a new generation of policymakers. Looking forward, he singles out the following factors as molding economic developments in Africa: (i) stronger democracy and better governance; (ii) more jobs and economic diversification; (iii) managing the rise of China; (iv) adapting to climate change; and (v) building strong education and health systems.

Taken together, Radelet's roster constitutes a forward-looking agenda for economics and politics in Africa with modern-day challenges on climate change and China thrown in. I shall focus on three points in the economic agenda that do not receive sufficient prominence. First, I shall discuss the post-HIPC–MDRI saga of Ghana to illustrate that what Radelet (2010, p. 15) calls the "end of the debt crisis" actually heralds new challenges as low-income countries begin to tap the international capital markets.[4] Second, while Africa's good growth performance of recent years is reason for hope, one must make a distinction between policies which *raise output levels* and those which *raise growth rates* substantially for prolonged periods of time. Africa is more likely to be in the first category. Third, the need for higher investment rates, public and private, which low-income countries may find difficult to self-finance, has implications for aid or official development assistance (ODA). I shall illustrate the latter two points by reverting to Kenya's experience and presenting arguments for a different approach to delivering aid.

## Ghana: Goodbye Debt Relief, Hello Eurobonds![5]

Ghana's government debt was slashed from 78 percent of GDP in 2005 to 42 percent in 2006 after official creditors wrote down their claims via the HIPC–MDRI program. In September 2007, the government issued a ten-year, $750 million Eurobond at an interest rate of 8.5 percent. The amount borrowed was a significant 5 percent of Ghana's 2007 GDP and represented a coming of age. Ghana was moving from the protected, lenient environment of official funding to borrowing from the market, and why not? By the reckoning of most economists, including Radelet, it could probably have served as a poster child for low-income countries tapping the international capital markets for the first time. The IMF's April 2008 *Regional Outlook for Africa* lavished praise on the country, noting its capital account liberalization had begun, following "considerable debt reduction from HIPC and MDRI debt relief." It had managed to tilt the composition of inflows toward the longer term and was in the midst of a "gradual, well sequenced opening" of the capital account.[6] As noted by Radelet, Ghana had a good reputation. Its consistent track record in economic, institutional, and governance reform was reflected in an IDA Resource Allocation Index of 4.0 for 2007 compared to an average of 3.3 for all IDA borrowers for that year.[7] Furthermore, Ghana had discovered oil, with the promise of revenues coming on stream in 2011. The Eurobond was a way of increasing spending in anticipation of higher fiscal revenues, in line with the Permanent Income Hypothesis.[8]

Several other HIPC–MDRI beneficiaries, such as Uganda and Zambia, were in the queue for issuing Eurobonds when the collapse of Lehman

Brothers in September 2008 put their plans on hold—fortunately, as it turns out with the wisdom of hindsight. It would have been easy to argue in favor of Eurobonds. A prime argument for debt relief was the "fiscal space" this would release for spending on the social sectors and infrastructure in pursuit of faster growth and poverty alleviation. Borrowing from the international capital markets via Eurobonds would only augment resources available for the much-needed public investment. So then, are the World Bank, the IMF, and the donor community being spoilsports when they steadfastly argue that low-income countries benefiting from HIPC–MDRI must avoid prematurely accessing the international debt markets lest this lead to another debt crisis? Not really, as subsequent events in Ghana illustrate.

According to the analysis laid out in an August 2009 IMF report, the 2008 elections in Ghana contributed to the fiscal deficit's ballooning to 14.5 percent of GDP in 2008 from 9 percent the previous year. The current account deficit shot up to 19 percent of GDP from 12 percent the previous year.[9] Proceeds from the 2007 Eurobond and from the privatization of Ghana Telecom, a total of over 10 percent of GDP, were important sources of financing. Government debt, which had been lowered to 42 percent in 2006 after HIPC–MDRI, was projected to peak at 67 percent of GDP in 2010 before coming down slowly over the medium term.[10] Even though oil revenues were expected to come on stream in 2011, these are "on a relatively modest scale and for a fairly short period."[11]

This was the sobering assessment of the IMF (2010, p. 12) a year later in June 2010: "On current projections, public debt peaks at 65 percent of GDP at end-2010. This increase of more than 20 percentage points of GDP in just four years excludes domestic expenditure arrears projected at 5 percent of GDP and state-owned enterprise (SOE) liabilities to banks from past underpricing of energy products amounting to about 6 percentage points of GDP."[12] In short, the reduction in indebtedness obtained via HIPC–MDRI was being rapidly reversed, and the picture looked even worse once arrears and contingent liabilities from state-owned enterprises were included.

In early 2011, a press release following an IMF mission noted: "substantial payments arrears were again incurred in 2010, contrary to program targets, reflecting commitments in 2008 and earlier years which continue to drive spending outlays. Excluding the new domestic arrears, public debt rose from 39 to 41 percent of GDP over the year to end-2010."[13] How did public debt manage to come in at 41 percent of GDP at the end of 2010 when it was being projected at a much higher 65 percent just a few months earlier? The reason was a massive 70 percent upward revision of Ghanaian GDP which took effect before the end of 2010, not a miraculous turnaround in the government's debt dynamics. This alone would have reduced the projected debt ratio from 65 percent of GDP to 38 percent! In addition to the upward revision of its historical GDP statistics, Ghana's real GDP increased by close to 14 percent in 2011 as oil production came on stream. This too should have contributed to the containment of the government's debt-to-GDP ratio. Nevertheless, the recalculated government debt-to-GDP ratio rose from 34 percent of GDP in 2008 to 45 percent in 2011.

A country like Ghana should be encouraged to borrow provided the money is well used. Similarly, borrowing against future oil revenues, as exemplified by Ghana's 2007 Eurobond, is justifiable on the grounds of expenditure smoothing and the virtual certainty that future generations are going to be better off—*provided policy and institutional improvements are maintained*. Front-loaded spending financed by borrowing makes sense if it helps to build up human capital and public assets or helps to alleviate poverty in the current generation. The first acknowledges that oil is a nonrenewable asset so that its depletion needs to be compensated by investing in new assets as a way of sharing the wealth with the next generation. The second is a way of sharing oil wealth with those who have been left out so far. Had the money from the Eurobond been spent on better infrastructure, rural and urban, and in support of improved R&D for agriculture, one could have argued that the increase in the government's indebtedness would be offset by faster growth and more taxes in the future. Instead, initially for Ghana, election-related spending went up as did the public sector wage bill, demonstrating the political economy dilemmas created by oil and the need for institutional safeguards to ensure good outcomes.

It is in the latter positive direction that Ghana has been heading. The IMF's February 2012 country report applauds the steps taken since 2009 to reduce fiscal and current account deficits, lower inflation, and rebuild foreign exchange reserves. In April 2011, the Petroleum Revenue Management Act was passed, described in IMF (2012) as "a pivotal first step toward transparent and responsible revenue management. The PRMA establishes a strong legal framework for the collection, allocation, and management of petroleum revenue in a transparent and accountable manner."[14] Recognizing the crying need for more and better infrastructure, IMF (2012) also gives its blessing for Ghana to increase its stock of nonconcessional borrowing from a maximum of $800 million to $3.4 billion—which would accommodate a loan agreement negotiated with the China Development Bank for various public investment projects. But the report cautions that a stronger institutional framework for vetting public investments will be needed, and that keeping the public sector wage bill under control remains a major challenge.

All in all, Ghana was able to avoid a fiscal-cum-debt crisis and there is every indication that it has learned from its scare over 2007–9. The country is living up to its reputation as well governed. Nevertheless, the marked ups and downs Ghana has experienced after debt relief from HIPC–MDRI are a cautionary tale for all low-income countries thinking of accessing the international capital markets. Ghana's experience shows that moving from a low-income country to emerging market status is unlikely to be smooth. Low-income countries, especially those which have benefited from official debt write-offs, must be vigilant about slipping back into chronic debt sustainability problems. Once a country gets into this rut, extrication is hard and long. The emerging market world is far more difficult than low-income country world because the market is not as understanding or forgiving as official creditors.

This begs the question of when low-income countries which have been beneficiaries of HIPC–MDRI should access the international capital markets. Even though Kenya was not a HIPC–MDRI beneficiary, its experience usefully emphasizes three steps. First, lowering country risk and improving governance will help by reducing the cost of capital and lengthening business horizons for the private sector. Second, signaling the intention to place government debt on a good trajectory by raising primary surpluses as Kenya did will help. Third, policies to strengthen the microfoundations for growth through the micropolicy trio of hard budgets, competition, and competitive real exchange rates will increase incentives for firms to upgrade technology and become more efficient, raising TFP growth. This three-step package will reduce government indebtedness and unleash the private sector from the shackles of political risk and policy uncertainty, as Kenya accomplished between 2003 and 2007. Once confidence takes root that public money will be well spent, going to the capital markets to fund good public investments makes sense, although issuing bonds in local currency in the domestic markets might be preferable initially.

## Back to Kenya

Unlike Ghana, Kenya reduced its government debt-to-GDP ratio significantly between 2003 and 2007 without benefiting from debt relief. After the Goldenberg scandal, and with access to official concessional loans slashed, Kenya chose to raise primary fiscal surpluses and shift toward domestic borrowing rather than default, as described in Chapter 5. Its perseverance paid off when, as a result of reduced political risk following the successful presidential elections of December 2002, the government's debt dynamics improved abruptly, with falling real interest rates and faster growth *even as primary fiscal surpluses shrank*. This sequence illustrates that, for low-income countries, the initial benefit in reducing indebtedness (measured by the debt-to-GDP ratio) is more likely to come from faster growth and reduced real interest rates than higher primary surpluses. I shall sketch the analytical reason and link the process to the three steps set out above.

Official external debt is likely to account for a big chunk of the government debt of most low-income countries. Such debt is concessional and typically denominated in hard currency, say the US dollar. Its share in total government debt is going to be high to begin with. It was 80 percent of total government debt for Kenya in the mid-1990s and 60 percent in 2002/3. The real interest rate on this component of the debt is going to be low because of concessionality. Hence, the main factor determining its burden is the real exchange rate, with an appreciation lowering the burden, per the derivations in Box 5.2. In contrast, the real interest rate on domestically borrowed debt is usually a market-determined interest rate driven by interest parity augmented with default and devaluation risks, as in equation (5.1). The latter risks are driven by perceptions of political instability and poor governance.

A government which improves governance and lowers political risk will cut risk premia and lower the cost of capital. This will induce the private sector to invest more and increase the size of the optimal capital stock. It will raise the steady-state level of output—but not the growth rate. Similarly, the government's resolve to place its debt on a downward trajectory will help private investment by reducing macroeconomic uncertainty and giving banks more incentive to lend to the private sector. This too will give a one-time boost to output, but is unlikely to boost growth rates. However, the micro-policy trio will boost growth rates by pushing the private sector to become more efficient and innovative. Low-income countries are well within the global technology frontier à la Philippe Aghion and Peter Howitt (recall Chapters 2 and 3). Hence, innovation by imitation could become a source of self-sustaining endogenous growth.

Notice the benefits of this package for government debt sustainability. Interest rates on domestic debt will fall as political risk declines. TFP growth will support real appreciation as an equilibrium phenomenon by maintaining competitiveness. This will reduce the burden of official debt. The very same three-step package will boost growth rates. The simultaneous reduction in real interest rates and faster growth will magnify the reduction in the government's debt-to-GDP ratio, thus creating genuine fiscal space for additional borrowing for public investments. For Kenya, the positive impact of reduced political risk on accelerating growth, falling real interest rates, and real appreciation resulted in government debt dynamics switching from an *increase* of 1.5 percentage points of GDP per year over the period 1996/7 to 2002/3 to a *decrease* of 5 percentage points of GDP *per year* over the period 2003/4 to 2006/7![15]

Kenya's experience encapsulates the particular challenge many low-income countries face in lowering political risk and promoting social cohesion. The benefits in terms of better debt dynamics and longer business horizons are likely to be substantial, as Kenya discovered, until the fiasco of the December 2007 presidential elections. Taken together, the experiences of Ghana and Kenya stress caution in accessing the international capital markets prematurely while maximizing the benefits from concessional official external debt via reforms to spur productivity growth and lower political risk. Easier said than done; but this is a prime lesson for low-income countries.

## The Aid Agenda

Radelet makes several suggestions for donors in his 2010 book, of which the most interesting is the recommendation that they concentrate on the "emerging countries" he identifies so as to propel them further and ensure a more productive use of aid. I like this agenda, which can be expressed in three points: a big push on infrastructure, especially electricity and transportation, which constitutes a serious barrier to private investment in many low-income countries; managing volatility, which economic studies show to be harmful to long-run growth—not just from external sources, but also from internal shocks stemming from ethnic and social conflict, corruption scandals, and botched elections, as set out in chapter 3; and skills—empirical studies show that it is cognitive skills, rather than the years of schooling, that make the difference in increasing labor productivity. These ideas were expressed in a speech Ngozi Okonjo-Iweala made at Harvard University in 2010.[16] The implications for donors are stark and I cannot do better than to quote her:

> A big push in infrastructure is the obvious solution. The trouble is how to finance this. President Obama noted in his interview with Bono that the G8, and I quote: "needed to honour the aid commitments that are critical to development, and that we also look at: …how we can foster the innovations that can be the game-changers in development." Here's one game-changing idea: let African countries securitize a small portion of their aid.
>
> In 2009, DAC bilateral donors gave $27 billion in net disbursements of aid to sub-Saharan Africa. Imagine that instead of doling out the money in small annual contributions, DAC donors decided to give a big push to Africa. They could issue African Development Bonds in New York, with a yield that matches the US 30-year Treasury bond rate, currently averaging around 4.5% per year. The payments on such a bond (principal plus interest) would amount to a little more than 6 cents for each dollar raised. There should be no additional risk premium because payments would be made directly by the Treasuries of the US, UK and other rich donors. This means that if donors agreed on paying out just $6 billion a year in cash towards debt service on African Development bonds—less than a quarter of what is currently given and less than the shortfall in the Gleneagles promise to Africa, African countries could receive $100 billion in cash immediately….*Most importantly, issuing a bond like this could change perceptions overnight about Africa as a place to do business.* Faced with secure financing of $100 billion, private firms across the world would line up to provide infrastructure in Africa.

Eventually, low-income countries will have to self-finance their growth; but, as Radelet emphasizes, they need help exiting the low income-low savings-low growth trap they find themselves in. A key aspect is to get growth going so that savings rates go up as the country becomes richer. Governments can set a good example by increasing public saving through cuts in recurrent spending and greater domestic revenue mobilization based on lowering tax rates and broadening tax bases as Kenya did. Lowering country risk while strengthening incentives for private investors to innovate and enter new areas will lower government indebtedness, as outlined in this chapter on Kenya, creating genuine fiscal space for public investments. Donors can help launch this process through a big push on infrastructure via the front-loading of aid suggested in Okonjo-Iweala (2010).

But pinning one's hopes on front-loaded aid might ring a little hollow in light of the burgeoning public debt in the USA and Japan and the debt crisis in the Euro periphery, not to mention slowing growth and stubbornly high unemployment in key donor countries. The realist would point out that even during good times for the donor countries aid has been fragmented and vola-tile, as documented by Homi Kharas (2008). Besides, attempts to front-load aid are likely to fall victim to the annual budgetary appropriations processes in donor countries, which creates a predisposition toward fragmentation. But this does not lessen the validity of front-loading aid as a genuine game changer.

This book is not the place to delve into how to change the international aid architecture;[17] but realities suggests that low-income countries will have to increasingly take economic matters into their own hands and craft their own destiny. Homegrown initiatives like *The New Partnership for African Development*, or NEPAD, sponsored by the African Union, are therefore highly encouraging in that they indicate a willingness to do precisely this.[18] This includes resolving challenges like the regional integration of markets and regional infrastructure projects to compensate for the small size of many low-income countries, topics that would take me far from this chap-ter's goal, which is to highlight what low-income countries could learn from emerging markets about sovereign debt and growth. So let me proceed to a summing-up.

## Summing Up the Lessons from Emerging Markets

First of all, avoid public debt sustainability problems linked to bad policy. Low-income countries which have received debt relief must ensure that any new borrowing pays for itself through explicit linkage with a long-run growth strategy, and incorporate such linkage in their vision statements. A useful starting point would be to raise public saving; to the extent this is negative, public borrowing is actually financing current spending and this is usually hard to justify. Low-income countries also need to approach market-based borrowing cautiously, as underlined by the Ghanaian experience and the contrasting experience of Kenya, which took determined steps to lower its government debt-to-GDP ratio, initially by raising primary fiscal surpluses as official concessional loans retrenched, and then by savoring the benefits of lowered political risk and faster productivity growth after 2002, until the election debacle of December 2007.

The vision statements should also recognize that debt sustainability is not a purely macroeconomic quest. The interdependence between the government intertemporal budget constraint and the microfoundations of growth needs to be carefully managed by hardening budgets for the government, firms, and banks, and promoting competition.

Second, the initial steps that need to be taken to boost growth are not as mysterious as might appear. The key is to raise the expected private return to capital while lowering the cost of capital. The private return to capital can be raised by improving institutions which protect private property rights and uphold contracts; reducing corruption and red tape; investing in infrastructure; and lowering marginal tax rates while expanding the bases through better tax policy and administration. Lowering the cost of capital requires political stability and social harmony, which would lower country risk and hence interest rates. The combination will lengthen private investment horizons and increase the wedge between the marginal private return to capital and international borrowing costs, spurring investment and faster growth.

Such an agenda has much in common with Radelet's roster; but one needs to make a distinction between a step up from the miserable record of the past and the self-sustaining growth needed to catch up with the likes of China and India (possibly involving these countries in the process via foreign direct investment). This is a deeper challenge that requires low-income countries in Africa and elsewhere to raise TFP growth rates and levels by setting in train forces that will lead to self-sustaining endogenous growth based on technological and skill upgrading. Only then will they stand a chance of catching up with emerging markets. The reform agenda then runs the gamut of hard budget constraints, competition, competitive real exchange rates, and reasonable real interest rates based on a foundation of macroeconomic stability linked to a solid government intertemporal budget constraint.

Third, there are no quick fixes, so don't expect quick results. Long lags are likely to be involved as a result of path dependence, as illustrated by the experience of countries as diverse as Kenya and India. What are the practical implications? Three. (i) Staying the course is vital because credibility takes time to establish; besides, reforms may be need to be started on a few key reinforcing fronts. (ii) Some deterioration in the public finances and debt dynamics is likely as costs of reform are incurred upfront, with benefits in terms of faster growth and taxes only coming later. This is why it is all the more important to raise the quality of public expenditure while exploring avenues for greater revenue mobilization, which, in many low-income countries, can be achieved while lowering marginal tax rates—a powerful instrument—and by taking measures to increase tax compliance. (iii) Policies to harden budgets and increase competition for firms and banks are of the essence in order to raise TFP while creating incentives for firms to increase efficiency and become more innovative in pursuit of self-sustaining growth.

Fourth, because of the long lags involved, the absence of convincing evidence that capital account liberalization boosts productivity and growth and the growing concern about myopic international capital markets, low-income countries will need to manage capital account liberalization prudently. They should, at a minimum, do the following: (i) keep public debt dynamics sustainable and thereby limit the issuance of new debt, be it in the domestic market or externally. The smaller the volume of Treasury bills issued in the domestic market, the lower the chances of a sudden stop even if nonresidents hold a large fraction of the issued debt; (ii) monitor private external borrowing by firms, especially those in the non-traded sector; (iii) ensure commercial banks also minimize external borrowing and that the banking system remains largely deposit-based with prudent loan–deposit ratios; and (iv) take steps to avoid currency mismatches on the balance sheets of the private sector, including households, to minimize vulnerability to external shocks that typically call for a real depreciation as part of the adjustment process. Taking steps (ii) to (iv), which derive from the broader self-insurance agenda of emerging markets, is going to require better financial reporting systems and central bank supervision.

Fifth, managing volatility is crucial. There are few excuses for low-income countries not to control domestic sources of volatility such as those which have hurt growth prospects in Kenya. Domestic shocks in low-income countries could emanate from poor economic management, corruption, and internal social conflict, oftentimes violent. One hopes the improvement in policies and institutions over the past decade has taken a bite out of domestic volatility in low-income countries; but external sources of volatility are going to continue to be important in the foreseeable future as the world recovers from the global financial crisis and the follow-on sovereign debt and banking crisis in advanced Europe. Donors have a major role to play here, in ensuring better coordination among themselves and in adopting countercyclical modes of aid delivery. But realities strongly suggest that low-income countries will have to assume primary responsibility for their own future.

## Finale

So there you are, having completed your 30th year at the World Bank, facing an expectant audience of country leaders who want to know what they should do to make their countries grow faster. What do you say when the applause dies down? This is what I would say, with considerable conviction.

Based on growth theory and country experience, developing countries are going to have a hard time converging to income levels in rich countries. But the gulf is so vast that developing countries, especially low-income countries, can do much to improve their growth performance and begin the process of catching up. In order to raise investment rates and eventually bridge the technological gap with rich countries, developing countries will need to: (i) ensure a healthy intertemporal budget constraint for the government; (ii) implement the micropolicy trio of hard budgets, competition, and competitive real exchange rates; and (iii) manage volatility better, especially from domestic sources.

These goals are interlinked, requiring the design of an appropriately broad policy package. Good governance and strong fiscal, financial, and judicial institutions must be simultaneously pursued. The logical place to start is with the public finances, as Box 3.6 on Nigeria vividly illustrated. A government which falters on the public finances is not going to get far on anything else because it will have no credibility. The micropolicy trio will inevitably involve taking on vested interests and incumbent firms and banks. Implementing it is a tough political proposition. And managing volatility well goes beyond economics. Social and ethnic peace must be nurtured.

Eventually, low-income countries will need to self-finance a big chunk of their investment, extrapolating from emerging market experience. They will also need to self-insure—not just by building up foreign exchange reserves and adopting flexible exchange rates, but in a comprehensive manner that includes placing public debt on a sustainable course while also limiting contingent liabilities from the private sector. The journey is long and much of the response has to be homegrown.

## Postscript

Toward the middle of 2013, new challenges appeared for emerging markets, as noted in Chapter 1. With the US Federal Reserve Board approaching the point of beginning to taper its massive asset purchases, emerging markets, which were earlier contending with the unwanted largesse of capital inflows, began facing the prospect of shrinking capital inflows. Countries with large current account deficits and low reserves relative to external financing requirements have been particularly vulnerable—and Turkey is one of these. It has become hostage to international market sentiment, with huge external financing requirements and a national savings rate that is just 16 percent of GDP. Turkey's growth slowed from the 9 percent range in 2010 and 2011 to a mere 2.2 percent in 2012 for a country which, by 2008, had slashed public debt and reduced inflation to single-digit levels while boasting healthy banks and solid growth prospects, pointing to the crying need for more self-financing. At the same time, growth fundamentals have deteriorated in major emerging markets including India, Brazil, and China. While the global financial cycle defined by the policies of the major central banks has been a definite factor, homegrown reasons have also been important. Brazil has been marked by a high degree of government intervention and a growing share of credit from public banks over the past few years, while the Chinese growth model of export- and investment-led growth appears to be running out of steam.

The economic challenges emerging markets now face will have to be addressed in a much more interconnected and volatile global economic environment than at the beginning of the millennium. No doubt their ongoing adjustment will provide fertile soil for several PhD dissertations. But one thing I am convinced of: these countries will have to continue to pay close attention to the government intertemporal budget constraint, the micropolicy trio, and opportunities for self-financed growth even as they find ways to cope with much greater volatility. These crucial insights from the two episodes covered in this book, the transition in Central and Eastern Europe and the emerging market crises of 1997–2001 and their aftermath, will continue to remain of high relevance in the unfolding next episode, which I leave to the next generation of country economists.

## Notes

1. The astute reader will ask, "What about real interest rates?" As mentioned in Chapter 3, well-managed public finances will enable both reasonable real interest rates and competitive real exchange rates, which are linked by interest parity.
2. For details, see Aizenman and Pinto (2011, 2013) and the references therein.
3. Ghana was recently upgraded to a "lower-middle-income" country by the World Bank. However, its experience remains relevant for low-income countries with limited access to the international capital markets—indeed, it is still an IDA-only country (IDA is the concessional loan wing of the Bank) at the time of writing, suggesting it is not yet regarded as creditworthy for IBRD (which charges interest rates closer to what the market would).
4. Recall from Chapter 1 that HIPC–MDRI refers to the program whereby official creditors wrote off a substantial part of their claims on several low-income countries starting around 2005.
5. With apologies to Carlos Diaz-Alejandro (1985).
6. IMF (2008, pp. 57–64).
7. The IDA Resource Allocation Index runs from a low of 1 to a high of 6 and is an important input into how much money low-income countries receive from the World Bank's soft-loan arm, the International Development Association (IDA). See: <http://web.worldbank.org/WBSITE/EXTERNAL/EXTABOUTUS/IDA/0,,contentMDK:20052347~menuPK:2607525~pagePK:51236175~piPK:437394~theSitePK:73154,00.html>.
8. The permanent income hypothesis posits that consumption should be determined not by current income but by the present value of lifetime income. In the Ghanaian government's case the latter would be increased by the oil discovery.
9. IMF (2009, p. 27), paragraphs 7 and 11 and Table 1.
10. IMF (2009, p. 28, table 2A).
11. *IMF Executive Board Concludes Article IV Consultation with Ghana.* Public Information Notice (PIN) No. 09/86, July 17, 2009, IMF.
12. IMF (2010).
13. IMF (2011a). A footnote at the end of this quote points out that the debt ratios reflect the upward revision to GDP by 70 percent as part of a rebasing exercise.
14. IMF (2012).

15. Recall Table 5.2, items 2, 3, and 4. Appendix 4 of IMF (2011b) shows that primary surpluses were insignificant in the reduction of gross public debt-to-GDP ratios in low-income countries between 1980 and 2010. The lion's share was attributable to the real interest rate-growth differential, as in the case of Kenya between 2003 and 2007; and debt relief (which was not a factor in Kenya).

16. Okonjo-Iweala (2010), emphasis added.

17. For instance, front-loading might be more palatable to donors if combined with Radelet's focus on countries with a track record, like the 17 emerging countries he identifies; or an entirely different approach to aid based on the present value of total aid needed to meet certain objectives, such as the Millennium Development Goals, and a minimum level of infrastructure in a given low-income country, while making it clear to that low-income country that this is all that is available and aid is not going to be open-ended. (Time inconsistency problems can be minimized by treating humanitarian aid separately.)

18. For information on NEPAD see <http://www.nepad.org/>.

# Annexes

# ANNEX I: KEY FEATURES OF NEOCLASSICAL GROWTH

Box 2.1 in Chapter 2 lists the three main features of neoclassical growth models and I sketch these out algebraically here.[1] Let us start with a Cobb–Douglas production function for gross domestic product, $Y$, where $K$ and $L$ are the capital stock and labor force respectively, and $0 \leq \alpha \leq 1$, that is, there are diminishing marginal returns to capital:

$$Y = A(t)K^{\alpha}L^{1-\alpha}, \tag{A1}$$

In equation (1), $A$ stands for technological progress or total factor productivity (TFP) and is shown as a function of time to capture its exogenous nature in the neoclassical Solow–Swann growth model. Let's divide both sides of the equation by $L$ to get:

$$y = Ak^{\alpha}, \tag{A2}$$

where $y \equiv Y/L$ is output per worker and $k \equiv K/L$ is the capital-to-labor ratio. Assume, to begin with, that technology is constant and that TFP growth is zero (that is, $dA/A = 0$). In this case, growth in output per worker can be written:

$$\hat{y} = \alpha\hat{k}, \tag{A3}$$

where a "^"or "hat" over a variable denotes a proportional change or growth rate. Assuming a closed economy so that investment equals saving, $\hat{y}$ can be written:

$$\hat{y} = \alpha\left[sA^{\frac{1}{\alpha}}y^{\left(\frac{\alpha-1}{\alpha}\right)} - (n+\delta)\right], \tag{A3'}$$

where $s$ is the savings rate, $n$ the growth rate of the work force, and $\delta$ the rate of depreciation of capital.[2] Since $y$ has a negative exponent, it follows that $\partial\hat{y}/\partial y < 0$, that is, that the growth rate of output per worker (which equals the growth rate of per capita income if the workforce is a constant share of population) falls as output per worker goes up. In other words, richer countries would tend to grow slower and poorer countries faster, leading to a convergence in per capita income levels. This is the so-called *Convergence Hypothesis*.

In this simple setup, there is a unique steady state to which all countries will converge. I shall express the right-hand side of (A3') in terms of the capital–labor ratio, $k$, which will serve as a bridge to two of Robert Solow's key insights:

$$\hat{y} = \alpha\left[sAk^{\alpha-1} - (n + \delta)\right]. \tag{A3''}$$

By comparing (A3) and (A3''), we see that $\hat{k} = sAk^{\alpha-1} - (n + \delta)$. The first expression on the right-hand side of this equality falls as $k$ increases because $\alpha - 1 < 0$, while the second, $n + \delta$, is constant. Eventually, the two will become equal, so that the growth rate of capital per worker, $\hat{k}$, goes to zero. In this case, $k$ will reach a steady state and so will $y$. (A3'') shows that we need diminishing marginal returns to capital (that is, $a$ positive but less than 1) in order to reach a steady-state level for $k$ (that is, $\hat{k} = 0$). This yields the two key results of neoclassical growth: (a) the steady-state rate of per capita output growth will be zero in the absence of exogenous TFP growth, that is, $\hat{y} = 0$ unless $\hat{A} > 0$. And (b) a rise in the savings rate will lead to a higher *level* of income but not to a permanent increase in the growth rate. That is, if $s$ rises, $\hat{y}$ will increase temporarily (since $\partial \hat{y}/\partial s > 0$) until $k$ reaches a new, higher steady-state level, but then revert to zero unless $\hat{A} > 0$.[3]

### Questioning Convergence

As Paul Romer points out in his 1994 survey, the convergence hypothesis is not supported by the empirical evidence, leading to questions about the validity of the model itself. These questions arise because the model leads to implausible inferences about the level of savings and investment rates in rich countries relative to poorer ones; but I will first provide another equation before I explore this further. The marginal product of capital is given by (you can check that $\partial Y/\partial K = \partial y/\partial k$):

$$MPK \equiv \frac{\partial y}{\partial k} = \alpha Ak^{\alpha-1}, \tag{A4}$$

from which it is clear that there are diminishing marginal returns to capital, since $\dfrac{\partial MPK}{\partial k} < 0$.

Let us compare an advanced economy and a developing country. In 1960, as Romer (1994) notes, output per worker in the Philippines was about a tenth of that in the USA. Based on equation (A2) with labor's share in national income $(1-a) = 0.6$, Romer goes on to say that this would imply that the capital–labor ratio in the USA was over 300 times that in the Philippines, suggesting an implausibly high level of savings and investment in the USA.

I am going to focus on the MPK instead in an attempt to tease out some development implications. Putting equations (A2) and (A4) together, these same numbers imply that the MPK in the Philippines would have been 31.6 times that in the USA in 1960! In this case, we would have witnessed an exodus of capital from the USA to the Philippines until the MPKs and hence $k$'s are equalized. This would also imply an equalization of $y$'s—that is, a convergence of income levels (as equation (A2) would tell us).

In trying to resolve these implausible results, there are two parameters up for grabs: $1-a$ and $A$. Since $(1-a)$ comes from the national income statistics, let us focus on $A$. The expressions for the ratios of output per worker and MPKs in the two countries are given by:

$$\frac{y_P}{y_U} = \left(\frac{A_P}{A_U}\right)\left(\frac{k_P}{k_U}\right)^{\alpha} ; \qquad (A5)$$

and

$$\frac{MPK_P}{MPK_U} = \left(\frac{A_P}{A_U}\right)\left(\frac{k_P}{k_U}\right)^{\alpha-1}, \qquad (A6)$$

where $P$ denotes the Philippines and $U$, the USA. Now consider the following thought experiment. Assume that the capital–labor ratio in the USA is 10 times that in the Philippines (rather than over 300 times) and further, that, since the USA is technologically more advanced, it is three times as efficient, that is, $\frac{A_P}{A_U} = 0.33$. Then equations (A5) and (A6) tell us that output per worker in the Philippines is 13 percent that of the USA but its MPK is 31 percent higher ( $\frac{MPK_P}{MPK_U} = 1.31$ ). These results are more plausible!

Suppose capital flows are liberalized, spurring an outflow from the USA to the Philippines until the MPKs were equalized. According to equation (A6), this would mean that the capital–labor ratio in the Philippines would go up from 10 to 16 percent of that of the USA, while its output per worker would rise from 13 percent to 16 percent of that in the USA. Obviously, the Philippines would grow faster than the USA until this new equilibrium is reached. But convergence in income *levels* does not occur, unlike in the previous case when identical technology (i.e., $\frac{A_P}{A_U} = 1$ ) was assumed. Thus, while the liberalization of capital flows will equalize marginal returns to capital, it will not lead to a convergence of income levels unless there is rapid technological catch-up, providing the point of departure for endogenous growth and highlighting the criticality of technology and human capital as discussed in Chapter 2.

Figure A1.1 shows how this might happen. The marginal product of capital for the USA is denoted by curve U, and that for the Philippines, P. The starting points are $U_1$ and $P_1$, while the post-capital account liberalization equilibrium is given by $U_2$ and $P_2$. While the capital–labor ratio in the Philippines rises, it, and the level of output per worker, remain below those in the USA in the new equilibrium. If the level of TFP in the USA were sufficiently high (corresponding to the curve U' or above), the capital account liberalization would lead to flows in the "wrong" direction!

## TFP and Growth Accounting

Algebraically, $A = \frac{Y}{K^{\alpha}L^{1-\alpha}}$, which is simply output per unit of input measured as a geometric average of $K$ and $L$. Hence, TFP is a generalized measure of productivity or efficiency. Its growth rate is computed through a so-called ***growth accounting exercise*** using equation (A1), which can be easily manipulated to get:

$$g \equiv \frac{dY}{Y} = \frac{dA}{A} + \alpha\frac{dK}{K} + (1-\alpha)\frac{dL}{L}. \qquad (A7)$$

In (A7), g, $dK/K$, and $dL/L$ can be obtained from the national income accounts and labor market statistics. Once we assume a value for $(1-a)$—which is simply the share of national income

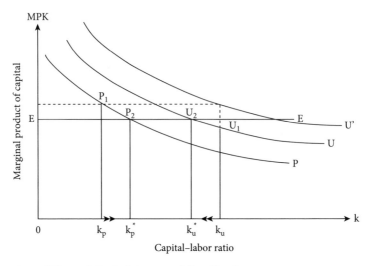

**Figure A1.1** Effects of Capital Account Liberalization

going to labor under perfect competition—equation (A7) can be solved for the growth rate of TFP. I am skirting a whole host of complications and controversy encountered in TFP growth calculations (see Caselli (2008))!

Paul Krugman (1994) captures the practical significance of TFP in his polemic questioning whether the rapid East Asian growth from 1960 to 1990 constituted a genuine miracle, that is, was a result of growing productivity or simply a matter of increasing inputs: "Mere increases in inputs, without an increase in the efficiency with which those inputs are used—investing in more machinery and infrastructure—must run into diminishing returns; input-driven growth is inevitably limited" (p. 67). He uses the output of a growth accounting exercise of the sort described earlier in this Annex to conclude that since "the remarkable record of East Asian growth has been matched by input growth so rapid that…[it] ceases to be a mystery" (p. 76).[4]

## Notes

1. If you really know neoclassical growth, you don't need this annex. I draw heavily on Paul Romer's 1994 survey, Robert Solow's seminal 1956 paper, and a 1990 NBER working paper by Xavier Sala-i-Martin.

2. Note that $\hat{k} = \hat{K} - \hat{L}$, with $\hat{L} = n$. Assuming a closed economy, the net increase in the capital stock $\dot{K} = sY - \delta K$, which gives $\hat{K} = \dfrac{sY}{K} - \delta$. Use this together with (A1) and (A3) to derive equation (A3').

3. See pages 10–12 of Sala-i-Martin (1990) and his Figure 1. NB: There will be no steady-state level either for income or capital per worker if $\hat{A} > 0$. However, there will be a steady-state solution for output per *effective* worker defined as $\tilde{y} = \dfrac{Y}{\tilde{L}}$, where $\tilde{L} \equiv BL$ and $B \equiv A^{\frac{1}{(1-\alpha)}}$. In this case, the

steady-state rate of growth of output per worker $y$ and that of capital per worker $k$ will both

equal $\dfrac{\hat{A}}{(1-\alpha)}$ along a so-called "balanced growth path" (output and capital grow at the same

rate). See also Lucas (1988).

4. For a rebuttal, see Bhagwati (1996). And see Chapters 2 and 3 for a policy-oriented discussion of accumulation versus TFP in growth.

# ANNEX 2: ASSESSING GOVERNMENT DEBT SUSTAINABILITY

Debt sustainability analysis became a routine exercise at the World Bank and IMF only in 2004 following the emerging market crises of 1997–2001 and the realization that low-income countries had excessive debt burdens. The goal in this Annex is to equip you with basic formulas and spell out caveats about standard approaches to examining government debt sustainability.

### Basic Formulas

Let $D$ denote nominal government debt. Abstracting from printing money, privatization proceeds, and bank bailout costs, the increase in $D$ is equal to the fiscal deficit, $FD$. The deficit is expenditure minus revenues. Expenditure includes capital and current expenditure and interest payments. Revenues consist of taxes, including income tax, VAT, import duties, and the like, as well as nontax revenue, which include profits transferred from the central bank (essentially, a portion of seigniorage). In addition to these explicit revenues, governments also benefit from implicit revenues, a prominent source in some developing countries being financial repression, which enables governments to borrow at below-market interest rates.

In examining a government's debt dynamics, it is convenient to partition expenditure into two components: interest payments on government debt; and the rest, referred to as primary expenditure. Hence, the deficit can be written as primary expenditure minus revenues, or the primary deficit, plus interest payments. This gives us:[1]

$$\dot{D} = FD = PD + iD, \tag{A8}$$

where $PD$ is the primary deficit and interest payments are given by the nominal interest rate, $i$, times nominal debt. The key variable in debt dynamics is the ratio of government debt to GDP, which we shall denote $d \equiv D/Y$, with $Y$ representing GDP. Let $g^N \equiv \dot{Y}/Y$ denote nominal GDP growth. It is easy to show that $\dot{d} = \dfrac{\dot{D}}{Y} - g^N d$. Combining this with (A8) gives:

$$\dot{d} = pd + \left(i - g^N\right)d, \tag{A9}$$

where $\dot{d}$ is the change in the government debt-to-GDP ratio and $pd$ is the ratio of the primary deficit to GDP. If we denote inflation (based on the GDP deflator) by $\pi$, then (A9) can be equivalently written:

$$\dot{d} = pd + (r - g)d, \tag{A9'}$$

where $r \equiv (i - \pi)$ is the real interest rate and $g \equiv (g^N - \pi)$ is the real growth rate.

But typically governments borrow in local currency and foreign currency ("dollars"). In this case, $D = D_d + xD_\$$, where $D_d$ is local, or domestic, currency debt, $D_\$$ is dollar debt, and $x$ is nominal exchange rate in local currency per dollar. The expression for the change in nominal debt now becomes: $\dot{D} = [PD + i_d D_d + i_\$ D_\$ x] + \dot{x}D_\$$, where $i_d$ and $i_\$$ are the interest rates on local currency and dollar debt respectively. The expression in square brackets is just the fiscal deficit, as in (A8). The expression tacked on at the end is the capital gain or loss on dollar debt as a result of nominal exchange rate movements: a depreciation against the dollar increases the burden of dollar debt while an appreciation lowers it. Defining $w \equiv D_d / D$ as the share of local currency debt and $\hat{x} \equiv \dot{x}/x$ as the rate of depreciation of the nominal exchange rate, we can derive:[2]

$$\dot{d} = pd + \left( \left[ wi_d + (1-w)(i_\$ + \hat{x}) \right] - g^N d \right) \tag{A10}.$$

A comparison with equation (A9) shows that the nominal interest rate is now replaced by a weighted average of the nominal interest rate on local currency debt, and that on dollar debt translated into a local currency equivalent by reflecting the depreciation/appreciation of the exchange rate, an expression the reader will recognize as ex post interest parity. I shall now derive the counterpart of equation (A9').

Let $\pi^*$ denote US inflation and $R \equiv P / xP^*$ represent the bilateral real exchange rate, where $P$ and $P^*$ are the price levels at home and in the USA respectively. The real exchange rate is defined in accordance with IMF convention, namely, an upward movement means a real appreciation or equivalently that $\rho \equiv \dfrac{dR}{R} = (\pi - \pi^* - \hat{x}) > 0$.[3]

Back to equation (A10). Consider the expression in round brackets on the right-hand side. By adding and subtracting $\pi$ and $(1-w)\pi^*$ and collecting terms appropriately, we get:

$$\left[ wi_d + (1-w)(i_\$ + \hat{x}) \right] - g^N = w(i_d - \pi) + (1-w)(i_\$ - \pi^*)$$
$$+ (1-w)(-\pi + \pi^* + \hat{x}) - (g^N - \pi).$$

Noting that $r_d = (i_d - \pi)$ and $r_\$ = (i_\$ - \pi^*)$, and recalling the definitions of real growth and real appreciation, gives us the equation we are after:

$$\dot{d} = pd + \left( \left[ wr_d + (1-w)(r_\$ - \rho) \right] - g \right)d \tag{A10'}.$$

We have now built a bridge to equations (5.2) and (5.3) and Box 5.2 in the Kenya chapter.

## Concepts and Insights

The government has a *debt sustainability problem* if the prevailing mix of primary fiscal balances, real interest rates, and growth rates would place the debt-to-GDP ratio on a path unacceptable to the market: for emerging markets, the market is the final arbiter of debt sustainability. For example, if the primary deficit is positive and the real interest rate exceeds the growth rate, then the debt-to-GDP ratio will be on an unsustainable, explosive path unless the primary fiscal surplus is raised or interest rates fall or growth picks up or all three happen. Procrastination could lead to a crisis or the need for a much bigger future fiscal compression to restore sustainability.

A *solvency problem* exists if the market believes that the government will be unable to mobilize the primary fiscal surpluses needed to fully service its debt and may have to default on its obligations. Technically, the present value of future primary surpluses as a ratio of GDP, with the discount rate equal to the real interest rate minus the growth rate, is less than the initial debt-to-GDP ratio. When there is a solvency problem, debt will be trading at a significant discount, with high spreads on dollar-denominated debt relative to the US government, and high real interest rates on local currency debt to compensate for default and devaluation risks, as seen in Chapter 7 on Russia.

An important conceptual distinction is that if a government has a solvency problem, it has a sustainability problem; but the converse is not true, as a sustainability problem can be potentially corrected by generating higher primary surpluses in the future, thereby ensuring that the present value of expected future primary fiscal surpluses equals or exceeds initial debt. However, in practice, there is no hard and fast rule for distinguishing between sustainability and solvency. A combination of sustainability problems and a myopic market may produce effects similar to solvency problems, that is, the market would be signaling its concern about default and devaluation risk in the way it priced the debt issued by the government, and there is a risk that new loans could dry up. See Box 3.1 in Chapter 3.

## A Numerical Example of Unsustainable Debt

The purpose of the numerical example is to illustrate the difference between unsustainability in debt *levels* versus *dynamics* on the one hand, and the high costs of *procrastination* in addressing unsustainable debt dynamics on the other. Go back to equation (A9'). Assume an initial debt-to-GDP ratio $d=60$ percent, real interest rate $r=6$ percent, real growth rate $g=2$ percent, and a primary deficit of 3 percent of GDP. In this case, the debt-to-GDP ratio will increase by *at least* 5.4 percentage points per year (the primary deficit of 3 percent plus the real interest rate minus the growth rate multiplied by the starting debt-to-GDP ratio, that is, 6 percent minus 2 percent times 60 percent = 2.4 percent). This is clearly unsustainable. In the absence of timely corrective action, $d$ will approach 77 percent at the end of year 3 based on (A9').

This is where a problem of *sustainability in debt levels* may also arise: suppose the market imposes a credit ceiling, as in the example of Sargent and Wallace (1981), of 75 percent of GDP. Then the country is likely to experience a crisis in the form of an inflationary burst, default, or both before it gets to the end of year 3, *unless* the primary surplus is raised to hold $d$ at 75 percent. The needed primary surplus $ps^*$ can be calculated by setting the change in the debt-to-GDP ratio equal to zero in equation (A9') to get the result:

$$ps^* = (r - g)d. \qquad (A11)$$

Plugging $d=75$ into formula (A11) yields $ps^*=3$ percent. But since there is a primary *deficit* of 3 percent to start with, a heroic fiscal effort equal to 6 percentage points of GDP will be needed to stabilize $d$ at 75 percent—which might not be feasible in short order. Therefore, to avoid a crisis, the government will need to start implementing a fiscal retrenchment well *before* the ceiling of 75 percent is reached. Investors will see the train wreck coming and real interest rates will begin to rise, making the retrenchment even harder.

Now imagine the government realizes it may need a borrowing cushion to deal with the fiscal costs of unanticipated shocks and decides to aim for $d=60$ percent. If it waits until $d$ reaches 75 percent, it will need a one-time jump in the primary surplus to 18 percent to return $d$ to 60 percent: *procrastination is costly*. After $d$ returns to 60 percent, a more modest primary surplus of 2.4 percent will suffice to keep $d$ at 60 percent.

## Pitfalls in Assessing Debt Sustainability

Three caveats are worth remembering. First, rules of thumb based either on prudential debt levels like the Maastricht criterion of 60 percent for the debt-to-GDP ratio or derived from cross-country regressions have not worked well in practice.[4] Russia was well within the Maastricht criterion of a debt-to-GDP ratio of 60 percent in early 1998, yet suffered a huge debt crisis that year. India has had debt-to-GDP levels well in excess of 75 percent for three decades, yet has never suffered a major crisis and grew rapidly from 2003 to 2008.

Second, debt sustainability is inherently forward looking. Calculating sustainable debt levels based on historical trajectories of the primary surplus or real interest rates and growth rates is therefore of limited use, except possibly in serving as a starting point.

This brings us to the third and most important caveat. For emerging market countries, the debt markets play a decisive role in deciding what level of debt is sustainable, indicating that market signals be taken seriously in addition to economic fundamentals, a topic to which I now turn.

## Fundamentals and Market Signals

Table A2.1 lists a set of indicators a country economist might use in assessing economic fundamentals, market signals, and the adequacy of international liquidity. Four comments are in order.

First, although history matters in terms of how a country reached a particular debt-to-GDP ratio as well as its track record on inflation and default, debt sustainability by nature is forward looking. An increase in the fiscal deficit is not always bad if sound public investments (as opposed to the "road to nowhere") are being made.

Second, what debt threshold is appropriate for a given country? Looking at market signals is inescapable in answering this question. If the government debt-to-GDP ratio is 50 percent but the bond spread is 700 basis points relative to the US government, this is telling us the market is uncomfortable *even though* indebtedness is below the 60 percent stipulation of Maastricht. Similarly, if the real interest rate on local currency Treasury bills is 25 percent, as in Russia in May 1998, this could a signal that the market is concerned about both devaluation and default. Both devaluation and default are last-resort ways of making government debt more sustainable but could be costly in terms of reputation and future borrowing costs.

Third, good fundamentals notwithstanding, there is reason to believe that markets are fickle and prone both to myopia and herd behavior. This is why the table highlights

**Table A2.1**  Fundamentals, Market Signals, and International Liquidity

| Area | Indicators | Comments |
|---|---|---|
| Fiscal/debt fundamentals | • size of deficit<br>• government savings<br>• expenditure composition<br>  o public investment<br>  o current expenditure | – If the deficit is high, one would like to know why—e.g., is it because of infrastructure investments with a high payoff in terms of future growth and taxes, or an increase in civil service wages? |
| | • revenue mobilization<br>  o tax composition<br>  o average effective tax rates<br>    and marginal tax rates | – Many developing countries have high marginal tax rates with small bases. If tax administration and compliance improve, marginal rates can be lowered while actually raising average effective tax rates. |
| | • debt dynamics | – This requires looking at both the "obvious" determinants: primary deficits, real interest rates, and growth; as well as the "less obvious": whether the real exchange rate is in equilibrium, contingent fiscal liabilities in the private sector, and the micro foundations of growth. |
| Growth fundamentals and micro–macro linkages | • competitive firms and banks<br>• real interest rates and real exchange rates | – Good micro means high future growth and revenues, helping fiscal solvency.<br>– Sustainable debt dynamics means lower cost of capital for private investment. Competitive real exchange rates help exports. |
| Market signals | • real interest rates on T-bills<br>• EMBI bond spreads | The information contained in these signals can be used to extract the devaluation and default risk premia being demanded by the market (as illustrated in Chapter 7). |
| International liquidity (a buffer against shifting market sentiment) | • Ratio of foreign exchange reserves to short-term external debt<br>• Ratio of foreign exchange reserves to broad money | Studies have identified both these variables to be strong indicators of vulnerability. |

*Notes:* The indicator list is meant to be illustrative, not exhaustive. Monetary policy is not explicitly discussed, although inflation expectations can be influenced by debt sustainability à la Sargent and Wallace (1981).

*international liquidity*—to avoid situations of self-fulfilling speculative attacks—although it is hard to pinpoint an instance of an exchange rate crisis in emerging markets unrelated to fiscal fundamentals.[5]

Fourth, even though there is a strong, almost exclusively macroeconomic bias in looking at debt sustainability, there are critical macro–micro linkages which the table attempts to bring out in the context of the growth fundamentals. The chapters on India and Russia are both compelling examples.

## Notes

1. Recall Box 3.2. I shall work in continuous time, which is less clunky. For discrete time derivations, see the technical appendix in Aizenman and Pinto (2005).

2. Hint: get an expression for $\dfrac{\dot{D}}{Y} = pd + i_d \dfrac{D_d}{D}\dfrac{D}{Y} + i_\$ \dfrac{xD_\$}{D}\dfrac{D}{Y} + \dfrac{\dot{x}}{x}\dfrac{xD_\$}{D}\dfrac{D}{Y}$ and then proceed, using the definitions of $d$, $w$, and $\hat{x}$ .

3. $\dfrac{dp}{p} \equiv \pi$ and $\dfrac{dp*}{p*} \equiv \pi*.$

4. See Gill and Pinto (2005) for a survey.

5. Even in the case of the East Asian countries, which have traditionally had low fiscal deficits, contingent fiscal liabilities (bailouts of banks and corporates), the buildup of which may have been encouraged by government policy, played a role, as argued in Burnside, Eichenbaum, and Rebelo (2001) and Frankel and Wei (2005).

# ANNEX 3: THE RUSSIAN AND ARGENTINE DEBT SWAPS

The main features of the Russian GKO–Eurobond swap of July 1998 were as follows: (a) it was voluntary and market-based; (b) all GKOs maturing before July 1, 1999 were eligible, with a *face value* of $39.3 billion, and a *market value* of $32.3 billion at prevailing exchange rates.[1] Excluding the 60 percent share believed held by the central bank and the state-owned savings bank, Sberbank, which were barred from participating, the market value of eligible GKOs dropped to about $13 billion, held by nonresidents and Russian commercial banks. (c) Those wanting to convert would receive an equal amount by market value of 7-year and 20-year dollar Eurobonds, and could bid by quoting a spread in basis points over the respective US Treasury benchmark bonds.

The bid results were announced on July 20, 1998. Even though the maximum spread of 940 basis points chosen by MOF was much higher than the prevailing spread on the benchmark Russian Eurobond, only $4.4 billion of GKOs by market value was tendered for exchange. This suggested that the holders of GKOs preferred to hold on to their short-dated paper and take the risk of a devaluation—mitigated by the prospect of a large official rescue package—than swap into long-term Eurobonds at highly attractive spreads, indicating anxiety about default risk.

Box A3.1 describes the Argentine swap. Argentina had little short-term debt; but its projected financing requirements were $22 billion per year over 2001–2005 *provided* primary fiscal surpluses were raised to at least 4 percent of GDP in order to stabilize the public debt to GDP ratio, which was not credible given the fiscal track record. A $29.5 billion debt swap ("mega-canje") was orchestrated in June 2001 to extend maturities and was greeted enthusiastically by investors.

The mega-swap would have enabled Argentina to postpone over $16 billion in debt service payments between 2001 and 2005; but this was small relative to financing requirements of $110 billion over this period. Above all, the swap was done at a spread of 1100 basis points, whereas according to Mussa (2002), calculations showed that, at spreads of over 1000 basis points, Argentina's debt dynamics were "virtually hopeless." After the swap, meltdown set in, as bond spreads rose even higher, tax collections continued to flag, and bank runs intensified as depositors rushed to convert their pesos into dollars before the constitutionally mandated exchange rate peg collapsed.

In contrast to the enthusiasm which greeted both swaps, ex post reviews were uniformly skeptical:

- Commenting on the Russian swap, Stanley Fischer, then First Deputy Managing Director of the IMF, expressed skepticism that a "market-friendly restructuring alone can fundamentally change a country's debt dynamics. Such restructurings take place at market prices, and thus almost by definition, do not significantly change the present value of the country's debt obligations…"[2]

- Calvo, Izquierdo, and Talvi (2002) observed that "the [Argentine] government engineered a massive debt swap in June 2001 to extend the maturity of the debt profile, but ended up validating extremely high interest rates which, in turn, confirmed expectations about an unsustainable fiscal position."

- Fischer's comment on the Russian swap is echoed by Lesson 8 of the ten lessons distilled by the Independent Evaluation Office (IEO) in its July 2004 evaluation of the IMF's role in Argentina, quoted in Box 7.4 of Chapter 7.

The fundamental insight from both cases was that market-based debt swaps will not lower the present value of the government's debt burden *because* market investors will not less this happen voluntarily. To the contrary, the additional compensation investors could exact for

---

**Box A3.1**  Argentina's Mega-Swap

The Argentine debt swap was concluded after months of concern about fiscal fundamentals.[a] Public debt stood at 55 percent of GDP at the end of 2000, but would have been much higher if corrected for real exchange rate overvaluation; recall how the unsustainable real appreciation of the ruble over 1995–7 helped Russia mask its unsustainable debt dynamics. In late 2000, Argentine sovereign bond spreads were 750 basis points above US treasuries and broke through 1000 basis points by March 2001. Market analysts were openly discussing default by late 2000. A $40 billion IMF package had been negotiated in December 2000 to stave off default and restore market confidence; but growth faltered, with the market appearing to have concluded that the fiscal and debt situation was not salvageable.

Against this background, $29.5 billion in bonds was swapped over June 1–4, 2001 for $31 billion of new bonds to extend maturities.

Under the mega-swap, existing bonds (Brady bonds, Eurobonds, and local securities) were exchanged for five new instruments. (i) A $11.5 billion, 7-year global bond[b] with a 7 percent coupon for the first three years and 15.5 percent after the fourth year, maturing in 2008. (ii) A .9 billion, 7-year global bond with a 10 percent coupon for the first three years and 12.4 percent after the fourth year, maturing in 2008. (iii) A $7.5 billion, 17-year global with a 12.25 percent coupon, maturing in 2018 with 15 years' interest capitalization.[c] (iv) A $8.5 billion, 30-year global with a 12 percent coupon, maturing in 2031, with 5 years' interest capitalization. And (v) a $2.1 billion, 5-year local bond with floating interest rates, maturing in 2006, with 2 years' interest capitalization.

---

[a] Mussa (2002), Servén and Perry (2005), and de la Torre, Levy Yeyati, and Schmukler (2003).
[b] Global bonds can be traded both in the US capital market and Euromarket.
[c] Interest capitalization refers to an increase in principal by addition, instead of payment, of accrued interest.

letting the government "reprofile" its debt would end up making matters worse. Fiscal fundamentals and market signals rule supreme.

## Notes

1. Please refer to the discussion in Chapter 7 on Russia. This annex draws on Pinto and Tanaka (2005).
2. "Comments and Discussion", Kharas, Pinto, and Ulatov (2001, p. 63).

# ANNEX 4: THREE GENERATIONS OF CRISIS MODELS

The three generations of crisis model all have to do with the collapse of a fixed exchange rate.[1] What differs across the models are the range of policy response options open to the government, how these are affected by actions taken by investors in the asset markets, and what happens to private sector balance sheets in the real and financial sectors. Fiscal considerations, actual or contingent, play a critical role in all three cases.

## First Generation

In 1979, Paul Krugman published a seminal paper in the *Journal of Money, Credit and Banking* on balance of payments crises. His so-called *first generation* model featured a government financing its fiscal deficit by credit from the central bank in the presence of a fixed exchange rate. The rate of inflation is equal to the rate of depreciation of the currency and is therefore zero initially. With the demand for money (which is a function of inflation) fixed to begin with, the credit created to finance the fiscal deficit spills over into current account deficits, depleting the central bank's foreign exchange reserves. At some point, domestic residents begin to suspect the authorities will run out of foreign currency, forcing the government to abandon the fixed peg and float the currency—the "crisis." This leads to a jump in the equilibrium inflation rate, which, post-crisis, is simply the rate of depreciation needed for the government's fiscal deficit to be financed by the inflation tax.

The beauty of Krugman's model is that the switch to a float happens before reserves actually reach zero. It happens when remaining reserves are exactly equal to the reduction in the demand for money (the home currency) that will occur at the point the float is adopted; the demand for money falls because at that point, the rate of inflation jumps from zero to the level needed to finance the government's fiscal deficit. Domestic residents simply buy up or "attack" the remaining reserves *at the pre-crisis fixed exchange rate*, forcing a float of the currency. Therefore, no one suffers a capital loss, since, in this model, domestic residents can calculate exactly when the switch to a float will take place and the exchange rate itself does not jump at that point. The inputs for this calculation include the pre-attack rate of reserve depletion (determined by the size of the fiscal deficit and related credit creation), the function linking money demand to inflation, and the post-float inflation rate needed to finance the deficit by the inflation tax.[2]

## Second Generation

In Krugman's model, the speculative attack on reserves is spurred by inconsistent fundamentals: a fiscal deficit financed by credit is not consistent with a fixed exchange rate (zero inflation). But in a 1994 paper heralding the *second generation crisis model*, Maurice Obstfeld argued that Krugman's model could not fully explain the Exchange Rate Mechanism (ERM) crisis of 1992–3 and the experience of Sweden in particular; Box A4.1 contains a brief description of this crisis. Industrial European countries could always augment reserves by borrowing, and "fiscal profligacy" in the shape of a fiscal deficit financed by credit from the central bank may or may not be part of the picture. But other factors come into play, such as the impact of high interest rates and politically unacceptable levels of unemployment, which might create a conflict between the interest-rate defense of a currency peg and bringing unemployment down.

Obstfeld's central idea is that the government has policy options to deal with actual or perceived unsustainability in macroeconomic policies. Its eventual response is driven by a political calculus in which it balances the *pain* of holding on to a fixed peg (for example, high interest rates leading to pressures on private sector balance sheets or the exacerbation of high unemployment) with the *gain* of letting it go (the pain will be avoided without a big effect on the government's credibility either because other important countries have acted similarly or the move will be seen as "sensible"). The ambiguity about how the government will eventually respond gives rise to "multiple equilibria." Market expectations, in turn, are molded by perceptions of which policy option the government will choose and the anticipated impact on asset prices. This would then affect positions taken by investors which could force the hand of the government. This circular logic could lead to a crisis as a *self-fulfilling prophecy* of shifting market sentiment even as fiscal fundamentals remain unchanged. Such models are often referred to as *second generation* models.

## Third Generation

The *third generation* crisis model was motivated by the East Asian experience of 1997–8. This highlighted balance sheet mismatches on currencies and maturities (short-term dollar debt financing long-term local currency assets), international illiquidity (insufficient reserves), and moral hazard (the private sector makes bad investment decisions but is confident the government will bail it out). As a result, even if the government is not *currently* running large fiscal deficits, *prospective* deficits may be high on account of contingent liabilities related to the fiscal costs of bailing out banks and private firms. The possible collapse of the fixed exchange rate is heightened by international illiquidity, manifested in a high ratio of short-term external debt to foreign exchange reserves and/or a high ratio of broad money to reserves. This configuration makes a country susceptible to shifts in market sentiment regarding a devaluation or a reversal of capital flows. If interest rates are raised to make domestic currency assets more attractive, this would put a strain on banks' balance sheets by increasing nonperforming loans; if the exchange rate is allowed to collapse, the real burden of dollar-denominated debt rises on corporate balance sheets, forcing them into bankruptcy, which hurts the banks as well. This makes it impossible to defend the peg against speculative attacks, forcing its abandonment as well as a costly bailout, as a wholesale bankruptcy of the corporate and financial sectors would be politically unacceptable.[3]

**Box A4.1**  The ERM Crisis of 1992–3

What was the ERM crisis of 1992–3? In a nutshell, the EU countries at that time were under a system to coordinate monetary and exchange rate policies with the goal of restricting exchange rate movements under the ERM as part of a transition to full monetary union and a single currency. Currency realignments were not permitted after 1987, and capital accounts were fully liberalized in 1990 as part of this process. In effect, the currencies of the other European countries in the system became pegged to the German mark since the Bundesbank was the most credible among the participating country central banks.[a]

The catalyst for the crisis was the reunification of East and West Germany in 1990. This involved major additional public expenditure on infrastructure and social benefits, swelling the German fiscal deficit and forcing the Bundesbank to hike interest rates. These developments were in line with the predictions that German real interest rates would need to rise to attract the necessary capital inflows and that a real appreciation of the mark would occur. The rise in interest rates put downward pressure on the other currencies in the system and what happened to the UK pound is a good illustration.

The UK happened to be in a recession at that point, with unemployment above 10 percent. Had the Bank of England (BoE) raised interest rates to keep the exchange rate within its narrow bounds under the ERM, the recession and unemployment would have worsened. Sensing a conflict between keeping the fixed exchange rate and preventing unemployment from going even higher, speculators—famously, George Soros—attacked the pound, borrowing it and converting the proceeds into German marks. On September 16, 1992, BoE was finally forced to hike its policy interest rate from 10 percent to 12 percent with a threat to hike further to 15 percent. With inflation running at just 3 percent, this was a massive hike in real terms. But BoE continued to haemorrhage foreign exchange reserves and the UK eventually withdrew from the ERM, abandoning its peg to the mark and making the bet made by the speculators a self-fulfilling prophecy. This decision enabled BoE to halve its interest rate and help the economy.

In his 2009 book on depression economics, Paul Krugman argues that with or without Soros, the pound would have had to be devalued, and that the speculators simply moved up the timetable. In fact, he argues that the speculators did the UK a favor by forcing the abandonment of its currency peg, thereby increasing its international competitiveness and allowing it to cut interest rates. But he also observes that speculators' actions in forcing self-fulfilling speculative attacks are not always beneficial, the East Asian crisis of 1997–1998 being a case in point (Krugman 2009, pp. 122–31).

---

[a] Eichengreen and Wyplosz (1993).

## Common Features

All three model generations are marked by fixed exchange rates, an open capital account, and low foreign exchange reserves. The second generation brings in market psychology and a conflict between external (maintaining exchange parity) and internal (e.g., keeping unemployment at politically acceptable levels) goals. Not knowing how the government will react brings in the possibility of multiple equilibria: the new equilibrium depends upon which goal the government chooses to pursue. For emerging markets, there is not going to be much of a choice: where there is a conflict between external and internal imbalance, the external constraint will typically dominate the internal one. This dominance holds particularly when the balance sheet problems associated with the third generation model are present. I now discuss this.

### External versus Internal Balance

Suppose an emerging market has an external financing constraint, which, in extreme form, would be manifested in a sudden stop in capital inflows. The standard way to address this would be to let the real exchange rate depreciate. Although a real depreciation should help relieve the external constraint via both the income effect and price effect (by reducing aggregate demand *and* shifting it toward domestic goods), it could lead to a costly recession when currency mismatches are present: with assets denominated in local currency and liabilities in foreign currency, the depreciation could lead to an increase in nonperforming loans and a bank credit squeeze. Alternatively, consider an emerging market which lowers its interest rate to deal with an unemployment problem. If the capital account is open, this could lead to an exodus from the domestic currency, forcing a depreciation which could create havoc in the presence of currency mismatches. Textbook prescriptions thus fail and may even backfire when the capital account is open and currency mismatches are present. Hence, the dominance of the external over internal balance is more likely to prevail when the capital account is open and firms and banks have currency mismatches on their balance sheets, as in the third generation model.[4]

Summing up, the "three generations" have two critical implications for emerging markets: first, it is not enough to look simply at fiscal and growth fundamentals; one also needs to pay attention to the market's signals on devaluation and default risk. Second, the third generation model has important implications for the government intertemporal budget constraint owing to contingent fiscal liabilities from potential bailouts of the private sector. Its message is clear: watch out for private external debt and currency mismatches.

## Notes

1. The exchange rate does not have to be literally fixed. Managed pegs, crawling pegs, and even inflation-targeting regimes (see Kumhof, Li, and Yan 2007) all fall into the category of regimes vulnerable to speculative attack and collapse.
2. An elegant exposition of this model—on which I have relied—is contained in Calvo (1996). See pp. 7–13 and Figure 1.
3. Various aspects of the third generation model were inspired or developed by Dooley (2000), Krugman (1999), Chang and Velasco (2000), and Burnside, Eichenbaum, and Rebelo (2001). See also Claessens (2005), Frankel and Wei (2005), and Diaz-Alejandro's seminal paper (1985).
4. A compelling account is contained in the annex to Frankel and Wei (2005), from which I have borrowed.

# ANNEX 5: THE SOVEREIGN DEBT RESTRUCTURING MECHANISM (SDRM)

A spate of high-profile crises beginning in the mid-1990s in large emerging markets like Mexico, Thailand, Indonesia, South Korea, Russia, Argentina, and Turkey (in chronological order) sparked a debate in the early 2000s about an efficient resolution mechanism that would benefit both creditors and countries. The IMF proposed the Sovereign Debt Restructuring Mechanism (SDRM) in 2001 "to ensure the orderly and timely restructuring of unsustainable sovereign debts" and reach agreement with a "diffuse group of creditors...to agree collectively to a restructuring that reduces the net present value of its obligations to a manageable level."[1]

Two potential benefits were emphasized: the SDRM would help overcome the collective action problems that contribute to delays in debt restructuring by making the decisions of a qualified majority of creditors binding on all. (It was argued that coordination problems with a multitude of bondholders would be far greater than for a few large creditor banks, as during the1980s debt crisis.) Second, it would provide a more predictable and timely process compared to the current system.

The following concerns were raised at the time: first, debt coverage was limited to external debt even though domestic debt was growing in importance throughout the 1990s. Second, the SDRM process may not have been more predictable as legal challenges could never be ruled out. Third, if, as proposed, the activation of the SDRM were left to the debtor country, the same incentives that lead to procrastination and costly delays in admitting unsustainability (as in Russia in 1998 and Argentina in 2000–01) might apply. Fourth, without some automaticity, for example, linking secondary market prices to apportioning a haircut among different creditor groups, it was not clear how the resolution would be hastened or made more transparent.

The proposal was eventually shelved because strong support from creditor groups and debtor countries alike did not materialize.

## Note

1. Krueger (2002).

# ANNEX 6: IMF'S FLEXIBLE CREDIT LINE

The IMF's Flexible Credit Line (FCL) is an insurance program against confidence shocks: where the emerging market has good fiscal fundamentals and sufficient international liquidity but is vulnerable to contagion or a spillover from an external shock.[1] In other words, it is being protected against a slowdown or sudden stop in capital flows triggered by an event which is no fault of its own. As the FCL Factsheet notes, the program "was designed to meet the increased demand for crisis-prevention and crisis-mitigation lending from countries with very strong policy frameworks and track records in economic performance."

A prime example, which we have become familiar with during the global financial crisis is the so-called safe-haven effect, whereby capital tends to flow to the rich countries when investors become more risk averse; this was starkly captured by opposite movements in bond yields. The yield on the ten-year US Treasury note *fell* substantially between mid-2007 and March 2009 (the nadir of the global financial crisis in the USA), while the spread on the EMBI global composite (a proxy for dollar-denominated emerging market sovereign debt) *rose* substantially over the same period *even though the crisis originated in the financial sector of the USA*. It was not a coincidence that the FCL was unveiled on March 24, 2009, when prospects for exiting the crisis were at their bleakest.

The FCL Factsheet elaborates: "A key objective of the lending reform is to reduce the perceived stigma of borrowing from the IMF, and to encourage countries to ask for assistance before they face a full blown crisis." The eligibility criteria include sustainable public debt and external positions as well as absence of vulnerability to a systemic banking crisis. Countries can borrow between 500 and 1000 percent of quota on a precautionary basis and pay a commitment fee of 24–27 basis points, which is refunded if they decide to draw on the loan, on which the interest rate would be a lot lower than on a market borrowing of the same size.

So far, three countries have signed on: Poland, Mexico, and Colombia; but none has actually drawn upon FCL resources, indicating the insurance nature of the facility. Their respective access would roughly be $10–20 billion for Poland, $23–46 billion for Mexico, and $6–12 billion for Colombia—certainly not the sums these countries could access easily from the market at reasonable interest rates during a confidence shock.

In the same spirit, the Federal Reserve of the US extended swap lines to Brazil, Mexico, and Singapore to enhance dollar liquidity in October 2008; these were to expire on April 30, 2009, but were extended to October 30 of that year.

## Note

1. Information as of September 27, 2012. <http://www.imf.org/external/np/exr/facts/fcl.htm>.

# REFERENCES

Acemoglu, Daron and James Robinson. 2012. *Why Nations Fail: The Origins of Power, Prosperity, and Poverty*. New York: Random House.

Acemoglu, Daron, Simon Johnson, James A. Robinson, and Yunyong Thaichoren. 2003. "Institutional Causes, Macroeconomic Symptoms: Volatility, Crises and Growth." *Journal of Monetary Economics* 50(1): 49–123.

Acharya, Shankar. 2001. "India's Macroeconomic Management in the Nineties." Indian Council for Research on International Economic Relations, New Delhi.

Acharya, Shankar. 2002a. "Macroeconomic Management in the Nineties." *Economic and Political Weekly*, April: 1515–38.

Acharya, Shankar. 2002b. "India's Medium-Term Growth Prospects." *Economic and Political Weekly*, July: 2897–906.

Aghion, Philippe and Olivier Blanchard. 1994. "On the Speed of Transition in Central Europe." Cambridge, MA: NBER Working Paper 4736.

Aghion, Philippe and Steven Durlauf. 2007. "From Growth Theory to Policy Design." Paper written for the Growth Commission. Available at: <http://www.growthcommission.org/storage/cgdev/documents/aghion-durlauf-wbapr3fin.pdf>.

Aghion, Philippe, Olivier Blanchard, and Robin Burgess. 1994. "The Behavior of State Firms in Eastern Europe Pre-Privatization." *European Economic Review* 38: 1327–49.

Aghion, Philippe, Robin Burgess, Stephen Redding, and Fabrizio Zilibotti. 2005. "Entry Liberalization and Inequality in Industrial Performance." *Journal of the European Economic Association* 3(2–3): 291–302.

Ahluwalia, Montek S. 2002a. "India's Vulnerability to External Crisis: An Assessment." In *Macroeconomics and Monetary Policy: Issues for a Reforming Economy. Essays in Honor of C. Rangarajan*, ed. Montek Ahluwalia, S. S. Tarapore, and Y. V. Reddy. Oxford: Oxford University Press.

Ahluwalia, Montek S. 2002b. "Economic Reforms in India since 1991: Has Gradualism Worked?" *Journal of Economic Perspectives* 16: 67–88.

Aizenman, Joshua and Brian Pinto. 2005. *Managing Economic Volatility and Crises: A Practitioner's Guide*. Cambridge: Cambridge University Press.

Aizenman, Joshua and Brian Pinto. 2011. "Managing Financial Integration and Capital Mobility. *Vox*. Available at: <http://www.voxeu.org/index.php?q=node/7058>.

Aizenman, Joshua and Brian Pinto. 2013. "Managing Financial Integration and Capital Mobility: Policy Lessons from the Past Two Decades." *Review of International Economics* 21, 4: 636–53.

Aizenman, Joshua, Kenneth M. Kletzer, and Brian Pinto. 2005. "Sargent-Wallace Meets Krugman-Flood-Garber, or: Why Sovereign Debt Swaps Don't Avert Macroeconomic Crises." *Economic Journal* 115, April: 343–67.

Aizenman, Joshua, Brian Pinto, and Artur Radziwill. 2007. "Sources for Financing Domestic Capital: Is Foreign Saving a Viable Option for Developing Countries?" *Journal of International Money and Finance* 26(5): 682–702.

Akerlof, George and Robert Shiller. 2009. *Animal Spirits: How Human Psychology Drives the Economy, and Why It Matters for Global Capitalism.* Princeton, NJ: Princeton University Press.

Balcerowicz, Leszek. 1994. "Economic Transition in Central and Eastern Europe: Comparisons and Lessons." *Australian Economic Review* 27(1): 47–59.

Bandiera, Luca, Praveen Kumar, and Brian Pinto. 2008. "Kenya's Quest for Growth: Stabilization and Reforms—But Political Stability?" Washington DC: World Bank Policy Research Working Paper WPS 4685.

Belka, M., S. Estrin, M. Schaffer, and I. J. Singh. 1995. "Enterprise Adjustment in Poland: Evidence from a Survey of 200 Private, Privatized, and State-Owned Firms." London School of Economics, Centre for Economic Performance Discussion Paper 233,

Bernanke, Ben S. 2004. "The Great Moderation." Remarks by Governor Ben S. Bernanke at the meetings of the Eastern Economic Association, Washington DC. Available at: <http://www.federalreserve.gov/boarddocs/speeches/2004/20040220/default.htm>.

Bhagwati, Jagdish. 1996. "The Miracle that Did Happen: East Asia in Comparative Perspective." Keynote speech, delivered at conference in honor of Professors Liu and Tsiang, Cornell University, May 3.

Blanchard, Olivier. 2005. "Fiscal Dominance and Inflation Targeting: Lessons from Brazil." In *Inflation Targeting, Debt, and the Brazilian Experience, 1999 to 2003,* ed. Francesco Giavazzi, Ilan Goldfajn, and Santiago Herrera. Cambridge, MA: The MIT Press.

Blanchard, Olivier. 2010. "Institutions, Markets, and Poland's Economic Performance." Speech delivered in Krakow, Poland, June 10.

Bruno, Michael and William Easterly. 1998. "Inflation Crises and Long-Run Growth." *Journal of Monetary Economics* 41: 3–26.

Budina, Nina and Norbert Fiess. 2004. "Public Debt and Its Determinants in *Market Access Countries: Results from 15 Country Case Studies.*" Washington DC: PRMED, the World Bank.

Budina, Nina, Gaobo Pang, and Sweder van Wijnbergen. 2007. "Nigeria's Growth Record: Dutch Disease or Debt Overhang?" Washington DC: World Bank Policy Research Working Paper 4256.

Buiter, Willem H. and Urjit R. Patel. 1992. "Debt, Deficits and Inflation: An Application to the Public Finances of India." *Journal of Public Economics* 47: 171–205.

Burnside, Craig. 2005. *Fiscal Sustainability in Theory and Practice: A Handbook.* Washington, DC: The World Bank.

Burnside, Craig, Martin Eichenbaum, and Sergio Rebelo. 2001. "Prospective Deficits and the Asian Currency Crisis." *Journal of Political Economy* 109: 1155–98.

Caballero, Ricardo J. 2003. "On the International Financial Architecture: Insuring Emerging Markets." NBER Working Paper 9570. Cambridge MA: National Bureau of Economic Research.

Calderon, Cesar, William Easterly, and Luis Servén. 2004. "Infrastructure Compression and Public Sector Solvency in Latin America." In *The Macroeconomics of Infrastructure*, Regional Study, Latin America and Caribbean Region, ed. William Easterly and Luis Servén. Washington, DC: The World Bank.

Calvo, Guillermo A. 1996. "Why is 'The Market' so Unforgiving? Reflections on the Tequilazo." University of Maryland. Available at: <http://drum.lib.umd.edu/bitstream/1903/4031/1/ciecrp4.pdf>.

Calvo, Guillermo A., A. Izquierdo, and E. Talvi. 2002. "Sudden Stops, the Real Exchange Rate and Fiscal Sustainability: Argentina's Lessons." Inter-American Development Bank, Research Department, Mimeo.

Carlin, Wendy, Steven Fries, Mark Schaffer, and Paul Seabright. 2001. "Competition and Enterprise Performance in Transition Economies: Evidence from a Cross-Country Survey." Centre for Economic Policy Research Discussion Paper Series 2840.

Carroll, C., J. Overland, and D. N. Weil. 2000. "Saving and Growth with Habit Formation." *American Economic Review* 90(3): 341–55.

Caselli, Francesco. 2008. "Growth Accounting." In *The New Palgrave Dictionary of Economics*, ed. Steven N. Durlauf and Lawrence E. Blume. Basingstoke: Palgrave Macmillan.

Cerra, Valerie and Sweta Saxena. 2005. "Did Output Recover from the Asian Crisis?" *IMF Staff Papers* 52(1): 1–23.

Chamley, Christophe P. and Brian Pinto. 2011. "Why Official Bailouts Tend Not to Work: An Example Motivated by Greece 2010." *The Economists' Voice* 8(1): Article 3.

Chang, Roberto and Andres Velasco. 2000. "The Asian Financial Crisis in Perspective." In *Private Capital Flows in the Age of Globalization*, ed. Uri Dadush, Dipak Dasgupta, and Marc Uzan. Cambridge, MA: The MIT Press.

Claessens, Stijn. 2005. "Finance and Volatility." In *Managing Economic Volatility and Crises: A Practitioner's Guide*, ed. Joshua Aizenman and Brian Pinto. Cambridge: Cambridge University Press.

Corden, W. Max. 1989. "Debt Relief and Adjustment Incentives." In *Analytical Issues in Debt*. ed. Jacob A. Frenkel, Michael P. Dooley, and Peter Wickham. International Monetary Fund.

DeLong, Bradford J. 2011. "Economics in Crisis." *The Economists' Voice*, May.

DeLong, J. Bradford and Lawrence H. Summers. 1992. "Equipment Investment and Economic Growth: How Strong is the Nexus?" *Brookings Papers on Economic Activity* 2: 157–211.

Denison, Edward F. 1962. *The Sources of Economic Growth in the United States and the Alternatives Before Us*. New York: Committee for Economic Development (711 Fifth Avenue).

Dervis, Kemal. 2005. "Returning from the Brink: Turkey's Efforts at Systemic Change and Structural Reform." In *Development Challenges in the 1990s: Leading Policymakers Speak from Experience*, ed. Timothy Besley and Roberto Zagha. World Bank/Oxford University Press.

Diaz-Alejandro, Carlos. 1985. "Good-Bye Financial Repression, Hello Financial Crash." *Journal of Development Economics* 19(1–2): 1–24.

Dooley, Michael. 2000. "A Model of Crises in Emerging Markets." *The Economic Journal* 110: 256–72. Available at: <http://people.ucsc.edu/~mpd/EJCrisis.pdf>.

Dornbusch, Rudiger. 1980. *Open Economy Macroeconomics*. New York: Basic Books.

Dornbusch, Rudiger and Alejandro Werner. 1994. "Mexico: Stabilization, Reform and No Growth." *Brookings Papers on Economic Activity* 1: 253–315.

Dungey, Mardi, Renee Fry, Brenda Gonzalez-Hermosillo, and Vance Martin. 2006. "Contagion in International Bond Markets during the Russian and the LTCM Crises." *Journal of Financial Stability* 2: 1–27.

Easterly, William. 2001. *The Elusive Quest for Growth: Economists' Adventures and Misadventures in the Tropics*. Cambridge, MA: The MIT Press.

Easterly, William. 2005. "National Policies and Economic Growth: A Reappraisal." In *Handbook of Economic Growth*, ed. Philippe Aghion and Steven N. Durlauf. Elsevier.

Easterly, William and Ross Levine. 2001. "What Have We Learned from a Decade of Empirical Research on Growth? It's Not Factor Accumulation: Stylized Facts and Growth Models." *The World Bank Economic Review* 15(2): 177–219.

Easterly, William and Luis Servén. 2003. *The Limits of Stabilization: Infrastructure, Public Deficits, and Growth in Latin America*. Stanford Social Sciences/The World Bank.

Easterly, William, Roumeen Islam, and Joseph Stiglitz. 2000. "Shaken and Stirred: Explaining Growth Volatility." Paper presented at Annual World Bank Conference on Development Economics. Available at: <http://williameasterly. files.wordpress.com/2010/08/24_easterly_islam_stiglitz_explaininggrowthvolatility_prp.pdf>.

EBRD (European Bank for Reconstruction and Development). 1999. *Transition Report 1999: Ten Years of Transition*. London: European Bank for Reconstruction and Development. Available at: <http://www.ebrd.com/pubs/econo/4050.htm>.

Eichengreen, Barry and Charles Wyplosz. 1993. "The Unstable EMS." *Brookings Papers on Economic Activity* 1: 51–143.

Eichengreen, Barry, Ricardo Hausmann, and Ugo Panizza. 2002. "Original Sin: The Pain, the Mystery, and the Road to Redemption." Paper prepared for the conference "Currency and Maturity Matchmaking: Redeeming Debt from Original Sin." Washington, DC: IADB.

Feldstein, Martin and Charles Horioka. 1980. "Domestic Saving and International Capital Flows." *The Economic Journal* 90: 314–20.

Fischer, Stanley. 1993. "The Role of Macroeconomic Factors in Growth." *Journal of Monetary Economics* 32(3): 485–512.

Fischer, Stanley. 2001. "Exchange Rate Regimes: Is the Bipolar View Correct?" *Finance & Development* 38(2). Available at: <http://www.imf.org/external/pubs/ft/fandd/2001/06/fischer.htm>.

Fischer, Stanley, Ratna Sahay, and Carlos Vegh. 1996. "Stabilization and Growth in Transition Economies: The Early Experience." *Journal of Economic Perspectives* 10(2): 45–66.

Flood, Robert and Peter Garber. 1984. "Collapsing Exchange Rate Regimes: Some Linear Examples." *Journal of International Economics* 17, 1–13.

Fonseka, Daminda, Brian Pinto, Mona Prasad, and Francis Rowe. 2012. "Sri Lanka: From Peace Dividend to Sustained Growth Acceleration." World Bank Policy Research Working Paper 6192. Available at: <http://www-wds.worldbank.org/external/default/WDSContentServer/IW3P/IB/2012/09/06/000158349_20120906090938/Rendered/PDF/wps6192.pdf>.

Forbes, Naushad. 2002. "Doing Business in India: What has Liberalization Changed?" In *Economic Policy Reforms and the Indian Economy*, ed. Anne O. Krueger. Chicago: The University of Chicago Press.

Frankel, Jeffrey A. and Alan T. MacArthur. 1988. "Political vs. Currency Premia in International Real Interest Differentials: A Study of Forward Rates for 24 Countries." *European Economic Review* 32(5): 1083–114.

Frankel, Jeffrey A. and Shang-Jin Wei. 2005. "Managing Macroeconomic Crises: Policy Lessons." In *Managing Economic Volatility and Crises: A Practitioner's Guide*, ed. Joshua Aizenman and Brian Pinto. Cambridge: Cambridge University Press.

Frydman, Roman and Stanislaw Wellisz. 1991. "The Ownership-Control Structure and the Behavior of Polish Enterprises during the 1990 Reforms: Macroeconomic Measures and Microeconomic Response." In *Reforming Central and Eastern European Economies: Initial Results and Challenges*, ed. Vittorio Corbo, Fabrizio Coricelli, and Jan Bossak. Washington: World Bank Symposium.

Gaddy, Clifford G. and Barry W. Ickes. 1998. "Russia's Virtual Economy." *Foreign Affairs* 77(5): 53–67.

GC (Commission on Growth and Development). 2008. *The Growth Report: Strategies for Sustained Growth and Inclusive Development*. The World Bank. Available at: <http://siteresources.worldbank.org/EXTPREMNET/Resources/489960-1338997241035/Growth_Commission_Final_Report.pdf>.

Giavazzi, Francesco, Ilan Goldfajn, and Santiago Herrera. 2005. *Inflation Targeting, Debt, and the Brazilian Experience, 1999 to 2003*. Cambridge, MA: The MIT Press.

Gill, Indermit and Brian Pinto. 2005. "Sovereign Debt in Developing Countries with Market Access: Help or Hindrance?" In *Financial Crises: Lessons from the Past, Preparation for the Future*, ed. Gerard Caprio, James A. Hanson, and Robert E. Litan. Washington: Brookings Institution Press.

Giovannini, Alberto and Martha de Melo. 1993. "Government Revenue from Financial Repression." *American Economic Review* 83(4): 953–63.

Godbole, Madhav. 1997. "Pay Revision: High Cost of Total Surrender." *Economic and Political Weekly*, October: 2506–7.

Goldstein, Morris. 2003. "Debt Sustainability, Brazil, and the IMF." Institute for International Economics Working Paper 03-1.

Goldstein, Morris and Philip Turner. 2004. *Controlling Currency Mismatches in Emerging Markets*. Washington DC: Institute for International Economics.

Gourinchas, Pierre-Olivier and Olivier Jeanne. 2006. "The Elusive Gains from International Financial Integration." *Review of Economic Studies* 73, 715–41.

Gourinchas, Pierre-Olivier and Olivier Jeanne. 2007. "Capital Flows to Developing Countries: The Allocation Puzzle." Cambridge, MA: NBER Working Paper W13602.

Green, Russell and Tom Torgerson. 2007. "Are High Foreign Exchange Reserves in Emerging Markets a Blessing or a Burden?" Department of the Treasury, Office of International Affairs Occasional Paper 6.

Grossman, Gene M. and Elhanan Helpman. 1994. "Endogenous Innovation in the Theory of Growth." *Journal of Economic Perspectives* 8(1) Winter: 23–44.

Hausmann, Ricardo, Dani Rodrik, and Andres Velasco. 2005. "Growth Diagnostics." Available at: <http://ksghome.harvard.edu/~drodrik/barcelonafinalmarch2005.pdf>.

Hevia, Constantino and Norman Loayza. 2013. "Saving and Growth in Sri Lanka." World Bank Policy Research Working Paper 6300. Available at: <http://elibrary.worldbank.org/doi/pdf/10.1596/1813-9450-6300>.

Hnatkovska, Viktoria and Norman Loayza. 2005. "Volatility and Growth." In *Managing Economic Volatility and Crises: A Practitioner's Guide*, ed. Joshua Aizenman and Brian Pinto. Cambridge: Cambridge University Press.

IDA and IMF (International Development Association and International Monetary Fund). 2011. *Heavily Indebted Poor Countries (HIPC) Initiative and Multilateral Debt Relief Initiative (MDRI): Status of Implementation and Proposals for the Future of the HIPC Initiative*, November. Available at: <http://siteresources.worldbank.org/INTDEBTDEPT/ProgressReports/23063134/HIPC_MDRI_StatusOfImplementation2011.pdf>.

IDB (Inter-American Development Bank). 2007. *Living with Debt: How to Limit the Risks of Sovereign Finance*. Economic and Social Progress in Latin America 2007 Report.

IEO (Independent Evaluation Office of the IMF). 2004. *Report on the Evaluation of the Role of the IMF in Argentina, 1991–2001*, July. Available at: <http://www.imf.org/EXTERNAL/NP/IEO/2004/ARG/ENG/INDEX.HTM>.

IMF (International Monetary Fund). 2001. *Turkey: Sixth and Seventh Reviews under the Stand-By Arrangement; Staff Supplement; and Press Release on the Executive Board Discussion*. IMF Country Report No. 01/89, June.

IMF (International Monetary Fund). 2003. *World Economic Outlook: Public Debt in Emerging Markets*, September.

IMF (International Monetary Fund). 2004. *Kenya: Selected Issues and Statistical Appendix*. Issued as IMF Country Report No. 09/192, June 2009. Available at: <http://www.imf.org/external/pubs/ft/scr/2009/cr09192.pdf>.

IMF (International Monetary Fund). 2008. *World Economic and Financial Surveys. Regional Economic Outlook: Sub-Saharan Africa. APR08*. Washington, DC: International Monetary Fund.

IMF (International Monetary Fund). 2009. *Ghana: 2009 Article IV Consultation*. IMF Country Report No. 09/256, August. Available at: <http://www.imf.org/external/pubs/ft/scr/2009/cr09256.pdf>.

IMF (International Monetary Fund). 2010. *Ghana*. IMF Country Report No. 10/178. Available at: <http://www.imf.org/external/pubs/ft/scr/2010/cr10178.pdf>.

IMF (International Monetary Fund). 2011a. *Statement at the Conclusion of an IMF Mission to Ghana*. Press Release No.11/59, March 1, 2011. Available at: <http://www.imf.org/external/np/sec/pr/2011/pr1159.htm>.

IMF (International Monetary Fund). 2011b. *Fiscal Monitor: Addressing Fiscal challenges to Reduce Economic Risks*, September. Available at: <http://www.imf.org/external/pubs/ft/fm/2011/02/pdf/fm1102.pdf>.

IMF (International Monetary Fund). 2012. *Ghana: Fifth Review under the Three-Year Arrangement under the Extended Credit Facility—Staff Report*. IMF Country Report No. 12/36. Available at: <http://www.imf.org/external/pubs/ft/scr/2012/cr1236.pdf>.

IMF (International Monetary Fund). 2013. *India: 2013 Article IV Consultation*. IMF Country Report No. 13/37, February. Available at: <http://www.imf.org/external/pubs/ft/scr/2013/cr1337.pdf>.

India, Planning Commission. 2002. *Tenth Five Year Plan 2002–2007*, vol. 1: *Dimensions and Strategies*. New Delhi. Available at: <http://planningcommission.nic.in/plans/planrel/fiveyr/10th/volume1/10th_vol1.pdf>.

Jeanne, Olivier. 1999. "Comment." In *Essays in Honor of Robert P. Flood, Jr.*, ed. Peter Isard, Assaf Razin, and Andrew K. Rose. Kluwer Academic.

Jorion, Philippe. 2000. "Risk Management Lessons from Long-Term Capital Management." *European Financial Management* 6: 277–300.

Kharas, Homi. 2008. "Measuring the Cost of Aid Volatility." The Brookings Institution, Wolfensohn Center for Development Working Paper 3. Available at: <http://www.brookings.edu/~/media/research/files/papers/2008/7/aid%20volatility%20kharas/07_aid_volatility_kharas.pdf>.

Kharas, Homi and Brian Pinto. 1989. "Exchange Rate Rules, Black Market Premia and Fiscal Deficits: The Bolivian Hyperinflation." *Review of Economic Studies* 56: 435–48.

Kharas, Homi, Brian Pinto, and Sergei Ulatov. 2001. "An Analysis of Russia's 1998 Meltdown: Fundamentals and Market Signals." *Brookings Papers on Economic Activity* 1.

Kletzer, Kenneth and Renu Kohli. 2001. "Financial Repression and Exchange Rate Management in Developing Countries: Theory and Empirical Evidence for India." IMF Working Paper WP/01/103.

Kornai, János. 1986. "The Soft Budget Constraint." *Kyklos* 39(1): 3–30.

Krueger, Anne. 2002. "New Approaches to Sovereign Debt Restructuring: An Update on Our Thinking." Paper prepared for the conference "Sovereign Debt Workouts: Hopes and Hazards," Institute for International Economics, Washington, April 1.

Krugman, Paul. 1979. "A Model of Balance-of-Payments Crises." *Journal of Money, Credit and Banking* 11: 311–25.

Krugman, Paul. 1988. "Financing versus Forgiving a Debt Overhang." *Journal of Development Economics* 29: 253–68.

Krugman, Paul. 1994. "The Myth of Asia's Miracle." *Foreign Affairs* 73(6): 62–78. Available at: <http://web.mit.edu/krugman/www/myth.html>.

Krugman, Paul. 1999. "Balance Sheets, the Transfer Problem, and Financial Crises." In *International Finance and Financial Crises: Essays in Honor of Robert P. Flood, Jr.*, ed. Peter Isard, Assaf Razin, and Andrew K. Rose. Kluwer Academic.

Krugman, Paul. 2009. *The Return of Depression Economics and the Crisis of 2008*. New York: Norton.

Kumhof, Michael, Shujing Li, and Isabel Yan. 2007. "Balance of Payments Crises under Inflation Targeting." *Journal of International Economics* 72: 242–64. Available at: <http://www.stanford.edu/~kumhof/jie2007-kly.pdf>.

Laeven, Luc and Fabian Valencia. 2008. "Systemic Banking Crises: A New Database." IMF Working Paper WP/08/224.

Lin, Justin Yifu and David Rosenblatt. 2012. "Shifting Patterns of Economic Growth and Rethinking Development." World Bank Policy Research Working Paper 6040. Available at: <https://openknowledge.worldbank.org/bitstream/handle/10986/6043/WPS6040.pdf?sequence=1>.

Lipton, David and Jeffrey Sachs. 1990a. "Creating a Market Economy in Eastern Europe: The Case of Poland." *Brookings Papers on Economic Activity* 1: 75–133.

Lipton, David and Jeffrey Sachs. 1990b. "Privatization in Eastern Europe: The Case of Poland." *Brookings Papers on Economic Activity* 2: 293–341.

Lucas, Robert E., Jr. 1988. "On the Mechanics of Economic Development." *Journal of Monetary Economics* 22: 3–42.

Lucas, Robert E., Jr. 1990. "Why Doesn't Capital Flow from Rich to Poor Countries?" *American Economic Review* 80(2): 92–6, Papers and Proceedings of the Hundred and Second Annual Meeting of the American Economic Association (May).

McKinnon, Ronald, I. 1993. *The Order of Economic Liberalization: Financial Control in the Transition to a Market Economy*. Baltimore, MD: Johns Hopkins University Press.

Mankiw, N. Gregory, David Romer, and David N. Weil. 1992. "A Contribution to the Empirics of Economic Growth." *Quarterly Journal of Economics* 107(2): 407–37.

Mody, Ashoka, Anusha Nath, and Michael Walton. 2011. "Sources of Corporate Profits in India: Business Dynamism or Advantages of Entrenchment?" IMF Working Paper WP/11/8. Available at: <http://www.imf.org/external/pubs/ft/wp/2011/wp1108.pdf>.

Mohan, Rakesh. 2004. "Finance for Industrial Growth." *RBI Bulletin*, March.

Mohan, Rakesh. 2011. *Growth with Financial Stability: Central Banking in an Emerging Market*. Oxford: Oxford University Press.

Mor, Nachiket, R. Chandrasekhar, and Diviya Wahi. 2006. "Banking Sector Reform in India." In *China and India: Learning from Each Other. Reforms and Policies for Sustained Growth*, ed. Jehangir Aziz, Steven Dunaway, and Eswar Prasad. International Monetary Fund. Available at: <http://www.imf.org/External/Pubs/FT/seminar/2006/ChiInd/Eng/chiind1.pdf>.

Mussa, Michael. 2002. *Argentina and the Fund: From Triumph to Tragedy*. Washington, DC: Institute for International Economics.

Myers, Stewart. 1977. "The Determinants of Corporate Borrowing." *Journal of Financial Economics* 5, 147–75.

OECD. 2006. *OECD Economic Surveys Brazil*. Vol. 2006/18, November.

Okonjo-Iweala, Ngozi. 2008. "Nigeria's Shot at Redemption: Turning Nigeria's Oil Windfall into a Blessing." *Finance & Development*, December: 42–4.

Okonjo-Iweala, Ngozi. 2010. "What's the Big Idea? To Position Africa as the Fifth BRIC—a Destination for Investment, Not Just Aid." Harvard Kennedy School, May 14. Available at: <http://www.africacncl.org/(ipw4ooekvaqsb4vrffjltwva)/blobdnld.aspx?6b6c47e9-df6e-4cc6-902c-5e70ca236ef5>.

Okonjo-Iweala, Ngozi. 2012. *Reforming the Unreformable: Lessons from Nigeria*. Cambridge, MA, and London: The MIT Press.

Oura, Hiroko. 2007. "Wild or Tamed? India's Potential Growth." IMF Working Paper WP/07/24.

Pack, Howard. 1994. "Endogenous Growth Theory: Intellectual Appeal and Empirical Shortcomings." *Journal of Economic Perspectives* 8(1), Winter: 55–72.

Pang, Gaobo, Brian Pinto, and Marina Wes. 2007. "India Rising: Faster Growth, Lower Indebtedness." World Bank Policy Research Working Paper WPS 4241.

Parks, Richard. 1978. "Inflation and Relative Price Variability." *Journal of Political Economy* 86(1): 79–95.

Pinto, Brian. 1987. "Nigeria During and After the Oil Boom: A Policy Comparison with Indonesia." *The World Bank Economic Review* 1(3): 419–45.

Pinto, Brian. 1990. "Black Market Premia, Exchange Rate Unification and Inflation in Sub-Saharan Africa." *World Bank Economic Review* 3(3): 321–38.

Pinto, Brian. 1991. "Black Markets for Foreign Exchange, Real Exchange Rates and Inflation." *Journal of International Economics* 30: 121–35.

Pinto, Brian. 1996. "Russia after Yeltsin's Re-Election: An Economic Report." International Finance Corporation, Mimeo.

Pinto, Brian and Sweder van Wijnbergen. 1995. "Ownership and Corporate Control in Poland: Why State Firms Defied the Odds." CEPR Discussion Paper Series 1273.

Pinto, Brian and Farah Zahir. 2004. "Why Fiscal Adjustment Now." *Economic and Political Weekly*, March 6: 1039–48.

Pinto, Brian and Shinsuke Tanaka. 2005. "Sovereign Debt Swaps with Private Creditors." The World Bank, PREM Anchor PRMED Note.

Pinto, Brian and Sergei Ulatov. 2012. "Financial Globalization and the Russian Crisis of 1998." In *The Evidence and Impact of Financial Globalization*, ed. Gerard Caprio. Academic Press/Elsevier.

Pinto, Brian, Marek Belka, and Stefan Krajewski. 1992. "Microeconomics of Transformation in Poland: A Survey of State Enterprise Responses." World Bank Policy Research Working Paper WPS 982.

Pinto, Brian, Marek Belka, and Stefan Krajewski. 1993. "Transforming State Enterprises in Poland: Evidence on Adjustment by Manufacturing Firms." *Brookings Papers on Economic Activity* 1: 213–70.

Pinto, Brian, Vladimir Drebentsov, and Alexander Morozov. 2000a. "Dismantling Russia's Nonpayments System: Creating Conditions for Growth." World Bank Technical Paper 471.

Pinto, Brian, Vladimir Drebentsov, and Alexander Morozov. 2000b. "Give Macroeconomic Stability and Growth in Russia a Chance: Harden Budgets by Eliminating Non-Payments." *Economics of Transition* 8(2): 297–324.

Pinto, Brian, Evsey Gurvich, and Sergei Ulatov. 2005. "Lessons from the Russian Crisis of 1998 and Recovery." In *Managing Economic Volatility and Crises: A Practitioner's Guide*, ed. Joshua Aizenman and Brian Pinto. Cambridge: Cambridge University Press.

Poddar, Tushar and Eva Yi. 2007. "India's Rising Growth Potential." Goldman Sachs Global Research Centres, Global Economics Paper 152.

Prasad, Eswar S., Raghuram G. Rajan, and Arvind Subramanian. 2007. "Foreign Capital and Economic Growth." *Brookings Papers on Economic Activity* 1: 153–209.

Raddatz, Claudio. 2007. "Are External Shocks Responsible for the Instability of Output in Low-Income Countries?" *Journal of Development Economics* 84: 155–87.

Radelet, Steven. 2010. *Emerging Africa: How 17 Countries are Leading the Way*. Center for Global Development.

Ramey, Garey and Valerie A. Ramey. 1995. "Cross-Country Evidence on the Link between Volatility and Growth." *American Economic Review* 85(5): 1138–51.

Rangarajan, C. and D. K. Srivastava. 2005. "Fiscal Deficits and Government Debt: Implications for Growth and Stabilisation." *Economic and Political Weekly*, July: 2919–33.

Reinhart, Carmen and Kenneth Rogoff. 2010a. "Growth in a Time of Debt." *American Economic Review: Papers and Proceedings* 100: 573–8.

Reinhart, Carmen and Kenneth Rogoff. 2010b. "Debt and Growth Revisited." *VOX*, August 11.

Reinhart, Carmen, Kenneth Rogoff, and Miguel Savastano. 2003. "Debt Intolerance." *Brookings Papers on Economic Activity* 1: 1–74.

Reserve Bank of India. 2002. *Report on Currency and Finance 2000–01*. Mumbai: RBI.

Richter, Tomas. 2011. "Tunneling: The Effect—and the Cause—of Bad Corporate Law." *Columbia Journal of European Law* 17(1): 23–55.

Rodrik, Dani. 1999. "Where Did All the Growth Go? External Shocks, Social Conflict and Growth Collapses." *Journal of Economic Growth* 4(4): 385–412.

Rodrik, Dani. 2008. "Spence Christens a New Washington Consensus." *The Economists' Voice* 5(3): Article 4.

Romer, Paul. 1994. "The Origins of Endogenous Growth." *Journal of Economic Perspectives* 8(1): 3–22.

Romer, Paul. 1986. "Increasing Returns and Long-Run Growth." *Journal of Political Economy* 94(5): 1002–37.

Sachs, Jeffrey. 1989. "The Debt Overhang of Developing Countries." In *Debt, Stabilization and Development: Essays in Memory of Carlos Diaz-Alejandro*, ed. Guillermo Calvo, Ronald Findlay, Pentti Kouri, and Jorge Braga de Macedo. Oxford: Blackwell.

Sachs, Jeffrey. 1990. "Introduction." In *Developing Country Debt and Economic Performance*, vol. 2: *The Country Studies: Argentina, Bolivia, Brazil, Mexico*, ed. Jeffrey Sachs. Chicago: The University of Chicago Press.

Sala-i-Martin, Xavier. 1990. "Lecture Notes on Economic Growth (I): Introduction to the Literature and Neoclassical Models." Cambridge, MA: NBER Working Paper 3563.

Sargent, Thomas J. and Neil Wallace. 1981. "Some Unpleasant Monetaristic Arithmetic." *Federal Reserve Bank of Minneapolis Quarterly Review* Fall: 1–17.

Servén, Luis. 2007. "Fiscal Rules, Public Investment and Growth." World Bank Policy Research Working Paper WPS 4382.

Servén, Luis and Guillermo Perry. 2005. "Argentina's Macroeconomic Collapse: Causes and Lessons." In *Managing Economic Volatility and Crises: A Practitioner's Guide*, ed. Joshua Aizenman and Brian Pinto. Cambridge: Cambridge University Press.

Soderbom, M. 2004. "Productivity, Exports and Firm Dynamics in Kenya 1999–2002." University of Oxford, Department of Economics, Centre for the Study of African Economies, CSAE Paper.

Solow, Robert M. 1956. "A Contribution to the Theory of Economic Growth." *Quarterly Journal of Economics* 70(1): 65–94.

Solow, Robert M. 1957. "Technical Change and the Aggregate Production Function." *Review of Economics and Statistics* 39(3): 312–20.

Solow, Robert M. 1994. "Perspectives on Growth Theory." *Journal of Economic Perspectives* 8 (1): 45–54.

Srinivasan, T. N. 2002. "India's Fiscal Situation: Is a Crisis Ahead?" In *Economic Policy Reforms and the Indian Economy*, ed. Anne O. Krueger. Chicago: The University of Chicago Press.

Steeves, Jeffrey. 2006. "Presidential Succession in Kenya: The Transition from Moi to Kibaki." *Commonwealth & Comparative Politics* 44(2): 211–33.

Sturzenegger, Federico and Holger Wolf. 2004. "Developing Country Debt: An Overview of Theory, Evidence, Options." The World Bank, PREM Anchor Background Paper.

Topalova, Petia. 2004. "Overview of the Indian Corporate Sector: 1989–2002." IMF Working Paper 64.

Topalova, Petia and Amit Khandelwal. 2011. "Trade Liberalization and Firm Productivity: The Case of India." *Review of Economics and Statistics* 93(3): 995–1009.

Tornell, Aaron and Philip R. Lane. 1999. "The Voracity Effect." *American Economic Review* 89(1): 22–46.

Torre, Augusto de la, Eduardo Levy Yeyati, and Sergio Schmukler. 2003. "Living and Dying with Hard Pegs: The Rise and Fall of Argentina's Currency Board." Universidad Torcuata di Tella, Centro de Investigacion en Finanzas Working Paper. Available at: <http://www.utdt.edu/Upload/CIF_wp/wpcif-032003.pdf>.

Van Wijnbergen, Sweder and Nina Budina. 2001. "Inflation Stabilization, Fiscal Deficits and Public Debt Management in Poland." *Journal of Comparative Economics* 29: 293–309.

Van Wijnbergen, Sweder. 1984. "The 'Dutch Disease': A Disease After All?" *The Economic Journal* 94(373): 41–55.

Warutere, Peter. 2005. "The Goldenberg Conspiracy: The Game of Paper Gold, Money and Power." The Institute for Security Studies Occasional Paper 177, September. Available at: <http://www.issafrica.org/static/templates/tmpl_html.php?node_id=318&slink_id=381&slink_type=12&link_id=28>.

Williamson, John. 1990. "What Washington Means by Policy Reform." In *Latin American Adjustment: How Much Has Happened?* ed. John Williamson. Washington DC: Institute for International Economics.

Williamson, John. 2000. "What Should the World Bank Think of the Washington Consensus?" *The World Bank Research Observer* 15(2): 251–64.

Williamson, John. 2002. "Is Brazil Next?" *International Economics Policy Brief 02-7*. Washington, DC: Institute of International Economics.

Williamson, John. 2008. "Letter: The Spence Commission and the Washington Consensus." *The Economists' Voice* 5(4): Article 4.

World Bank. 2003a. *India: Sustaining Reform, Reducing Poverty*, World Bank Development Policy Review. New Delhi: Oxford University Press.

World Bank. 2003b. *Kenya: Investment Climate Assessment*. Washington, DC: World Bank.

World Bank. 2006. *Inclusive Growth and Service Delivery: Building on India's Success*. Basingtoke: Palgrave Macmillan.

World Bank. 2007. *Kenya: Investment Climate Assessment*. Washington, DC: World Bank.

Young, Alwyn. 1995. "The Tyranny of Numbers: Confronting the Statistical Realities of the East Asian Growth Experience." *Quarterly Journal of Economics* 110(3): 641–80.

# INDEX

Note: "n." after a page reference indicates the number of a note on that page

1980s debt crisis  6, 36–8, 47, 225
1997–2001 crises  38, 176, 178
   *see also* crises of 1997–2001
   *see also* emerging market crises of 1997–2001

Abacha, Sani  1
accumulation  30
Acemoglu, Daron  14 n. 3, 48, 49
Acharya, Shankar  113 n. 5, 114 n. 9
Africa  187, 188, 194, 196
   *see also specific countries*
African Development Bonds  194
African Union  195
Aghion, Philippe  26, 42–3, 45, 60, 70, 113, 114
   n. 16, 193
Ahluwalia, Montek S.  113 n. 5, 114 n. 6
aid  188, 193–5, 198
Aizenman, Joshua  37, 40, 48, 52 n. 8, 87, 137 n.
   15, 137 n. 16, 162, 175, 176, 180 n. 8, 180 n.
   13, 180 n. 14, 200 n. 2, 216 n. 1
Akerlof, George A.  1, 14 n. 1
arap Moi, Daniel  77–8, 83, 85–6, 89, 90, 91
Argentina
   balance sheet mismatches  145
   debt crisis  3, 7, 12, 38, 52 n. 4, 98, 100, 141
   debt swap  132, 133–4, 186, 217–18
   exchange rate regime  12, 60, 72, 145, 180 n. 4
   government debt sustainability
      problems  172
   inflation  150
   lessons  163, 166
   second generation models  143
   self-insurance  112
   unsustainable debt dynamics  145
arrears
   Ghana  189
   Russia  116, 117, 118, 124, 128, 129
Asian growth miracle  25–6

balance sheet currency mismatches  100
Balcerowicz, Leszek  56, 57, 61, 74, 75 n. 4

Bandiera, Luca  88, 89
Bank of England (BoE)  223
banks  192, 197
   Brazil  199
   Ghana  189
   India  100, 107
   Kenya  82
   Poland  64, 65, 67–8, 69, 70, 72
   Turkey  163, 164, 166
barter, Russia  9–11, 116–17, 118, 122, 124, 128,
   129, 133
Belka, Marek  61, 63, 70, 73, 75 n. 1, 75 n. 7,
   75 n. 8
Berlin Wall  6
Bernanke, Ben  14 n. 5
Bhagwati, Jagdish  209 n. 4
black market exchange rate  6, 7, 47
   Nigeria  8
   Poland  56, 57
Blanchard, Olivier  55, 56, 70, 75 n. 3, 158, 161
   n. 16, 180 n. 11
Blustein, Paul  135
Brady deals  6, 37
Brazil  6, 152–9
   binding constraint to growth  38, 40–1, 42
   credit and inflation history  186
   creditworthiness  167, 186
   debt crisis  3, 6, 7, 12, 141
   exchange rate regime  145
   Federal Reserve's swap lines  228
   financial engineering  153–6
   fiscal space  153, 156–9
   global financial crisis  4
   government debt sustainability
      problems  171
   growth fundamentals  199
   primary surpluses  83
   self-insurance  112, 171
   sovereign credit rating  162
Bruno, Michael  136 n. 2

Budina, Nina 51, 75, 76 n. 15, 114 n. 11
Buiter, Willem H. 100, 113 n. 3
Bundesbank 223
Burgess, Robin 70
Burnside, Craig 37, 160 n. 6, 216 n. 5, 224 n. 3
Bush, George W. 135

Caballero, Ricardo J. 169, 170
Calderon, Cesar, 151–2
Calvo, Guillermo A. 218, 224 n. 2
capital account liberalization 19–22, 29, 207, 208, 111–12, 197
 India 97, 101, 159, 186
 *see also* open capital accounts
capital controls, India 110
capital flight 52 n. 4
 Russia 130
capital intensity 21, 22
capital–labor ratios 19, 21, 25, 26
Carlin, Wendy 76 n. 14
Carroll, Christopher 30
Caselli, Francesco 208
catalytic approach to a capital account
 crisis 134
CBR 121
Central Statistical Office, Poland (GUS) 62
Cerra, Valerie 160 n. 1
Chamley, Christophe P. 132, 137 n. 14
Chandrasekhar, R. 107
Chang, Roberto 160 n. 5, 160 n. 6, 224 n. 3
Chile 147
China 196
 and African economic developments 187
 growth fundamentals 199
 national savings and growth 26, 27
 political stability and social cohesion 92
 productivity 22
 savings rates 178, 183
China Development Bank 191
Cienski, Jan 75 n. 2
Claessens, Stijn 160 n. 5, 160 n. 6, 224 n. 3
Clark, Lindley H. Jr. 76 n. 13
closed economy 176
collateralized debt obligations (CDOs) 169
Colombia 227
Commission on Growth and Development
 (GC) 33–5, 36
competition 17, 183, 184–5, 191, 197, 198
 governance 183
 growth policy package 42, 43, 44, 45, 50
 Poland 60, 71, 72, 74
 savings rates and TFP growth 183
 *see also* import competition; micropolicy trio
competitive real exchange rates 17, 183, 185, 191, 198
 1980s debt crisis 38
 growth policy package 42, 43, 44–5, 46, 52
 Poland 59, 60, 71, 72, 73
 Russia 121
 savings rates and TFP growth 184

self-insurance 174, 179
 *see also* micropolicy trio
compulsory dividend, Poland 58, 59, 62, 64
contagion, Russia 135
contingent bonds 169
contingent liabilities
 Ghana 189
 self-insurance 170, 171, 173
conventional wisdom 8, 32, 53, 95
 Russia 117
Corden, W. Max 37
corruption 32
 Kenya 77, 80, 93
cost of capital 192
 Kenya 83–5, 90, 91
Cottarelli, Carlo 180 n. 11
Council of Mutual Economic Assistance
 (CMEA) 61, 63, 64, 66, 67, 68, 72, 73, 74
country economic analysis 6–13
crawling peg, Turkey 163, 165, 167
crises of 1997–2001 141, 145, 147–8
crisis literature 142
crisis of the 1980s 36–8, 47
Crockett, Andrew 176
Czech Republic 55, 71–2, 73

de Melo, Martha 114 n. 8
debt intolerance 139, 147–8, 149, 150–1, 160, 186
 Brazil 152, 153, 154, 158
 open capital accounts 159
 self-insurance 178
 Turkey 162
debt structure 149
 Brazil 153–4
decapitalization, Poland 58, 59, 63–4, 65
default risk premium, Russia 125–7, 129
DeLong, Bradford J. 15 n. 7, 30, 90
Denison, Edward F. 19, 42
Dervis, Kemal 167–8
devaluation risk premium, Russia 125–6, 127, 129
development finance institutions (DFIs),
 India 106, 107
Diaz-Alejandro, Carlos 111, 145, 147, 160 n. 6, 200 n. 5, 224 n. 3
diminishing marginal returns 20, 205, 206
Dobbs, Michael 135
domestic financial liberalization, India 111–12
domestic volatility 47–9, 197–8
 Kenya 79
Dooley, Michael 160 n. 6, 224 n. 3
Dornbusch, Rudiger 14 n. 6, 46, 131, 136 n. 7, 164
Drebentsov, Vladimir 15 n. 9, 137 n. 11, 137 n. 12
Dungey, Mardi 137 n. 17, 137 n. 18
Durlauf, Steven 43
Dutch Disease 6, 7, 49, 51

East Asian crisis 3, 4, 6, 12, 52 n. 3, 141, 223
  balance sheet mismatches 145
  exchange rate regimes 145
  Russia 121–2
  self-insurance 171
  third generation models 143–5, 146, 147, 222
Easterly, William 14 n. 2, 31 n. 6, 48, 136 n. 2, 141, 151–2, 161 n. 17
economic fundamentals, Kenya 93
Economic Transformation Program (Poland) 56
Economist Intelligence Unit (EIU)
  Kenya 80
  Russia 121
Edwards, Sebastian 14 n. 6
effective tariff rate, India 106
Eichenbaum, Martin 160 n. 6, 216 n. 5, 224 n. 3
Eichengreen, Barry 148, 149, 161 n. 8
emerging market crises of 1997–2001 3, 5, 36, 38, 118–19, 145, 186, 200, 211
endogeneity 119
endogenous growth 20, 22–31, 40, 193, 196
entry barriers, India 108, 109
Eurobonds 188–9
  Ghana 188–92
  GKO–Eurobond swap 126–7, 132–4, 186, 217–18
  Kenya 77, 78
European Bank for Reconstruction and Development (EBRD) 76 n. 14
European Union
  Exchange Rate Mechanism crisis 142, 222, 223
  growth compared with that of the US 43
exchange rate-based stabilization, Turkey 164, 165, 166–7
Exchange Rate Mechanism (ERM) crisis 223
  second generation crisis models 142, 146, 222
exit strategy, Turkey 163
expropriation risks 32
external debt overhang 152, 161 n. 12
  growth policy package 36, 37
external volatility 47, 198

Federal Reserve
  Long-Term Capital Management 135
  swap lines 228
  taper 4, 5, 199
Feldstein, Martin 176
Feldstein–Horioka puzzle 176
Fiess, Norbert 114 n. 11
financial fragility 145, 147
financial globalization 175, 176
financial integration 175, 177
firm-level restructuring, India 106
first generation crisis models 142, 145, 146, 221, 223–4
fiscal credibility, Turkey 167
fiscal deficit identity 39
fiscal fundamentals 149, 150, 159–60, 186

fiscal profligacy 222
  India 96, 98, 101, 102
fiscal solvency 37, 119, 148
  problem 213
  Russia 120, 127, 131–2
  self-insurance 173–4
fiscal space 36, 41, 139, 142, 148, 150–2, 186, 193
  aid agenda 195
  Brazil 153, 156–9
  Eurobonds 189
  India 112
  self-insurance 178
Fischer, Stanley 12, 15 n. 14, 115, 118, 119, 120, 121, 122, 180 n. 6, 218
Fitch Ratings, Turkey 162, 180 n. 10
fixed exchange rate 145, 159
  third generation crisis models 144, 222
Flexible Credit Line (FCL) 174, 227–8
flexible exchange rates 38
  India 100
  self-insurance 173–4, 178
  Turkey 173
Flood, Robert 160 n. 2
Fonseka, Daminda 29
Forbes, Naushad 108
foreign direct investment (FDI) 196
  neoclassical growth economics 21, 22, 29
  Poland 60
  productivity gaps 177
foreign portfolio investors 177
Frankel, Jeffrey A. 94 n. 6, 146, 160 n. 6, 216 n. 5, 224 n. 3, 224 n. 4
Frydman, Roman 58–9, 63, 65, 75 n. 6

Gaddy, Clifford G. 10, 129
Garber, Peter 160 n. 2
Gazprom 10, 128
Germany
  reunification 223
  safe haven 174
Ghana 187–92, 193
  as emerging country 187
  lessons 196
Ghana Telecom 189
Giavazzi, Francesco 154, 158, 161 n. 14, 161 n. 15
Gill, Indermit 160 n. 7, 161 n. 9, 178–9, 180 n. 12, 181 n. 17, 216 n. 4
Giovannini, Alberto 114 n. 8
GKO–Eurobond swap 126–7, 132–4, 186, 217–18
global financial crisis 3, 142
  Brazil 162
  fiscal space 152
  Lehman Brothers bankruptcy 173
  Nigeria 51
  Poland 55
  recovery 198
  resilience of developing countries 4, 179

global financial crisis (*Cont.*)
  safe-haven effect 227
  self-insurance 168–70, 171
  Turkey 162
global technological frontier *see* technological
  frontier
Godbole, Madhav 114 n. 9
Goldenberg scandal 81–2, 85, 192
Goldfajn, Ilan 154, 158, 161 n. 14, 161 n. 15
Goldman Sachs 182
Goldstein, Morris 149, 157
Gore, Al 135
Gourinchas, Pierre-Olivier 21–2, 24,
  176, 177
governance 2, 183, 184, 192, 198
  Africa 187
  Ghana 191
  growth policy package 33, 47, 48, 50
  Kenya 77, 78, 79, 80, 90, 191
  managing volatility 47, 48, 50
  Poland 68, 71, 72
  privatization 71, 72
government debt dynamics
  Kenya 79, 86–8, 91, 92
  Russia 117, 122, 123, 125, 126, 128, 130,
    131–2, 133
government intertemporal budget constraint
  (GIBC) 13, 18, 139, 196, 198, 199
  Brazil 154
  growth policy package 33, 35–42, 47, 49, 50, 52
  India 97, 111, 113
  Kenya 84
  managing volatility 47
  Russia 117, 119, 120, 133
  second generation models 143
  self-insurance 170, 171, 172, 173, 174, 179
  sustainable government debt dynamics 185,
    186
  third generation crisis models 224
  Turkey 167, 168
gradual nature of Indian reforms 106
Greece 132
Green, Russell 180 n. 9
Gross National Income (GNI) 147, 180 n. 5
Gross National Product (GNP) 147, 149, 164,
  166, 180 n. 5
Grossman, Gene M. 23–4, 31 n. 5
growth accounting 119, 207–8
Growth Commission (GC) 33–5, 36
growth diagnostics 38, 40–1, 52 n. 2
growth policy packages 30–1, 32–52, 174–5
  government intertemporal budget
    constraint 35–42
  Growth Commission 33–5
  managing volatility 45–50
  micropolicy trio 42–5
growth takeoff, India 109
Guidotti–Greenspan rule 173
Gurvich, Evsey 137 n. 16

hard budget constraints 17, 44, 182, 184–5,
  191, 197, 198
  Brazil 156, 157, 158
  governance 183
  growth policy package 42, 43–4, 45, 50
  Kenya 79, 90–1
  Poland 59, 60, 64, 67–9, 70, 71, 72, 73, 74,
    131
  Russia 121, 129, 131, 133, 135, 136
  savings rates and TFP growth 183, 184
  self-insurance 174, 179
  *see also* micropolicy trio
Hausmann, Ricardo 38, 40–1, 52 n. 2, 52 n. 6,
  148, 149, 153, 159, 161 n. 8
Heavily Indebted Poor Countries Initiative *see*
  HIPC–MDRI
Helpman, Elhanan 23–4, 31 n. 5
Herrera, Santiago 154, 158, 161 n. 14, 161 n. 15
Hevia, Constantino 29
HIPC–MDRI 2, 5, 78, 189, 191
  Ghana 187, 188, 191
Hnatkovska, Viktoria 49
Horioka, Charles 176
Howitt, Peter 26, 42–3, 45, 60, 193
Hudson, Alexandra 180 n. 1
human capital
  growth policy package 50
  neoclassical growth economics 21, 25, 29
Hungary 55

Ickes, Barry W. 10, 129
IDA Resource Allocation Index 200 n. 7
  Ghana 188
Imai, Masaaki 91
imitation 42–3, 45
import competition
  growth policy package 44, 45, 50
  India 106, 108, 109
  Kenya 79
  Poland 59, 60, 61, 64, 67, 69, 70, 71, 73
  Russia 121
  savings rates and TFP growth 184
  self-insurance 174, 179
income convergence 1–2
  neoclassical growth economics 19–23, 29,
    184, 205–7
India 5, 95–114, 196
  avoidance of macroeconomic
    meltdown 100–1
  debt-to-GDP levels 214
  fiscal adjustment 159
  "fiscal profligacy" 9
  growth fundamentals 199
  import liberalization 60
  lessons 111–12
  long lags 197
  micropolicy trio 43, 45
  national savings and growth 26, 27
  Ninth Plan outcomes 101–6

political stability and social cohesion 92
public debt dynamics 185–6
reasons for growth in 2003 106–9
reforms of 1991 96, 98, 100, 101, 106–7
savings rates and TFP growth 178, 183, 184
self-insurance 171
solving the puzzle 109–11
India Planning Commission 114 n. 6
Indonesia 121, 126, 144, 145, 148, 164
infrastructure 32
foreign direct investment 22, 29
innovation 42–3, 45
insolvency
growth policy package 36, 37
India 97
institutions 2
managing volatility 47, 48, 49–50
Instituto Nacional de Estadística y Censos (INDEC) 150
interfirm payment arrears, Poland 58, 64, 68–9, 72
International Development Association (IDA) 200 n. 7
Resource Allocation Index 188, 200 n. 7
International Finance Corporation (IFC) 115
international financial institutions (IFIs)
fiscal space 151
original sin 149, 150
Russia 126, 127
self-insurance 169, 179
*see also* International Monetary Fund; World Bank
International Monetary Fund (IMF)
Argentina 134, 218
Brazil 158
currency mismatches 150
fiscal space 151
Flexible Credit Line 174, 227–8
Ghana 188, 189, 190, 191
HIPC–MDRI 189
India 95, 111, 113
Kenya 80
macroeconomic policy prescription 118
Nigeria 8
Poland 57, 75
public debt sustainability analysis 211
real exchange rate 212
resources 180 n. 12
Russia 124, 126, 127, 136
self-insurance 169
Sovereign Debt Restructuring Mechanism 225
Turkey 163, 167, 168, 173
Washington Consensus 35
Investment Climate Assessment (ICA), Kenya 89–90
investment grade, Brazil 167
Islam, Roumeen 48, 141

Izquierdo, A. 218

Japan 195
Jeanne, Olivier 21–2, 24, 146, 176, 177
Jorion, Philippe 137 n. 17
junior bondholders, Russia 127, 134

Kenya 5, 77–94, 188, 191, 192–3
conundrum 79–83
domestic volatility 197
economic data 53
economic improvement explanations 85–6
government debt dynamics 86–8
import liberalization 60
insights 90–2
lessons 196
long lags 197
micropolicy trio 43, 45
political risk, cost of capital, and private investment 83–5
private sector 88–90
public debt dynamics 185
savings rates and TFP growth 183, 184, 195
as threshold country 187
Vision 2030 13, 93, 182
Khandelwal, Amit 114 n. 16
Kharas, Homi 119, 123, 125, 126, 132, 136 n. 9, 137 n. 10, 137 n. 20, 195, 219
Kibaki, Mwai 78, 89
Kletzer, Kenneth M. 114 n. 8, 137 n. 15, 137 n. 16
Kohli, Renu 114 n. 8
Korea 47, 145
Kornai, János 43, 44, 71
Krajewski, Stefan 61, 63, 73, 75 n. 1, 75 n. 7, 75 n. 8
Krueger, Anne 225 n. 1
Krugman, Paul 10, 15 n. 10, 22, 37, 142, 146, 160 n. 4, 160 n. 6, 174, 208, 221–2, 223, 224 n. 3
Kumar, Praveen 88, 89
Kumhof, Michael 224 n. 1

Laeven, Luc 145
lagged effects, Indian reforms of 1991 96
Lane, Philip 48
Latin America
debt crises 6, 34, 35–6, 37, 47, 146
macroeconomic adjustment programs 151
leading edge innovation 42–3
learning-by-doing externalities 50
Lehman Brothers 51, 173, 188–9
Letter of Intent (Turkey) 163, 167
Levine, Ross 31 n. 6
Levy Yeyati, Eduardo 118
Li, Shujing 224 n. 1
Lin, Justin Yifu 52 n. 1
Lipton, David 55, 56, 58, 71, 76 n. 15

Loayza, Norman  29, 49
London Club  75, 136
long lags  160, 184, 197
    India  97, 109, 111, 159, 184, 197
    Kenya  90–1, 184, 197
Long-Term Capital Management (LTCM)  135
Lucas, Robert E., Jr.  21, 22, 24, 25, 29, 31 n. 1,
    32, 55, 95, 177, 209 n. 3
Lula da Silva, Luiz Inácio  157, 158

Maastricht criterion  12, 36, 214, 136 n. 8, 143
    Argentina  134
    Russia  125, 143
McCarthy, Alan T.  94 n. 6
McKinnon, Ronald  58, 60, 75 n. 5
macro–micro linkages  13–14, 179, 183
    growth policy package  33
    India  97, 113
    Kenya  79, 91
    Poland  71
    Russia  120, 128–9, 131, 133, 185
    self-insurance  174
    sustainable government debt dynamics  185
macro-prudential controls/regulations  172, 187
macroeconomic accounting  39–40
macroeconomic crises  22, 173
macroeconomic policy trilemma, Kenya  81
macroeconomic stringency, Poland  57–62,
    65, 71
Malaysia  145
managing volatility  18, 197–8
    aid agenda  194
    external versus domestic volatility  47–9
    growth policy package  33, 45–50, 52
    Kenya  79
    Russia  117
    self-insurance  175
    strengthening institutions  49–50
    themes  48
Mankiw, N. Gregory  22–4, 25, 27, 29, 31 n. 4
Manoel, Alvaro  161 n. 15
manufacturing sector (Poland)  58
Marcos, Ferdinand  1
marginal returns to capital  20, 21, 22, 24
market myopia, India  111
Mass Privatization Program (Poland)  58, 76
    n. 10
Mexico
    competitive real exchange rates  46
    crisis  6, 52 n. 4
    Federal Reserve's swap lines  228
    human capital  31 n. 1
    IMF's Flexible Credit Line  227
microfoundations for growth  119, 183, 184,
    185, 191, 196
    India  106–9
    Russia  116, 120, 122,, 186
micropolicy trio  17, 191, 193, 198, 199–200
    growth policy package  33, 42–5, 49, 52

India  113
    Poland  59, 60, 71, 72, 73, 75, 185
    pragmatic growth strategy  29–30
    Russia  117, 121, 185
    self-insurance  174, 178, 179
    sustainable government debt dynamics  185
    see also competition; competitive real
        exchange rates; hard budget constraints;
        import competition
Millennium Development Goals  201 n. 17
Minas Gerais affair  155–6
Ministry of Finance (MOF), Poland  68
Mody, Ashoka  108, 113, 114 n. 16
Mohan, Rakesh  107, 113
Moody's, Turkey  180 n. 10
Mor, Nachiket  107
moral hazard  146–7
    self-insurance  169
    third generation crisis models  144, 222
Morozov, Alexander  15 n. 9, 137 n. 11, 137 n. 12
Mugabe, Robert  1, 91
Multilateral Debt Relief Initiative (MDRI)  see
    HIPC–MDRI
multiple equilibria  142, 222, 223
    Brazil  157, 158
Mussa, Michael  60, 137 n. 16, 180 n. 4,  218
Myers, Stewart  161 n. 12

Nath, Anusha  108, 114 n. 16
National Bank of Poland  57, 67, 68, 69
national income identity  39
national saving identity  39
neoclassical growth economics  19–31, 205–9
    self-financed growth  177
    income convergence  184
neoclassical income convergence  55
network externalities  148, 161 n. 10, 169
New Partnership for African Development
    (NEPAD)  195
Nigeria
    Abacha  1
    Dutch Disease  6, 7
    oil prices  1, 48, 49, 50, 51
    public finances  198
    self-insurance  17
    Vision 2020  182
noncash settlements, Russia  117, 122, 129, 130,
    131, 137 n. 11

O'Shaughnessy, Arthur  182
Obama, Barack  194
Obstfeld, Maurice  142, 143, 158, 160 n. 4, 174,
    222
official development assistance (ODA)  188
oil  1, 38
    Ghana  188, 189, 190–1
    Russia  129–30, 136
    Turkey  164
    volatility of prices  47, 48, 49–50, 51

Okonjo-Iweala, Ngozi 51, 194, 195, 201 n. 16
one-way bet 165
open capital accounts 145, 159, 224
    India 111
    Turkey 166
    *see also* capital account liberalization
Organisation for Economic Co-operation and
    Development (OECD) 156, 159, 162
Organization of the Petroleum Exporting
    Countries (OPEC) 1, 38
original sin 139, 142, 147–50, 160
    Brazil 153
    self-insurance 169
Oura, Hiroko 110
Overland, Jody 30

Pack, Howard 24
Pang, Gaobo 51, 102, 105, 113 n. 2
Panizza, Ugo 148, 149, 161 n. 8
Paris Club 51, 74, 75
Parks, Richard 136 n. 2
Patel, Urjit R. 100, 113 n. 3
Permanent Income Hypothesis 200 n. 8
    Ghana 188
Perry, Guillermo 160 n. 3, 180 n. 4, 218
Petroleum Revenue Management Act (PRMA,
    Ghana, 2011) 190–1
Philippines 1, 52 n. 3, 145, 171, 206–7
Pinto, Brian 8, 15 n. 9, 37, 40, 48, 51, 52 n. 8,
    61, 63, 70, 73, 75 n. 1, 75 n. 7, 75 n. 8, 75 n.
    9, 76 n. 11, 87, 88, 89, 102, 104, 105, 113 n.
    2, 114 n. 6, 114 n. 7, 119, 123, 125, 126, 132,
    135, 136 n. 1, 136 n. 9, 137 n. 10, 137 n. 11,
    137 n. 12, 137 n. 13, 137 n. 14, 137 n. 15,
    137 n. 16, 137 n. 20, 160 n. 7, 161 n. 9, 162,
    175, 176, 178–9, 180 n. 8, 180 n. 12, 180 n.
    13, 180 n. 14, 181 n. 17, 200 n. 2, 216 n. 1,
    216 n. 4, 219
Poddar, Tushar 111
Poland 5, 7, 55–76
    hard budgets and competition 131, 185
    IMF's Flexible Credit Line 227
    lessons 71–3
    macroeconomic stringency 57–62
    micropolicy trio 43, 44–5
    SOE visits 62–71
    transition 98
Polish Central Statistical Office (GUS) 62
Polish Solidarity Movement 74
political instability 32
political risk 192, 193
    Kenya 83–5, 89, 90, 91–2, 93, 192, 193
    pragmatic growth strategy 30
political uncertainty, Kenya 79, 80
PPWW 58, 59, 62, 64, 67
pragmatic growth strategy 27–31
Prasad, Eswar S. 176–7
primary surpluses 15 n. 8, 148, 160
    Brazil 83, 154, 156–8

fiscal space 151
    growth policy package 36
    India 100
    Kenya 81, 82–3, 84, 85, 191, 192, 196
    self-insurance 178
    Turkey 83, 167, 168
principal–agent literature 58, 64–5
priors 53
private sector bailouts 144, 145, 222, 224
privatization
    Kenya 81
    Poland 58, 60, 61, 64, 69, 70, 71–2, 73
productivity 30
productivity gaps 177
public debt crises 3, 6–7, 11–12
public debt sustainability 3, 4, 211–16
    concepts and insights 212–13
    formulas 211–12
    fundamentals and market signals 214–16
    growth policy package 36, 37
    Kenya 192, 193
    numerical example 213–14
    pitfalls in assessment of 214
    self-insurance 171–2, 178–9

Raddatz, Claudio 47
Radelet, Steven 187–8, 193, 194, 196
Radziwill, Artur 175, 176, 180 n. 13, 180 n. 14
Rajan, Raghuram G. 176–7
Ramey, Garey 48
Ramey, Valerie A. 48
Rangarajan, C. 104
RAO UES 128
real appreciation 49–50
    Turkey 164, 165
real interest rates 200 n. 1
    Brazil 154, 156
    Kenya 192, 193
    Russia 116, 117, 118, 120, 122, 123, 124, 125,
        129, 130, 131
    Turkey 163, 166
Real Plan (July 1994) 152, 167
Rebelo, Sergio 160 n. 6, 216 n. 5, 224 n. 3
reform benefits, India 97
reform costs, India 97
reform-related revenue losses, India 109, 110
Reinhart, Carmen 11, 12, 15 n. 11, 100, 149,
    150, 151, 152, 161 n. 8, 161 n. 13, 162
Reserve Bank of India 114 n. 12
Richter, Tomas 76 n. 12
risk premium 36
Robinson, James 14 n. 3
Rodrik, Dani 34, 38, 40–1, 48, 52 n. 2, 52 n. 6,
    153, 159
Rogoff, Kenneth 11, 12, 15 n. 11, 100, 149, 150,
    151, 152, 161 n. 8, 161 n. 13, 162
Romer, David 22–4, 25, 27, 29, 31 n. 4
Romer, Paul 19, 20, 22, 24, 29, 206, 208 n. 1
Rosenblatt, David 52 n. 1

rules of thumb 11–12, 214
  India 112
Russia 5, 7, 53, 115–37
  barter 9–11
  credit and inflation history 186
  debt crisis 3, 7, 11, 12, 38, 52 n. 4, 98, 100,
    141, 166
  debt-to-GDP levels 214
  default and devaluation risk 97
  East Asian crisis 121–2
  exchange rate regime 13, 72, 145
  fundamental fiscal problem 122–4
  GKO–Eurobond swap 126–7, 132–4, 186,
    217–18
  government debt sustainability
    problems 171
  hard budgets and competition 185
  lessons 130–5, 163, 166
  macro–micro linkages 128–9
  market anxiety and the July 1998 rescue
    package 125–7
  micropolicy trio 43, 44–5, 46, 71
  oil prices 129–30
  privatization 72, 73
  public debt dynamics 186
  refining the textbook 118–21
  second generation models 143
  stabilization 164
  unsustainable debt dynamics 145
Rwanda 182
Ryan, Terry 94 n. 3

Sachs, Jeffrey 37, 38, 47, 52 n. 4, 55, 56, 58, 71,
  76 n. 15
safe-haven effect 227
Sahay, Ratna 120, 122
Sala-i-Martin, Xavier 208 n. 1, 208 n. 3
Sargent, Thomas J. 120, 213, 215
Savastano, Miguel 100, 149, 151, 152, 161 n. 8,
  161 n. 13, 162
savings rates 182, 183–4, 195–6
  aid agenda 194–5
Saxena, Sweta 160 n. 1
Sberbank 217
Schmukler, Sergio 218
Schumpeter, Joseph 44, 71
second generation crisis models 142–3, 145,
  146, 221, 222, 223–4
  Brazil 157
self-financed growth 139–40, 175–9, 194, 199, 200
self-fulfilling prophecy 143, 222
self-insurance 38, 142, 168–75, 187, 197, 199
  backstopping liquidity 173–4
  convergence to 171–3
  and growth policy 174–9
  India 112
  package 160, 172, 179
  Turkey 163, 168
  why it worked 170–1
senior creditors, Russia 127

Servén, Luis 151–2, 160 n. 3, 161 n. 17, 180 n. 4, 218
Shiller, Robert 1
Singapore 228
social cohesion 193
  Kenya 92, 93
social conflict 48
social fragmentation, Kenya 79, 91, 93
Soderbom, M. 94 n. 9
SOEs *see* state-owned enterprises
Solidarity Movement, Poland 74
Solow, Robert M. 2, 19, 20, 22, 23, 24, 42, 206,
  208 n. 1
Solow residual 119
solvency *see* fiscal solvency
Soros, George 223
South Korea 47, 145
sovereign credit ratings 162
sovereign debt 2–3, 5
Sovereign Debt Restructuring Mechanism
  (SDRM) 172, 225
Soviet Union, former 61
Sri Lanka 28–9
Srinivasan, T. N. 100, 113 n. 5, 114 n. 6
Srivastava, D. K. 104
stabilization 119, 120
  Russia 117, 118, 120, 124, 130, 131, 136, 185
  Turkey 163
Standard & Poor's
  Brazil 162
  Kenya 78
  Turkey 180 n. 10
state manufacturing sector (Poland) 58
state-owned enterprises (SOEs)
  Ghana 189
  managers, Poland 59–62, 63–5, 66, 68,
    69–70, 73, 74
  Poland 56, 57, 58, 59–71, 72, 73–4, 75
Steeves, Jeffrey 94 n. 2
Stiglitz, Joseph 48, 141
Sturzenegger, Federico 150
Sub-Saharan Africa 5, 194
Subramanian, Arvind 176–7
Suharto, President 121
Summers, Lawrence H. 30, 90
sustainable government debt dynamics 183,
  185–6, 195–6, 197
Sweden 142, 222

Talvi, E. 218
Tanaka, Shinsuke 219
Tanzania 78, 85
technological frontier 26, 193
  growth policy package 42–3
  Poland 60
  pragmatic growth strategy 30
technology 21, 23, 24, 25, 29
terms-of-trade (ToT) shocks
  Poland 72
  volatility 47
Thailand 3, 6, 145

third generation crisis models  143–5, 146, 147, 221, 222, 223–4
three generations of crisis models  160
    self-insurance  172, 173
    *see also* first generation crisis models; second generation crisis models; third generation crisis models
Topalova, Petia 114 n. 15, 114 n. 16
Torgerson, Tom 180 n. 9
Tornell, Aaron  48
Torre, Augusto de la  218
total factor productivity (TFP)  2, 26, 28–30, 42, 52, 119, 182, 183–4, 191, 193, 196, 197
    financial integration  177
    growth accounting  207–8
    India  111
    Kenya  80, 90
    neoclassical growth economics  19, 20, 21–2, 205–7
    self-insurance  178
trade liberalization, Poland  60, 61
transition  56
    micropolicy trio  43, 44–5
    Poland  56, 58, 71, 73, 98, 185
    Russia  133
Turkey  6, 163–8
    credit and inflation history  186
    debt crisis  3, 6, 7, 12, 100, 141
    exchange rate regime  13
    failure of the 2000 program  164–6
    global financial crisis  4
    government debt sustainability problems  172
    primary surplus  42, 83
    self-insurance  112, 171, 173
    sovereign credit rating  162
    turnaround  166–8
    vulnerability  199
Turner, Philip  149

Uganda  78, 85, 188
Ulatov, Sergei  123, 125, 126, 132, 135, 136 n. 9, 137 n. 10, 137 n. 13, 137 n. 16, 137 n. 20, 219
unindexed local currency debt, Brazil  154, 158
United Kingdom  223
United States
    Brady Plan  37
    Federal Reserve *see* Federal Reserve
    global financial crisis  152, 227
    growth compared with that of the EU  43
    human capital  31 n. 1
    inflation compared to that of Kenya  86
    interest rates  38
    neoclassical growth economics  25, 206–7
    public debt  195
    safe haven  174
    subprime mortgage crisis  85, 147
unsustainability
    debt dynamics  104, 110, 145

Indian government debt  96, 97, 98, 100
unsustainable trajectory, Indian government debt  100
"v-shaped" recovery  141
Valencia, Fabian  145
van Wijnbergen, Sweder  50, 51, 70, 75, 75 n. 1, 75 n. 9, 76 n. 11, 76 n. 15
VChK  129
Vegh, Carlos  120, 122
Velasco, Andres  38, 40–1, 52 n. 2, 52 n. 6, 153, 159, 160 n. 5, 160 n. 6, 224 n. 3
Venezuela  48
Vietnam  92, 145
virtual economy, Russia  10, 129
vision statements  182, 195, 196
volatility *see* managing volatility
voracity  48

Wahi, Diviya  107
Wallace, Neil  120, 213, 215
Walton, Michael  108, 114 n. 16
Wanjiru, Samuel Kamau  77
Warutere, Peter  94 n. 4
Washington Consensus  34–5, 36
Wei, Shang-Jin  146, 160 n. 6, 216 n. 5, 224 n. 3, 224 n. 4
Weil, David N.  22–4, 25, 27, 29, 30, 31 n. 4
Wellisz, Stanislaw  58–9, 63, 65, 75 n. 6
Werner, Alejandro 14 n. 6, 46, 131, 136 n. 7, 164
Wes, Marina  102, 105, 113 n. 2
Williamson, John  34–5, 157
Wolf, Holger  150
World Bank
    fiscal space  151
    Ghana  200 n. 3
    Growth Commission  33–5, 36
    HIPC–MDRI  189
    India  95, 96, 101
    International Development Association  200 n. 7
    International Finance Corporation  115
    Investment Climate Assessment (Kenya)  89–90
    Kenya  77, 79, 89–90, 93
    macroeconomic policy prescription  118
    Nigeria  8
    public debt sustainability analysis  211
    self-insurance  169
    Washington Consensus  34, 35

Yan, Isabel  224 n. 1
Yeltsin, Boris  115
Yi, Eva  111
Young, Alwyn  25, 29

Zahir, Farah  104, 113 n. 2, 114 n. 6, 114 n. 7
Zambia  188
Zimbabwe  1, 91
Zyuganov, Gennady  115